PICTORIAL SINO-KOREAN CHARACTERS

Fun with Hancha

PICTORIAL SINO-KOREAN CHARACTERS

Fun with Hancha

흥미 漢字學習

Text and Illustrations

By

PROF. JACOB CHANG-UI KIM

HOLLYM INTERNATIONAL CORP.

Elizabeth, New Jersey   Seoul

Pictorial Sino-Korean Characters

Copyright © 1988
by Jacob Chang-ui Kim

First published in 1988
Fourth printing, 2002
by Hollym International Corp.
18 Donald Place, Elizabeth, New Jersey 07208, USA
Tel:(908)353-1655   Fax:(908)353-0255
http://www.hollym.com

Published simultaneously in Korea
by Hollym Corporation; Publishers
13-13 Kwanchol-dong, Chongno-gu, Seoul 110-111, Korea
Phone: (02)735-7551~4   Fax:(02)730-5149, 8192
http://www.hollym.co.kr

Hard cover edition ISBN: 0-930878-58-2
Paperback edition ISBN: 1-56591-005-2
Library of Congress Catalog Card Number: 88-80723

Printed in Korea

In memoriam
my father Kim Hong-sŏk, deacon
who taught me *Hancha* and much more.

I would also like to dedicate this book to
the students of mine who have studied the
Korean language in mutual friendship and
enjoyment and who go out into this world
to uphold peace.

The whole earth was of one language,
and of one speech.   -*Genesis* 11:1-

其清如溪　So clear like stream
其淡如水　So fresh like water

By Shelling Hwong, Chinese Calligrapher

PREFATORY NOTE

This volume by Reverend Jacob Chang-ui Kim is a much needed work and is the outcome of Reverend Kim's extensive foreign language teaching, training and research in International Studies. His effort will be extremely beneficial to all students of the Korean language.

Defense Language Institute
Presidio of Monterey
Monterey, California

MONTE R. BULLARD
Colonel, U.S. Army
Commandant

PREFACE

This book is designed for those who are eager to learn the written Korean language and acquire a basic working ability to read and write it in their everyday communication.

Pictorial Sino-Korean Characters performs various aids for writing Korean, particularly the Sino-Korean characters known as *Hancha*.

In 1972, some 1,800 characters were prescribed by the Ministry of Education of the Republic of Korea and adopted by law as those most effective and essential for common use. These are here given with their origin, etymology, history, classification and signification. Each character is accompanied by a chart demonstrating the proper way to write it and pictographs. This is a purely practical guide for students of Korean to help them understand Sino-Korean and the Korean language wisely. While teaching at the Defense Language Institute in California, I had the difficult experience of trying to alleviate the frustrations and mental blocks which would develop in students who were having trouble picking up Sino-Korean characters.

I have proposed a pedagogic strategy that is based on the use of that which is appropriately relevant. The characters were selected on the basis of the frequency of their appearance in modern writings.

The McCune-Reischauer romanization is based on an attempt to use common English values of letters to represent Korean sounds in terms of the raw impressions they make on an American ear. This system was influenced by the Wade-Giles romanization of Chinese and the Hepburn romanization of Japanese. I have followed the McCune-Reischauer system with minor revisions and tried to make the transcription appear and sound as natural as possible.

I gratefully acknowledge the contributions of the Defense Language Institute, Library Director Mr. Gary D. Walter and the library of the Monterey Institute of Foreign Studies.

Thanks also to Professor Stewart W. Hobson of the Chinese Language Department faculty of Defense Language Institute, Monterey, California; for kindly proofreading my manuscripts. Also, for valuable help I am indebted to Mr. Chu Shin-won, Vice President at Hollym Corporation; Publishers.

I hope this book may be a good stepping stone for you to go on to more advanced reading, writing, and conversation.

I welcome any criticism which might help me to improve upon this book and lead to a better understanding of the use and meaning of "Sino-Korean."

Let's study together!

Monterey, California
August 9, 1987

Jacob Chang-ui Kim

CONTENTS

PART Ⅳ RADICALS (214 Characters)

PART V THEOLOGICAL AND
BIBLICAL TERMS

ILLUSTRATIONS

PART I

INTRODUCTION

Yongbiŏch'ŏn-ga (Songs of Flying Dragons), the early Yi dynasty panegyric eulogizing the virtue of the ancestors of the Yi founder comparing the Yi house to a deep rooted tree and a spring of deep waters.

源遠之水旱亦不竭流斯為川于海必達

根深之木風亦不扤有灼其華有蕡其實

ᄉᆡ미기픈므른ᄀᆞ마래아니그츨ᄊᆡ내히이러바ᄅᆞ래가ᄂᆞ니

불휘기픈남ᄀᆞᆫ ᄇᆞ라매아니뮐ᄊᆡ곶됴코여름하ᄂᆞ니

右第一章 ○總叙我朝王業之興皆由天命之佑先述其所以作歌之意也

1. Characters from China

The characters used in writing Sino-Korean originally came from China. However, we are dealing with them only in so far as they form part of the Korean language.

Chinese characters have a long history, the earliest discovered writings having been dated from about 14th century B.C. (甲骨文 Oracle bones, *chia-ku wen*). In 100 A.D. during the Han dynasty, this was modified by Hsu Sheng (許愼, 30–124 A.D.) in his 15-volume paleographical work, *Shuo-wen Chieh-tzu* (說文解字) or the explanation of writing and analysis of words. It lists 9,353 characters under 540 radical entries. Of this number, 364 were pictographic, 125 simple ideographic, 1,167 compound ideographic and 7,697 phonetic compounds.

The most complete collection is the *Kang Hsi Dictionary* (康熙字典) with about 50,000 characters of the Ching dynasty (清), done in 1716.

Since 1949, after the establishment of the People's Republic of China, the government had actively pursued language reform until the Cultural Revolution, 1966～76. They changed and simplified the characters from original letters. Variants include four main categories: (1) interposition of radical components, (2) partial change of radical components, (3) addition of a radical component, and (4) use of new characters.

For examples:
(1) Interposition of radical components
  a. Between left and right
    綿 (cotton) ＝縣   隣 (neighbor) ＝鄰
  b. Between vertical and horizontal radical components
    羣 (flock) ＝群   峯 (peak) ＝峰
    畧 (about) ＝略

(2) Partial change of radical components

熱(heat) ＝热   効(effect) ＝効

館(tavern) ＝舘

(3) Addition of a radical component

果(fruit) ＝菓   場(place) ＝塲

(4) Use of new characters

雙(double) ＝双   體(body) ＝体

人人(crowd) ＝衆

Modern Simplified Characters

ai	罢〔罷〕	备〔備〕	表〔錶〕	cai
呆〔獃〕	bai	贝〔貝〕	bie	才〔纔〕
〔騃〕	摆〔擺〕	bi	别〔彆〕	can
爱〔愛〕	ban	笔〔筆〕	bin	参〔參〕
碍〔礙〕	板〔闆〕	币〔幣〕	宾〔賓〕	蚕〔蠶〕
ang	办〔辦〕	毕〔畢〕	bing	灿〔燦〕
肮〔骯〕	bang	毙〔斃〕	并〔並〕	cang
ao	帮〔幫〕	bian	〔併〕	仓〔倉〕
袄〔襖〕	bao	边〔邊〕	bu	ceng
奥〔奧〕	宝〔寶〕	变〔變〕	卜〔蔔〕	层〔層〕
ba	报〔報〕	biao	布〔佈〕	chan
坝〔壩〕	bei	标〔標〕	补〔補〕	搀〔攙〕

	Happiness	Myriad	Upright	Eye	to defend	Heaven	Uniform	Corn	to obtain	Tiger	Moon	Sun
Ancient Images (about 19th cent. B.C.)												
Shell-and-Bone Characters (about 18th cent. B.C.)												
Ta-Chüan (about 17th–3rd cent. B.C.)												
Hsiao-Chüan (246–207 B.C.)												
Li-Shu (about 200 B.C.–A.D. 588)	福	萬	貞	目	衛	天	齊	禾	獲	虎	月	日
Changes after Han Dynasty (after A.D. 588)	福	萬	貞	目	衛	天	齊	禾	獲	虎	月	日

THE EVOLUTION OF CHINESE CHARACTERS

2. Sino-Korean to Japan

Many theories have been advanced since the end of the 19th century about the affinities of the Japanese language. Some linguists have classified Japanese with the language of neighbouring areas, such as Ryukyuan, Ainu, and Korean, while others have grouped it with Chinese, Tibetan, Burmese, Ural-Altaic, Malayan, and Polynesian. Still others maintain that Japanese is related to Greek, but this theory is not widely accepted.

This is only natural as Chinese culture has been disseminated widely and deeply.

Four kinds of writing systems are used in Japanese: Kanji (Chinese characters), Hiragana and Katakana (two phonetic syllabaries) and Romaji (the Roman alphabet). Chinese characters and Hiragana are used for the expression of all except words not of Chinese origin, which are expressed by Katakana.

The more complicated type is known as the Kanji. The Kanji serves generally to represent the principal words of specimen of writing in the Japanese language, and thus express the nouns, pronouns, nominalizers, and numbers. Also they are utilized in the roots of adjectives, verbs, and adverbs.

The simpler type of characters is known as Kana. This takes two forms, the Hiragana, which are relatively cursive in appearance, and the Katakana, which are relatively angular.

In fact, the Japanese language contains a large vocabulary based on the Chinese language. According to *The Vocabulary and Chinese Characters in Ninety Magazines of Today* (vol. III)—the analysis of the results published by The National Language Research Institute, the percentage of the vocabulary based on the Chinese is 41.3% of the total number. This ratio will increase in academic material.

The Japanese began to write their language, which they had known only as speech, when contact with Korea and China resulted in the importation of Chinese characters. This contact dates as far back as the first century A.D. Towards the end of third century, two Korean scholars; Wang In(王仁, Wa-ni in Japanese) and Ajikki(阿直岐) of Paekche dynasty came over to Japan and acted as teachers.

A Paekche Sinologist, Wang In is said to have presented a copy of the *Ch'ŏnjamun*(千字文, *Ch'ien-tzu Wen* in Chinese), *One Thousand Character Classic*, and 10 copies of the *Nonŏ* (論語, *Lun yu* in Chinese) as a tribute to the Emperor Ojin(應神). So, the Chinese characters were formally introduced to Japan as early as 285 A.D.

We can find evidence compiled in the early part of the eighth century, in both ancient recorded Korean history and Japanese history, especially the *Kojiki*(古史記), *Record of Ancient Matters*, compiled in the year of 712; *Nihonshoki*(日本書記), *Records of Japan*, compiled in the year of 720.

Moreover, The coming of Buddhism in 552 added impetus to the study of religious texts written in Chinese characters. It is said that Buddhism came to Japan with the introduction of Buddhist images and writings from Paekche on the Korean peninsula.

In addition to art, music, science of divination, medicine, and farming methods were also taught to the Japanese. Japan's Asuka culture and the development of an ancient nation were due to the diffusion of the culture of the Three Kingdoms of Korea.

3. Kanji Education in Japan

In Japanese also, they adopted the Chinese characters which

they call Kanji(Chinese letters). The basic number of Kanji for general use taught to all Japanese school children is 1,850.

In 1951, The Ministry of Education found it necessary to supplement the list of 1,850 characters with a list of 92 characters approved for use in personal names. By 1977, the number had increased to 1,950 basic characters, to be taught in grammar schools and up through high schools.

Since that time, the regulation has generally been observed in documents published by the government, in institutions of public education, in newspapers and magazines, etc. So, most publications and documents can be read with a knowledge of Tōyō-Kanji(the Kanji for daily use). In addition, both the Tōyō-Kanji and the Kyōiku-Kanji(the educational Kanji) have been revised a little on the basis of research on the actual use of Kanji.

However, Kanji are not so easy for Japanese students, either. They study Kanji for six years at elementary school, for three years at secondary school, and for three years at high school—a total of twelve years. Even so, there are rather few who can read and write all of the 1950 Tōyō-Kanji without mistakes when they enter the university.

Scholar E. Reischauer, the former American ambassador to Japan, once lamented that the Japanese language could not be mastered. If so, one of the reasons would certainly be the difficulties of learning Kanji.

4. The Combination Writing in Korean

The time of the importation of the Chinese writing system to Korea is uncertain. At least by the time of the warring states(403–221 B.C.), the existence of a Chinese writing system became known to Korea through Chinese itinerants and émigrés.

The difficulty the Koreans encountered in adapting the writing system of China is seen from the various methods of writing used in Korea prior to the invention of the alphabet by Sejong in 1443.

The first writings by Koreans were in ordinary Chinese. Despite the early contact with the Chinese script, the earliest securely dated inscription demonstrating that writing was used by the Koreans comes from 414 A.D. The writing is on a monument erected in honor of King Kwanggaet'o of Koguryŏ dynasty. It is written in ordinary Chinese.

A reading capability in the Han-gŭl alphabetic system alone is a limited literacy. Because many classic scholars and linguists use approximately 70% Hancha 30% Han-gŭl, it requires a strong knowledge of the Chinese characters to read most newspapers, journals, and textbooks. Thus dictionaries are written in the combination alphabet-Chinese character system.

The colleges and universities use this combination system almost exclusively. Knowledge of the Chinese characters continues to be of importance in Korea, yet many middle and high school students find difficulty in learning to read in the Sino-Korean.

Today a knowledge of about two thousand characters is adequate to read the newspaper. In accord with this policy, the newspaper publishers agreed in 1967 to limit the number of characters used in the newspapers.

Characters with the radical 金 (metal, gold)					
Gold	金	금 (kŭm)	Copper	銅	동 (tong)
Tin	錫	석 (sŏk)	Lead	鉛	연 (yŏn)
Silver	銀	은 (ŭn)	Iron	鐵	철 (ch'ŏl)

5. The Features of Sino-Korean

The Chinese characters are called *Hantzu* in Chinese, *Hancha* in Korean, and *Kanji* in Japanese, all meaning "Han characters (漢字)." These characters are used exclusively in Chinese writings, and in combination with the *Han-gŭl* alphabet in Korea and with the *Kana* syllabaries in Japan.

The Sino-Korean(Hancha), in written form, is a combination of three major elements: pictograms, ideograms and phonograms.

Most philologists have based their work upon the '*Sŏlmun*' (說文), a book of Chinese etymology. Hŏ Shin(許愼), as pronounced in Korean or Hsu Shen as pronounced in Chinese, classified the ancient characters under six categories of characters(六書). The Chinese usually speak of the "original roots of the six categories of Chinese characters(六書根源)," showing how they were constructed and how new ones based upon them could be formed.

The characters are divided into two great classes. In the first class known as *mun* or *wen*(文), there are the simple characters. In the second class known as *cha* or *tzu*(字), the compounds were placed. These two classes were in later further subdivided, into the six classes that we know now.

The six categories of Chinese characters:

1) The Pictograms 象形

Our system of writing is based primarily on pictographs. Its appeal is more to the eye than to the ear, and the aesthetic value exceeds that of phonetic scripts.

These are visual and primitive symbols, tracing out some familiar objects; they were drawn to be representative of their original shape as much as possible. However, the simple pictures were incapable of illustrating the great mass of abstract notions and hundreds of concrete words.

Therefore, during the Shang dynasty(商朝, 1765–1122 B. C.) of China about the time when Moses received the Ten Commandments, pictographs were greatly improved. They were already being artistically and skilfully drawn, as demonstrated by the Shang bronzes and Shang oracle bone inscriptions, which we have to examine today.

The image can be divided into five kinds: single, double, triple, combined and complex.

(1) Single figures:

Ch'a　車　수레 차 cart,

Il　日　날 일 sun, day,

(2) Double figures:

Pyŏng　竝　나란히 설 병 standing together,

(3) triple figures:

Sam　森　나무 빽빽할 삼 forest,

(4) Combined figures:

Sa　射　쏠 사 to shoot,

(an arrow, a bow and a hand)

(5) Complex figures:

Ki　箕　키 기 corn-flail or winnower,

(a corn-flail set on a stand)

2) Indicative Symbols 指事

This development was to add a little suggestion on to the pictographs to indicate their new meaning often by the idea of some motion:

Sŏl　舌　혀 설 tongue, 舌　　Mouth with something sticking out, or with a thousand tastes, represents "tongue."

Hap　合　합할 합 agree, 合　　Man with one mouth, represents "agree."

Chwa　坐　앉을 좌 sit, 坐　　Two men sitting on the earth or ground represent the character for "sit."

Myŏng 明 밝을 명 bright or clear, 明　A combination of sun and moon, which have in common the attribute of luminosity.

The characters listed in this category by the *Shuo-wen*(說文) are comparatively few. In form they are similar to those in the first category. In function they differ in being used exclusively for abstract description and the expression of imaginative ideas.

3) The Phonograms　形聲

This system is now known as phonetic compounds, which means that a basic character was borrowed, compounded and garnished with certain radicals. While it retained the same sound, it meant something else. For example, take the character *pang* 方 meaning "square."

To avoid complications and confusion, different radicals were added as component parts but still based on the sound of "*pang*" as a sign to support the compounded character. This differentiated its meaning yet brought it into logical relation with the character.

For example, utilizing the sound "*pang*" 方 we find:

肪 기름 방 *pang* with "flesh" radical, means "fat";

紡 길쌈 방 *pang* with "silk" radical, means "weave";

芳 꽃다울 방 *pang* with "grass" radical, means "fragrance";
防 막을 방 *pang* with "mound" radical, means "defence";
房 방 방 *pang* with "gate" radical, means "room."

4) The Ideograms 會意

The second supplementary principle was by means of ideographs or combinations, which means that one or more independent characters were put together to give a new meaning with an entirely new sound.

Take for example the character for the door, 門 문 문. Pictograph  and modern character 門.

問 물을 문 With the symbol "mouth" (口) at the door the character means "to ask or inquire."

聞 들을 문 With an ear(耳) at the door the character represents "news" or "to hear."

開 열 개 Two hands on the door becomes "open."

閉 닫을 폐 With a bolt or bar at the door becomes "close" or "closed."

農 농사 농 Originally it was written . You can see ⊕ representing "field" or "land" and  or  a "plough." To plough the land is symbolical of agriculture. In the second character there is, in addition, a sign() representing the human foot.

5) Converted Words 轉注

Their meanings are understood in an extended or derived sense, sometimes metaphorical or figurative, occasionally inverted or even directly opposite to the original. *Chŏn*(轉) means turning or transmitting, *chu*(注) means explaining or noting: together they signify "to explain by turning" or "to express by reciprocation." Thus two or more characters are constructed to explain one another. For example: *no* (老), meaning "old," if the final upward stroke is turned downward, becomes *ko* (考), meaning "examine" (youngsters are generally examined by their elders). *Chwa* and *u* (左 and 右) mean left and right respectively; the ancient characters are ✶ and ✦, the second being formed by reversing the first.

The characters *sang* and *ha* (上 and 下, ⸜ and ⸝ in ancient writing) mean "up" and "down"; but by extension they also stand for above and below, superior and inferior. There are many possible ways of interpreting the characters in this category and the best method is still in dispute.

6) Falsely Borrowed 假借

Another method to increase the Chinese characters was found by the development of the falsely borrowed character system.

In this system one character may have one or two pronunciations but yet two different meanings. For example: in Cantonese the character 長, *chong* means "long" but the same character pronounced *chaing* means "elder." In Korean it also means "long or elder," but the pronunciation is *chang*.

Sŏ (西) was, in ancient writing ⊗, ⊕ originally constructed out of a bird returning to its nest at sunset; but as the sunset towards the west, this character was permanently borrowed for the meaning "west."

PART II

WRITING HANCHA

An epitaph of Koryŏ dynasty. It was composed by Yi Sung-in, a famous scholar of the day, and was written by Kwon Chu, a master of the traditional calligraphic style of the time. It has been kept at Shillŭk Temple, Yŏju, Kyŏnggi-do.

以人 州 徒 教 願 至
飯 化 縱 銘 公 弓
諸 楮 史 懶 帳 劍
化 為 始 翁 記 忽
士 紙 自 塔 否 遺
終 釋 庚 慕 予 可
始 幻 申 久 益 勝
不 造 二 也 自 痛
息 墨 月 因 傷 我

1. Calligraphy

The calligraphy is a totally spontaneous, highly individualistic art. The writer feels that a man's handwriting accurately measures the extent of his cultural attainment and aesthetic sensibilities, and even betrays his physical appearance.

The quality of attention demanded of the calligrapher is different. A western calligrapher must pay attention to what he is doing, of course, but his work does not demand the absolute concentration and mental tranquility of his counterpart. The westerner can touch up small mistakes, while revision of oriental calligraphy is unthinkable. One mistake, and the whole piece is discarded.

Four treasures of the study: The oriental calligrapher has four basic tools, called "four treasures of the study" (文房四寶, 문방사보). They are brush, ink, inkstone and paper.

1) **Brush** : The Chinese brush is perfectly round, unlike the flat lettering brushes of western sign painters. It consists of three parts; holder, hair, and sheath. The holder, or handle, is a length of bamboo tube or a hollow wooden rod. The hair, or brush, is constructed in layers. A central bunch of deer or rabbit hair is surrounded by an outer circle of softer hairs taken from goats or hemp string.

2) **Inkstick** : A brush must be dipped in ink, though Chinese brushes never sink into bottles. Ink is stored and carried as a solid black bar, sometimes incised with decorations and characters traced in gold.

When ready to write, the calligrapher grinds the bar with a few drops of water on an inkstone until he has achieved his desired consistency.

The invention of ink is traditionally attributed to a calligrapher and inkmaker named Wei Tan, who lived during the

TRADITIONAL KOREAN STATIONERY

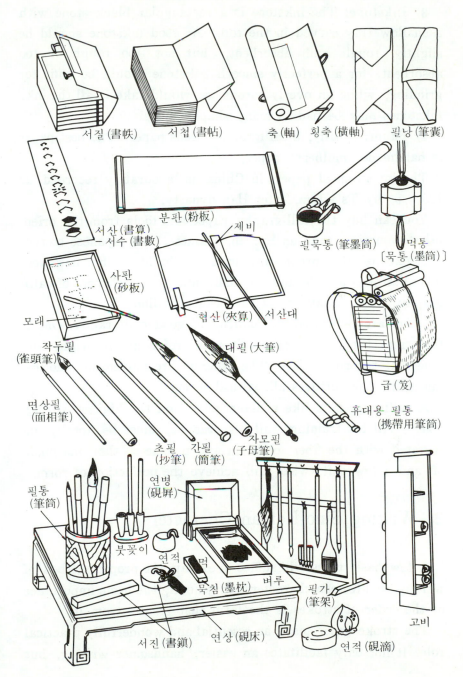

서질 (書帙)   서첩 (書帖)   축 (軸) 횡축 (橫軸)   필낭 (筆囊)

분판 (粉板)   제비

서산 (書算)   필묵통 (筆墨筒)   먹통
서수 (書數)   〔묵통 (墨筒)〕

사판
(砂板)

모래   협산 (夾算)   서산대

작두필
(雀頭筆)   대필 (大筆)

급 (笈)

면상필
(面相筆)   휴대용 필통
(携帶用筆筒)

초필   간필   자모필
(抄筆) (簡筆)   (子母筆)

연병
필통   (硯屏)
(筆筒)

붓꽂이   연적 먹   벼루   필가
묵침 (墨枕)   (筆架)

서진 (書鎭)   연상 (硯床)   고비
연적 (硯滴)

late Han dynasty around the third century A. D.

3) **Inkstone:** The inkstone is a rectangular black stone with a shallow tray carved in the top. A good inkstone should be slightly rough and absorbent, but not too rough or too absorbent, for a perfectly smooth inkstone would be unfit for grinding, while an overly porous one would take in all the ink. Inkstones may be had in many shapes and sizes.

4) **Paper:** Finally, a calligrapher needs paper. The best paper is handmade, mulberry paper.

The invention of paper in China is accurately recorded as 105 A. D. by Ts'a Lun, later Han dynasty.

You can buy the calligraphy paper and tools from the oriental stationeries, such as Korean, Chinese, and Japanese stores.

Strokes of the brush are used to build each character. These strokes are the most fundamental linear element of calligraphy, an art that exacts the beauty of line.

There are two essential qualities of good calligraphy. One is the strength of each stroke. Strength refers to the right emphasis at the right place. The other is life movement, the cosmic spirit that utilizes all natural forms.

A calligrapher is like a diver poised on the highest springboard. All his training, all his practice, must be totally integrated with the fiber of brain and muscle so that one push-off and a few deft twists will achieve the perfection of form.

2. Writing Sino-Korean Characters

A few basic rules will suffice to explain the proper method of writing Sino-Korean characters. In general, the basic importance of the order of strokes is the form that results from it.

The stroke order plays an essential and wonderfully practical role. It not only facilitates an easier, handsomer writing, but

BRUSH, INKSTICK AND INKSTONE

Brushes 붓

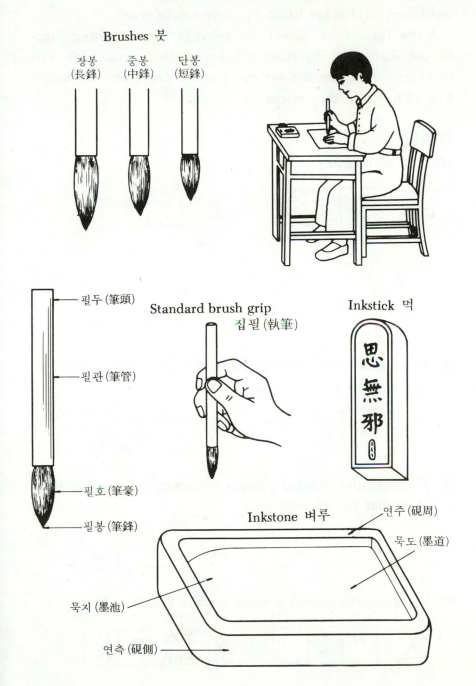

장봉
(長鋒)

중봉
(中鋒)

단봉
(短鋒)

필두(筆頭)

필관(筆管)

필호(筆豪)

필봉(筆鋒)

Standard brush grip
집필(執筆)

Inkstick 먹

思無邪

Inkstone 벼루

연주(硯周)

묵도(墨道)

묵지(墨池)

연측(硯側)

also gives you a guide when searching for letters in a dictionary, which are listed by their stroke order.

A few basic rules should be followed when writing Sino-Korean characters. By strictly following these rules, one will be able to recognize the various handwritten forms no matter how abbreviated they might be.

Writing order

(1) Top to bottom.

(2) Left to right

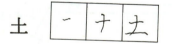

(3) Horizontal strokes usually precede perpendicular ones when two or more strokes cross.

(4) Perpendicular strokes precede horizontal ones when they touch but fail to cross.

(5) Right-to-left diagonal strokes precede left to right.

(6) Center first, then left and right.

水 [기 | 水 | 水]   小 [丿 | 小 | 小]

(7) Fill up before closing.

國 [冂 | 國 | 國]   田 [冂 | 用 | 田]

(8) The perpendicular line running thru center written last.

書 [マ | 聿 | 書]   事 [彐 | 彐 | 事]

(9) Complete one part before starting another part.

比 [上 | 比 | 比]   林 [木 | 村 | 林]

(10) There is one acute angle and sweep then the horizontal stroke is written last.

女 [人 | 乆 | 女]   母 [口 | 毋 | 母]

Frames for analyzing Sino-Korean characters

(1) ▢   日 날 **일**   date, sun

(2) ▢   材 재목 **재**   material

(3) ▢   男 사내 **남**   male

(4) ▢   回 돌아올 **회**   return

(5) ▢   能 능할 **능**   ability

(6)		術 재주 술	artistic
(7)		新 새 신	new
(8)		時 때 시	time
(9)		怒 성낼 노	angry
(10)		品 물건 품	article
(11)		變 변할 변	change
(12)		讀 읽을 독 귀절 두	read

3. The Eight Strokes with Possible Variations

(1) 點法 점법, 점쓰기

Dots made by slant of brush or pen, moving from top to bottom or left to right.

The "water" radical combination. Note that lower dot goes from bottom up anticipating the next stroke to come at right in the remainder of the character involved.

This is the popular "fire" radical.

(2) 橫法 횡법, 가로긋기

Horizontal line written from left to right.

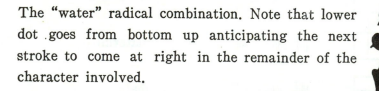

(3) 竪法 수법, 세로긋기
Vertical line made from top
downward.

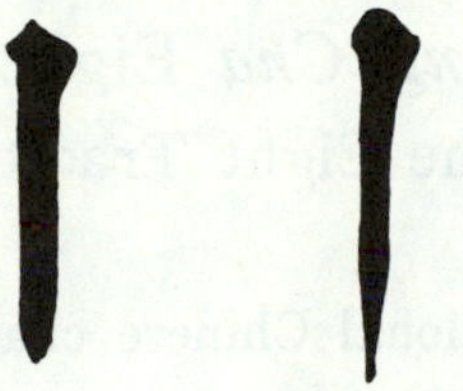

(4) 撇法 별법, 왼쪽으로 비껴 치는 획
Important stroke with many vari-
ations but always downward from
right to left— even if only slightly
inclined or curled.

(5) 捺法 날법, 오른쪽으로 비껴 치는 획
Sweeps downward to the right—some steeply and some
quite flat.

(6) 鉤法 구법, 끝을 꺾어친 획
Horizontal hooks
Vertical hooks

(7) 厥法 궐법, 굽혀친 획 Curve Hooks
Left and right
curve hooks

(8) 角法 각법 가운데 꺾어치기 획 Angles

Right angle   Left angle

Obtuse angle   Acute angle

4. *Yŏng Cha* Eight Strokes
(The Eight Traditional Brush Strokes)

Traditional Chinese characters are composed of eight stroke groups. The character *Yŏng* that follows means "eternal or everlasting" and is considered by the Chinese to contain all eight kinds of strokes. It was first designed by Che Ohng, Han dynasty. It is usually constructed with five strokes today, however. The five strokes are achieved by combining the central vertical stroke with the horizontal and the hook, and making left side wing as a single stroke. Both constructions follow.

Yŏng in traditional eight strokes

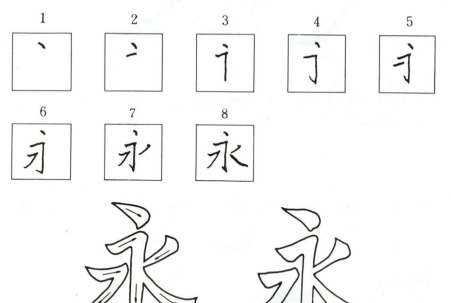

Yŏng Cha Eight strokes designed by Che Ohng
(漢나라 蔡邕이 고안한 「永字八法」)

Yŏng in current five strokes

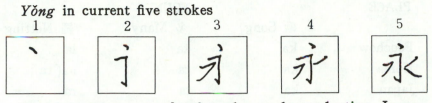

Here is another example of stroke number reduction. In constructing a simple box character that normally required strokes, the second and third strokes are combined as either a sharp angular turning stroke or as a rounded turning stroke.

In hand writing, the rounded top and right combined stroke is probably the most popular because it can be accomplished faster.

Ku in four strokes   *Ku* in current three strokes

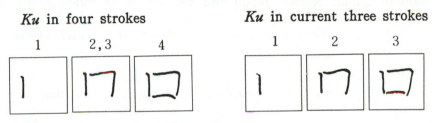

5. Comparison of Sounds

The Chinese system of writing was disseminated first to Korea, then to Japan and Vietnam (Annam) because of geographical propensities.

Most proper nouns were rendered into Chinese and pronounced in the dialects of the disseminators. Although those who carried the characters abroad came from various parts of China and many of those who went to Japan were Koreans, pronunciations of the four peoples are close even today.

The following comparison of sounds is taken from the Chinese translation of *The Chinese Language: An Essay on its Nature and History* by Bernhard Karlgren, a Swedish Sinologist. (Phonetic symbols are those of the International Phonetic Association.)

PLACE			SOUNDS		
	歌 Song		多 Many		羅 Netting
Foochow	ka		ta		la
Korea	ka		ta		na[ra]
Japan	ka		ta		ra
Vietnam	ka		da		la

Etymologically, Chinese characters are estimated to constitute more than 50 percent of all Korean words. The Japanese percentage is believed to exceed 40 and Vietnamese to be at least 33.

The pronunciation of a number of Chinese terms currently used in China, Korea, Japan and Vietnam is as follows:

	Chinese	*Korean*	*Japanese*	*Vietnamese*
注意 주의 attention	chu i	*chuŭi*	chui	chu y
古典 고전 classic	ku tien	*kojŏn*	koten	co dien
觀念 관념 concept	kuan nien	*kwannyŏm*	kannen	quan niem
討論 토론 discussion	tao lun	*t'oron*	toron	thao luan
農夫 농부 farmer	nung fu	*nongbu*	nofu	nong phu
旅館 여관 hotel	lu kuan	*yŏgwan*	ryokan	lu quan
模範 모범 model	mo fan	*mobŏm*	mohan	mo pham
父母 부모 parents	fu mu	*pumo*	fubo	phu mau
國會 국회 parliament	kuo hui	*kuk'oe*	kokkai	quoc hoi
公安 공안 public security	kung an	*kong-an*	koan	cong an

6. The Similarity of Ancient Letters

Now let us compare the ancient Egyptian and Babylonian script with the Chinese.

Ancient Babylonian:

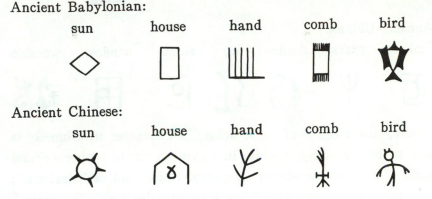

Ancient Chinese:

Between the first two pairs of characters there is a difference in the way of imagining the object. Both of the fourth pair have a connection with ladies, but in Babylonian the object is a comb while in Chinese it is a broom. The similarity of construction in the fifth pair is only very approximate. For convenience I will divide my comparisons into two groups.

(1) Similar in form and meaning:

Ancient Egyptian:

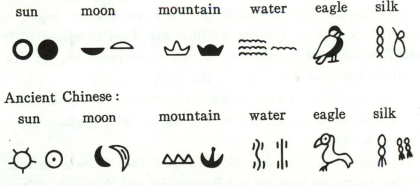

Ancient Chinese:

(2) Different in form but similar in meaning:

Ancient Egyptian:

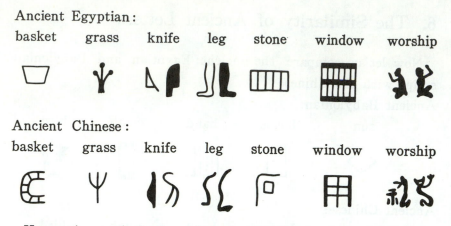

basket	grass	knife	leg	stone	window	worship

Ancient Chinese:

basket	grass	knife	leg	stone	window	worship

Here, the method of constructing a character in Chinese is seen to be "sketchy," while in Egyptian it is elaborate and exact. The one has strong simplified lines, and is "idealistic"; the other is "photographic," a kind of painting — "realistic." By the time that the Egyptian script had reached its greatest refinement, it had become inconvenient for writing, and incapable of modification to meet the requirements of daily use, it fell away. But the Chinese preserved a great capacity for development, and so it keeps its life, yet without ever losing touch with its very ancient origins.

Thus a whole literature has grown up, suggesting various places, chiefly Egypt and Babylon, as the points from which either from the Chinese people or their civilization began a migration to China. Chinese writing has been compared with both Egyptian and Babylonian, with the conclusion that it was certainly borrowed from one or the other.

I have myself been able to point out certain very interesting parallels between the structure of Chinese and Egyptian hieroglyphic writing.

The Chinese scholar Hua Shih-fu said that Chinese characters were derived from ancient Babylonian and Egyptian, "Kuo-Wen-T'an-So-I-Pan."

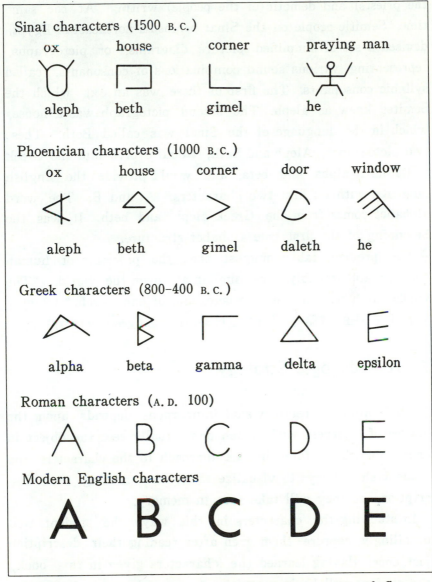

Sinai characters (1500 B.C.)

ox	house	corner	praying man
aleph	beth	gimel	he

Phoenician characters (1000 B.C.)

ox	house	corner	door	window
aleph	beth	gimel	daleth	he

Greek characters (800–400 B.C.)

| alpha | beta | gamma | delta | epsilon |

Roman characters (A.D. 100)

A   B   C   D   E

Modern English characters

A   B   C   D   E

When cuneiforms emerged, the Egyptians, west of Sumer, were still communicating words, syllables, and ideas with picture symbols called hieroglyphs. However, over the next 1500 years, hieroglyphs were gradually replaced by shorthand scribbles based on stylized hieroglyphs and called hieratic (of the priests) and demotic(of the people) writing. At the same time, Semitic people on the Sinai peninsula northeast of Egypt, devised a set of simplified picture diagrams, or pictographs, representing various sound combinations of consonants, called syllabic consonants. The first of these was an ox, which the Semites knew as aleph. The second pictograph was a house, which in the language of the Sinai was called Beth. These two pictographs, Aleph and Beth, would evolve into the Greek and Roman alpha and beta, and would provide the English language with its first two characters, A and B. The word alphabet comes from the Greek aleph and beth. It was the beginning of the first true alphabet structure.

The previous tables suggest that the processes of human thought are probably very similar all over the world. "The whole earth was of one language, and of one speech." (온 땅의 口音이 하나요 言語가 하나이었더라. (創世記 *Genesis 11 : 1*))

7. A Pedagogic Strategy

The ability to retain visual impressions depends upon the degree of clearness with which one actually sees the object in one's mind. Therefore, in this approach to the characters, the student should try to visualize them when reading their description, so they will take root in memory.

In studying the characters in this way, the student will unfailingly capture them even after reading their description just once. Having learned the characters given in this book, the student will be in a position to create his own pictures for any number of other Sino-Korean, Chinese, or Japanese characters that he may wish to learn.

This book applies sound theory. To create a strong foundation in the memory, learning and retention methodology has been systematically documented by many education specialists. *

For instance:

Word list	Stimulus figures	Reproduced figures	Letter

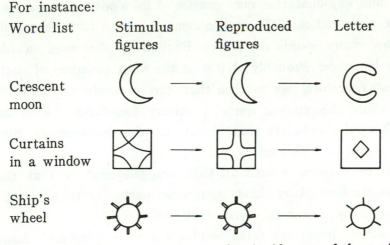

Crescent moon			
Curtains in a window			
Ship's wheel			

The author draws attention to the significance of the problem with which the student of oriental languages is faced. Obviously, the difficulty is magnified for those of a Germanic or Romance language background. If we look at this learning process objectively, several salient points emerge:

A. Writing characters that are readable is very difficult and requires a great deal of time in practicing form balance and stroke order.

B. Similarities of characters, little or no way to be sure of pronunciation, no way to determine meaning from appearance.

C. Need for constant practice and reinforcement.

D. Contact with native speaker is seldom or rare.

Nevertheless, these are not facts to be intimidated by, but rather a challenge to look forward to anxiously. There is beauty and simplicity behind that which initially looks complex and overwhelming. While the Chinese language used to boast

* Such as L. Carnichael, H.P. Hogan and A.A. Walter, F.C. Bantlett, Robert Gagne, Morris E. Eson; An experimental study of the effect of language on visually perceived form.

upwards of 50, 000 characters, they use 10, 000 in contemporary use, and any character may consist of from one, to as many as 30 or more radicals. These are some fearsome facts, yet look at how many words the native English speaker uses in his daily language. Probably 1, 000 at the most generous of estimates! Therefore, we can see that careful study of this book will afford the student quite a strong foundation, with an 1, 300 word vocabulary that include the five hundreds of biblical words and phrases.

The importance behind all this braggadoccio* is that the words are learned by their component parts, in other words character by character, even stroke by stroke.

The most important thing besides a good learning tool, however, is the concentration and time that is put into the learning process.

Over two decades ago these were the empirically proven facts:

A. Gouin says to learn a language takes 800~900 hours for basic course.

B. The Foreign Service Institute of the Department of State put the minimum professional proficiency:

① Average aptitude will take 1, 000 to 1, 200 hours (6 to 7 months of intensive study). That is for language in the Germanic and Romance families.

② Slavic languages take 15~18 months (2, 625 hours) most other languages, 18 months (3, 150 hours).

③ Amharic, Arabic, Chinese, Japanese, and Korean take 25 months of intensive study (4, 375 hours).

I cannot emphasize enough the possibilities which exist for a more speedy apprehension of these oriental languages, if the public world make use of the learning techniques and examples

* to be boastful

set forth by this book.

The Florida State University professor, Robert Gagne's *The Conditions of Learning* was drawn from often during the planning of this presentation. Exceptionally noteworthy are his 8 types of learning, rule learning principle which has much in common with the radical systems of these languages.

DECORATIONAL CHARACTERS

Pillow cases

Rice cake

壽 목숨 수 longevity   福 복 복 blessing   祝 빌 축 bless; pray

Pencil holder

Cushion

囍 쌍희 희 great joy

SEASON'S GREETINGS

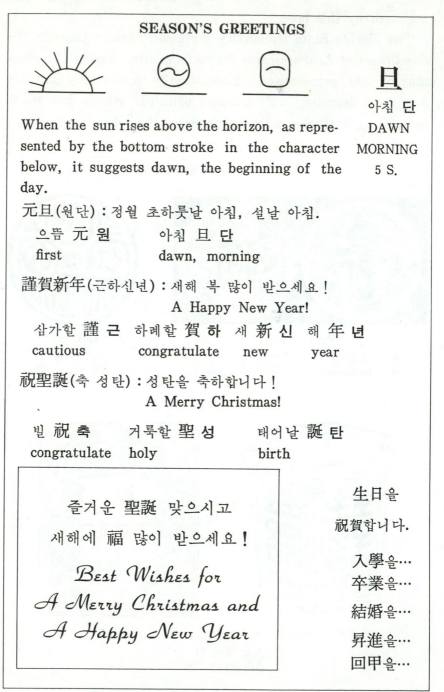

아침 **旦**
DAWN
MORNING
5 S.

When the sun rises above the horizon, as represented by the bottom stroke in the character below, it suggests dawn, the beginning of the day.

元旦(원단) : 정월 초하룻날 아침, 설날 아침.

으뜸 元 원　　　아침 旦 단
first　　　　　　dawn, morning

謹賀新年(근하신년) : 새해 복 많이 받으세요!
A Happy New Year!

삼가할 謹 근　하례할 賀 하　새 新 신　해 年 년
cautious　　　congratulate　　new　　　year

祝聖誕(축 성탄) : 성탄을 축하합니다!
A Merry Christmas!

빌 祝 축　　　거룩할 聖 성　　　태어날 誕 탄
congratulate　holy　　　　　birth

즐거운 聖誕 맞으시고
새해에 福 많이 받으세요!

Best Wishes for
A Merry Christmas and
A Happy New Year

生日을
祝賀합니다.

入學을…
卒業을…
結婚을…
昇進을…
回甲을…

PART III

CHARACTERS

A *Village School*. A small group of pupils were taught Chinese classics in olden times. Painted by Kim Hong-to (1745-?), Yi dynasty.

Explanatory Notes

On this page there appears an annotated sample of the character entry. It has been slightly modified from the actual entry in this book to show the full range of information provided for characters in the first character group.

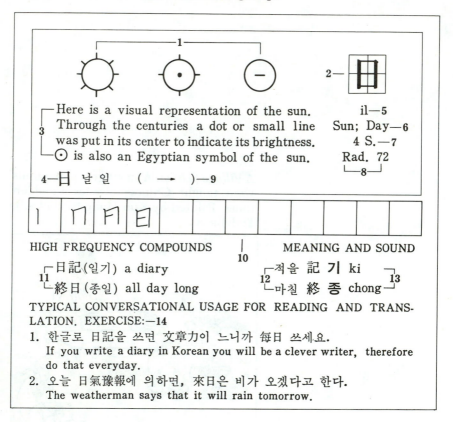

Here is a visual representation of the sun. Through the centuries a dot or small line was put in its center to indicate its brightness. ⊙ is also an Egyptian symbol of the sun.

il—5
Sun; Day—6
4 S.—7
Rad. 72

4—日 날 일   (→)—9

HIGH FREQUENCY COMPOUNDS | MEANING AND SOUND

10

日記(일기) a diary
終日 (종일) all day long

적을 記 기 ki
마칠 終 종 chong

TYPICAL CONVERSATIONAL USAGE FOR READING AND TRANSLATION. EXERCISE:—14

1. 한글로 日記을 쓰면 文章力이 느니까 每日 쓰세요.
   If you write a diary in Korean you will be a clever writer, therefore do that everyday.

2. 오늘 日氣豫報에 의하면, 來日은 비가 오겠다고 한다.
   The weatherman says that it will rain tomorrow.

Key:

1. The three steps are letter evolution of the pictograph.
2. The character
3. Etymological explanation
4. The character with Korean scripts
5. Pronunciation

6. Character definition
7. Stroke count
8. Radical information and number
9. Simplified character
10. Stroke order diagram
11. Frequency character compounds and meaning
12. New characters; meaning in Korean scripts
13. Pronunciation of compound characters. The Romanized transcription in this textbook is known as the "McCune-Reischauer Romanization" which is the transcription most widely used.
14. Exercise: Typical conversational usage for reading and translation. Especially this column utilized for useful application. For example, proverbs, maxims and Korean common sayings and the ability to understanding compositions.

The Division of Characters: Classified by the order of creation in the book of *Genesis*.

Abbreviations

   S. : Strokes

   Rad. : Radical

Take the character for day (日) and by adding one line try to make eight new characters.

目	눈 목 eye	田	밭 전 field
旦	아침 단 morning	由	말미암을 유 cause
㫤	오랠 구 old	甲	갑옷 갑 armour
白	흴 백 white	申	납 신 monkey; report

1. 宇宙 우주 The Universe

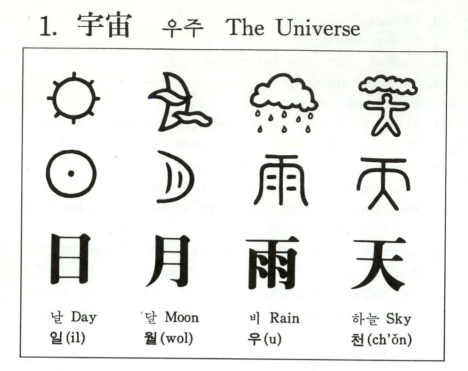

날 Day · 달 Moon · 비 Rain · 하늘 Sky
일 (il) · 월 (wol) · 우 (u) · 천 (ch'ŏn)

太初에 하나님이 天地를 創造하시니라. (創世記 1 : 1)

In the beginning God created the heavens and the earth.
(*Genesis* 1 : 1)

땅이 混沌하고 空虛하며 黑暗이 깊음 위에 있고 하나님의 神은 水面에 運行하시니라. 하나님이 가라사대 빛이 있으라 하시매 빛이 있었고 그 빛이 하나님의 보시기에 좋았더라. 하나님이 빛과 어둠을 나누사 빛을 낮이라 稱하시고 어두움을 밤이라 稱하시니라. 저녁이 되며 아침이 되니 이는 첫째 날이니라.
(創世記, *Gen.* 1 : 2~5)

하나님이 가라사대 하늘의 穹蒼에 光明이 있어 晝夜를 나뉘게 하라. 또 그 光明으로 하여 徵兆와 四時와 日字와 年限이 이루라. 또 그 光明이 하늘의 穹蒼에 있어 땅에 비춰라 하시고 하나님이 두 큰 光明을 만드사 큰 光明으로 낮을 主管하게 하시고 작은 光明으로 밤을 主管하게 하시며 또 별들을 만드시고 …
(創世記, *Gen.* 1 : 14~16)

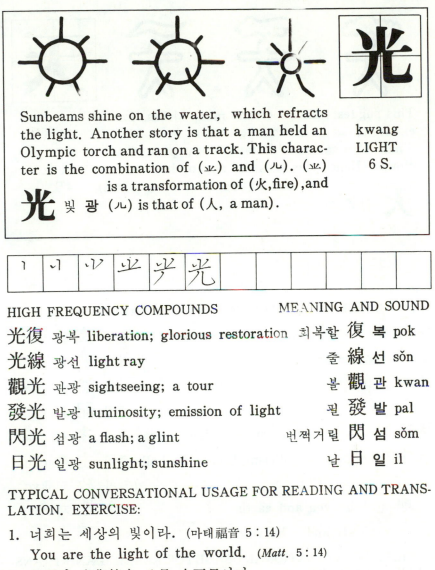

Sunbeams shine on the water, which refracts the light. Another story is that a man held an Olympic torch and ran on a track. This character is the combination of (火) and (儿). (火) is a transformation of (火, fire), and

光 빛 광 (儿) is that of (人, a man).

kwang
LIGHT
6 S.

HIGH FREQUENCY COMPOUNDS

MEANING AND SOUND

光復 광복 liberation; glorious restoration   회복할 復 복 pok

光線 광선 light ray   줄 線 선 sŏn

觀光 관광 sightseeing; a tour   볼 觀 관 kwan

發光 발광 luminosity; emission of light   필 發 발 pal

閃光 섬광 a flash; a glint   번쩍거릴 閃 섬 sŏm

日光 일광 sunlight; sunshine   날 日 일 il

TYPICAL CONVERSATIONAL USAGE FOR READING AND TRANSLATION. EXERCISE:

1. 너희는 세상의 빛이라. (마태福音 5 : 14)
   You are the light of the world. (*Matt.* 5 : 14)

2. 韓國의 光復節은 八月 十五日이다.
   Korea's Liberation Day is August fifteenth.

3. 民俗村에 外國觀光客들이 많았어요.
   There were a lot of foreign tourists in the Folk Village.

4. 여호와는 나의 빛이요 救援이시라. (詩篇 27 : 1)
   The Lord is my light and my salvation. (*Ps.* 27 : 1)

This suggests an important man, Moses, for example, as he is coming down from Mt. Sinai. One can see his face is up near the clouds. Hence the sense of sky or heaven.

ch'ŏn
SKY
HEAVEN
4 S.

(Exodus 20 : 16) *(Genesis* 1 : 6~8)

天 하늘 천

HIGH FREQUENCY COMPOUNDS

天文學 천문학 science of astronomy

天使 천사 an angel

天然記念物 천연기념물 a natural monument

天才 천재 a genius; a very brilliant person

天主教 천주교 Catholicism; Roman Catholic Church

天地 천지 heaven and earth

天下 천하 all under heaven

MEANING AND SOUND

글월 文 문 mun

부릴 使 사 sa

그럴 然 연 yŏn

기록할 記 기 ki

재주 才 재 chae

주인 主 주 chu

가르칠 教 교 kyo

땅 地 지 chi

아래 下 하 ha

TYPICAL CONVERSATIONAL USAGE FOR READING AND TRANSLATION. EXERCISE:

1. 하늘의 별 따기 : 성취하기 매우 어려움을 이르는 말.
   Plucking stars from heaven. (a very difficult work to do)

2. 心靈이 가난한자 자는 福이 있나니 天國이 저희 것임이요. (마태福音 5 : 3) Blessed are the poor in spirit, for theirs in the kingdom of heaven. (*Matt.* 5 : 3)

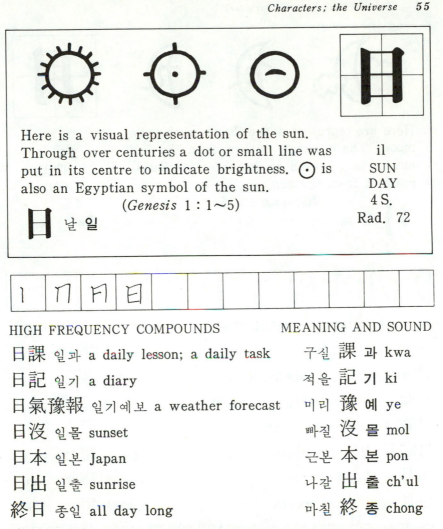

Here is a visual representation of the sun. Through over centuries a dot or small line was put in its centre to indicate brightness. ⊙ is also an Egyptian symbol of the sun.

(Genesis 1 : 1∼5)

日 날 일

il
SUN
DAY
4 S.
Rad. 72

HIGH FREQUENCY COMPOUNDS

日課 일과 a daily lesson; a daily task

日記 일기 a diary

日氣豫報 일기예보 a weather forecast

日沒 일몰 sunset

日本 일본 Japan

日出 일출 sunrise

終日 종일 all day long

MEANING AND SOUND

구실 課 과 kwa

적을 記 기 ki

미리 豫 예 ye

빠질 沒 몰 mol

근본 本 본 pon

나갈 出 출 ch'ul

마칠 終 종 chong

TYPICAL CONVERSATIONAL USAGE FOR READING AND TRANSLATION. EXERCISE:

1. 한글로 日記를 쓰면 文章力이 느니까 이제부터 그렇게 하세요. If you write a diary in Korean, you will be a clever writer, therefore do that from now on.

2. 오늘 日氣豫報에 의하면 이슬비가 온 후에 午後에는 개겠다고 한다. According to today's weather forecast, it is said that after a light drizzle in the morning there will be clearing in the afternoon.

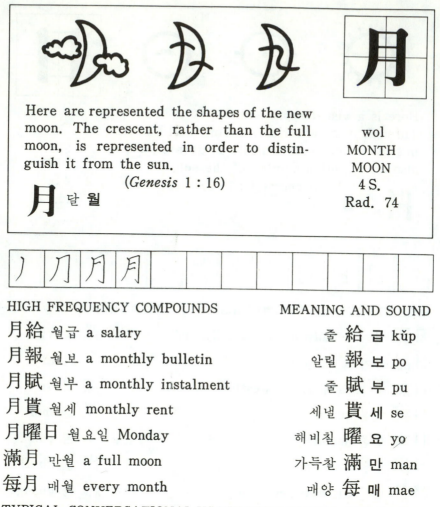

Here are represented the shapes of the new moon. The crescent, rather than the full moon, is represented in order to distinguish it from the sun.

(*Genesis* 1 : 16)

月 달 월

wol
MONTH
MOON
4 S.
Rad. 74

HIGH FREQUENCY COMPOUNDS

月給 월급 a salary

月報 월보 a monthly bulletin

月賦 월부 a monthly instalment

月貰 월세 monthly rent

月曜日 월요일 Monday

滿月 만월 a full moon

每月 매월 every month

MEANING AND SOUND

줄 給 급 kŭp

알릴 報 보 po

줄 賦 부 pu

세낼 貰 세 se

해비칠 曜 요 yo

가득찰 滿 만 man

매양 每 매 mae

TYPICAL CONVERSATIONAL USAGE FOR READING AND TRANSLATION. EXERCISE:

1. 달도 차면 기운다 : 세상의 온갖 것이 한번 성하면 다시 줄어든다는 말. The moon wanes when its brightest rays fade.

2. 月給장이는 生活이 맑은데, 목돈 구하기가 힘들다. A salary man's life is simple but it is difficult for him to accumulate a large sum of money

3. 歲月如流 (세월여류) : 세월은 흐르는 물과 같다. The months and years pass swiftly.

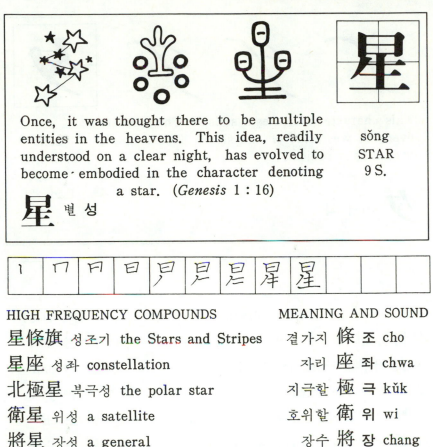

Once, it was thought there to be multiple entities in the heavens. This idea, readily understood on a clear night, has evolved to become embodied in the character denoting a star. (*Genesis* 1 : 16)

星 별 성

sŏng
STAR
9 S.

| 丨 | 冂 | 冃 | 日 | 旦 | 旦 | 旦 | 早 | 星 | | | |

HIGH FREQUENCY COMPOUNDS

星條旗 성조기 the Stars and Stripes

星座 성좌 constellation

北極星 북극성 the polar star

衛星 위성 a satellite

將星 장성 a general

彗星 혜성 a comet

MEANING AND SOUND

곁가지 條 조 cho

자리 座 좌 chwa

지극할 極 극 kŭk

호위할 衛 위 wi

장수 將 장 chang

비 彗 혜 hye

TYPICAL CONVERSATIONAL USAGE FOR READING AND TRANSLATION. EXERCISE:

1. 東方博士 세 사람이 별을 보고 아기 예수를 찾아가 敬拜했다.
   The three wise men of the east followed the star found the baby Jesus and worshipped Him.

2. 우리 나라에서 五星將軍이 누구인지 아십니까?
   Do you know who is the five star general in our country?

3. 天文學은 별과 모든 天體에 관한 것을 연구하는 學問이다.
   Astronomy is the study of stars, the sun, the moon and planets.

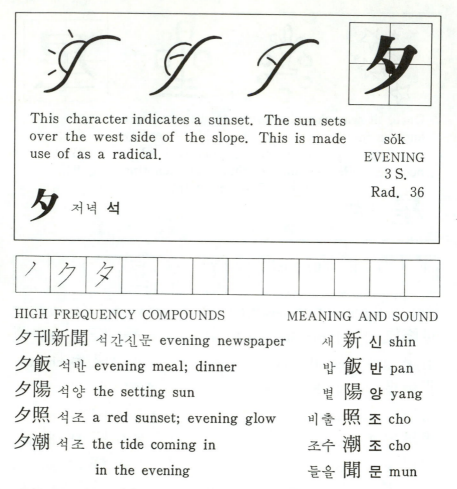

This character indicates a sunset. The sun sets over the west side of the slope. This is made use of as a radical.

sŏk
EVENING
3 S.
Rad. 36

夕 저녁 석

HIGH FREQUENCY COMPOUNDS

夕刊新聞 석간신문 evening newspaper

夕飯 석반 evening meal; dinner

夕陽 석양 the setting sun

夕照 석조 a red sunset; evening glow

夕潮 석조 the tide coming in

      in the evening

MEANING AND SOUND

새 新 신 shin

밥 飯 반 pan

볕 陽 양 yang

비출 照 조 cho

조수 潮 조 cho

들을 聞 문 mun

TYPICAL CONVERSATIONAL USAGE FOR READING AND TRANSLATION. EXERCISE:

1. 一朝一夕(일조일석) : 하루 아침이나 하루 저녁처럼 짧은 時日 In a brief interval.

2. 지금은 보통 夕飯대신 저녁이라고 많이 부른다. Now instead of being called *sŏkpan*, dinner is generally called *chŏnyŏk*.

3. 몬트레이 海岸은 물개의 서식처로도 有名하지만 해 지는 夕陽 의 경치도 퍽 아름답다. The Monterey beach is famous not only for being a habitat for seals but also the beauty of its setting sun.

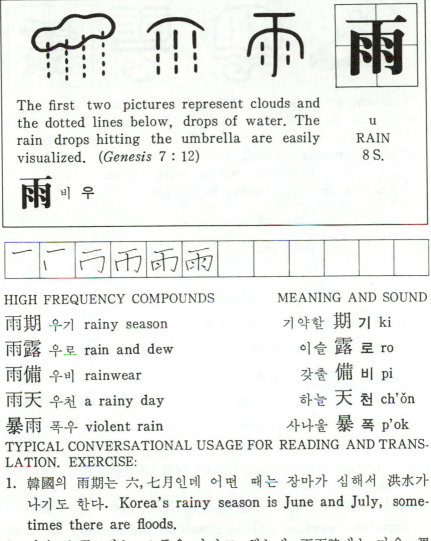

The first two pictures represent clouds and the dotted lines below, drops of water. The rain drops hitting the umbrella are easily visualized. (*Genesis* 7 : 12)

u

RAIN

8 S.

雨 비 우

HIGH FREQUENCY COMPOUNDS

雨期 우기 rainy season

雨露 우로 rain and dew

雨備 우비 rainwear

雨天 우천 a rainy day

暴雨 폭우 violent rain

MEANING AND SOUND

기약할 期 기 ki

이슬 露 로 ro

갖출 備 비 pi

하늘 天 천 ch'ŏn

사나울 暴 폭 p'ok

TYPICAL CONVERSATIONAL USAGE FOR READING AND TRANSLATION. EXERCISE:

1. 韓國의 雨期는 六, 七月인데 어떤 때는 장마가 심해서 洪水가 나기도 한다. Korea's rainy season is June and July, sometimes there are floods.

2. 다음 金曜日에는 소풍을 가기로 했는데 雨天時에는 다음 週로 연기하기로 했다. We have a plan to go on a picnic next Friday, but if it rains, we must postpone it next week.

3. 雨後竹筍 (우후죽순) : 비 온 뒤에 무럭무럭 여기저기 솟는 竹筍 ; 어떠한 일이 한때에 많이 일어남. Bamboo shoots after rain. (springs up like mushrooms after rain)

4. 風雨大作 (풍우대작) : 바람이 몹시 불고 비가 많이 옴.

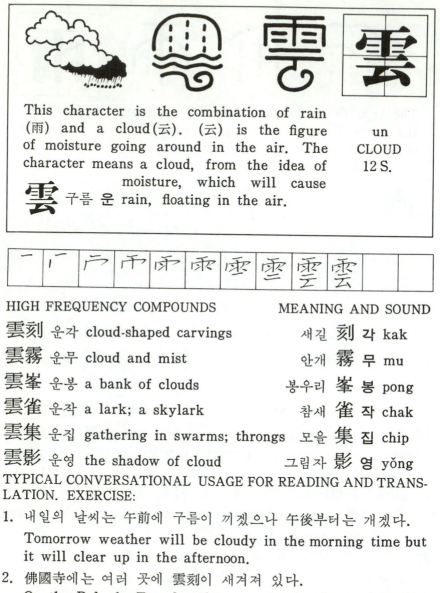

This character is the combination of rain (雨) and a cloud (云). (云) is the figure of moisture going around in the air. The character means a cloud, from the idea of moisture, which will cause rain, floating in the air.

un
CLOUD
12 S.

雲 구름 운

HIGH FREQUENCY COMPOUNDS

雲刻 운각 cloud-shaped carvings

雲霧 운무 cloud and mist

雲峯 운봉 a bank of clouds

雲雀 운작 a lark; a skylark

雲集 운집 gathering in swarms; throngs

雲影 운영 the shadow of cloud

MEANING AND SOUND

새길 刻 각 kak

안개 霧 무 mu

봉우리 峯 봉 pong

참새 雀 작 chak

모을 集 집 chip

그림자 影 영 yŏng

TYPICAL CONVERSATIONAL USAGE FOR READING AND TRANSLATION. EXERCISE:

1. 내일의 날씨는 午前에 구름이 끼겠으나 午後부터는 개겠다.

   Tomorrow weather will be cloudy in the morning time but it will clear up in the afternoon.

2. 佛國寺에는 여러 곳에 雲刻이 새겨져 있다.

   On the Pulguk Temple, there are many places decorated with cloud-shaped carvings.

3. 지난 土曜日에 國民學校 運動場에는 많은 사람들이 雲集했었다.

   Last Saturday, many people gathered on the elementary school playground.

This character calls to mind the experiment done by Ben Franklin, who introduced proof of electricity to westerners. This he did when one cloudy day the kite, with the key attached to it, drew sparks. The Korean kite's origin is traced to a general, Kim Yu-shin of the Shilla dynasty.

chŏn

ELECTRICITY
LIGHTNING
13 S.

電 전기 전
번개 전

ーーーーーーーーーーーー

HIGH FREQUENCY COMPOUNDS

電氣 전기 electricity

電氣工學 전기공학 electrical engineering

電力 전력 electric power

電報 전보 telegram

電子顯微鏡 전자현미경 electronic microscope

電池 전지 battery

電話 전화 telephone

MEANING AND SOUND

기운 氣 기 ki

장인 工 공 kong

힘 力 력 ryŏk

알릴 報 보 po

나타날 顯 현 hyŏn

거울 鏡 경 kyŏng

연못 池 지 chi

말할 話 화 hwa

TYPICAL CONVERSATIONAL USAGE FOR READING AND TRANSLATION. EXERCISE:

1. 새로 이사왔으니까 電話局에 가서 電話架設을 申請해야겠다.
   Because I have just moved, I have to go to the telephone office and request installation of a telephone.

2. 公衆電話가 어디 있는지 아세요?
   Do you know where the public phone is?

3. 電光石火(전광석화) : 번갯불과 돌을 쳐서 번쩍하는 불.

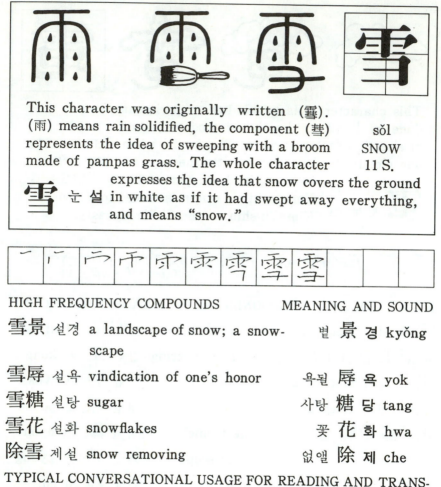

This character was originally written (霽).
(雨) means rain solidified, the component (彗)
represents the idea of sweeping with a broom
made of pampas grass. The whole character
expresses the idea that snow covers the ground
雪 눈 설 in white as if it had swept away everything,
and means "snow."

sŏl
SNOW
11 S.

HIGH FREQUENCY COMPOUNDS   MEANING AND SOUND

雪景 설경 a landscape of snow; a snow-   별 景 경 kyŏng
            scape

雪辱 설욕 vindication of one's honor   욕될 辱 욕 yok

雪糖 설탕 sugar   사탕 糖 당 tang

雪花 설화 snowflakes   꽃 花 화 hwa

除雪 제설 snow removing   없앨 除 제 che

TYPICAL CONVERSATIONAL USAGE FOR READING AND TRANS-
LATION. EXERCISE:

1. 눈이 많이 오는 것은 豊年이 든다는 表示이다. Abundant snow
   is the sign of a fruitful year; a snowy year, a rich year.

2. 雪糖은 重要한 輸入品目의 하나이다.
   Sugar is one of the important import items.

3. 雪霜加霜(설상가상) : 눈 위에 서리가 덮임 ; 불행한 일이 엎친
   데 덮치어서 거듭 일어남. Frost on the snow. (to make
   matters worse)

4. 北風寒雪(북풍한설) : 북쪽에서 불어오는 된바람과 차가운 눈.

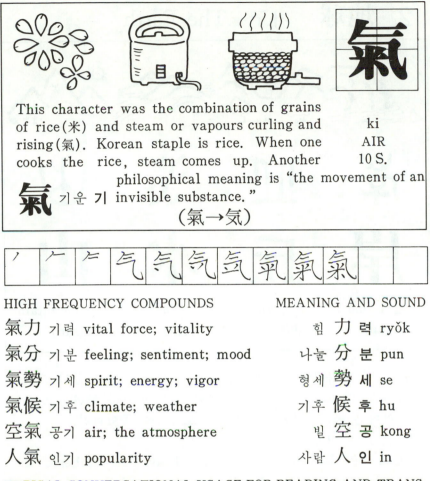

This character was the combination of grains of rice (米) and steam or vapours curling and rising (氣). Korean staple is rice. When one cooks the rice, steam comes up. Another philosophical meaning is "the movement of an invisible substance."

ki
AIR
10 S.

氣 기운 **기** invisible substance."

(氣→気)

/ 一 二 气 气 氕 氘 氙 氚 氣 氣

HIGH FREQUENCY COMPOUNDS

氣力 기력 vital force; vitality

氣分 기분 feeling; sentiment; mood

氣勢 기세 spirit; energy; vigor

氣候 기후 climate; weather

空氣 공기 air; the atmosphere

人氣 인기 popularity

MEANING AND SOUND

힘 力 력 ryŏk

나눌 分 분 pun

형세 勢 세 se

기후 候 후 hu

빌 空 공 kong

사람 人 인 in

TYPICAL CONVERSATIONAL USAGE FOR READING AND TRANSLATION. EXERCISE:

1. 나는 사철의 氣候가 변화되는 곳에서 사는 것을 좋아한다.
   I like to live in a place with the four seasons.

2. 空氣 맑고 바다 경치가 좋은 곳이 어디입니까?
   What place has clean air and a nice seascape?

3. 요즘은 누가 人氣있는 俳優인가?
   Who is the most popular actor in these days?

4. 氣盡脈盡(기진맥진) : 氣運과 精力이 다함.
   Complete exhaustion.

2. 地球 지구 The Earth

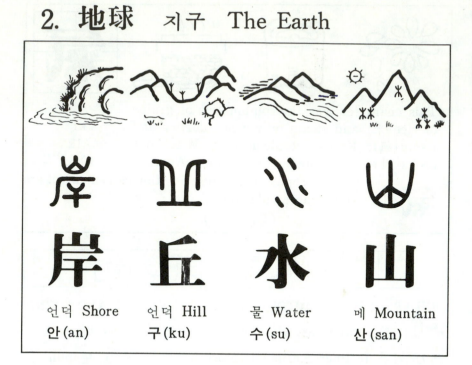

| 언덕 Shore | 언덕 Hill | 물 Water | 메 Mountain |
| 안 (an) | 구 (ku) | 수 (su) | 산 (san) |

하나님이 가라사대 天下의 물이 한 곳으로 모이고 뭍이 드러나라 하시매, 그대로 되니라. 하나님이 뭍을 땅이라 稱하시고 모인물을 바다라 稱하시니라. 하나님의 보시기에 좋았더라.
(創世記 1 : 9~10)

God said: Let the waters under heaven be gathered into one place and let the dry land appear; and it was so. God called the dry land earth and the gathering of the waters He called seas, and God saw that it was good.

(*Genesis* 1 : 9~10)

옷을 덮음같이 땅을 바다로 덮으시매 물이 山들 위에 섰더니⋯ 主께서 물의 境界를 定하여 넘치지 못하게 하시며 다시 돌아와 땅을 덮지 못하게 하셨나이다. 여호와께서 샘으로 골짜기에서 솟아나게 하시고 山 사이에 흐르게 하사 들의 各 짐승에게 마시우니 들 나귀들도 解渴하며 空中의 새들이 그 가에서 깃들며 나무가지 사이에서 소리를 發하는도다. (詩篇, *Psalms* 104 : 6, 9~12)

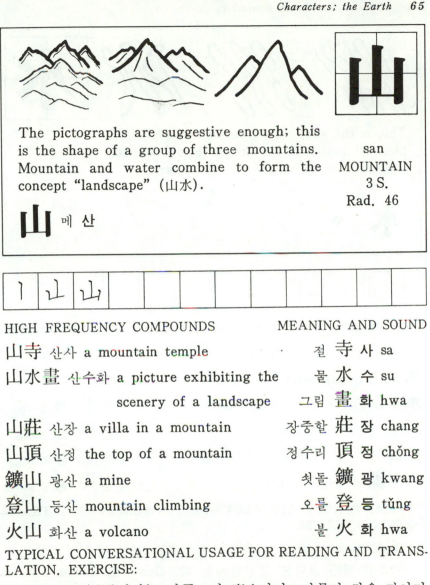

The pictographs are suggestive enough; this is the shape of a group of three mountains. Mountain and water combine to form the concept "landscape" (山水).

山 메 산

san
MOUNTAIN
3 S.
Rad. 46

丨	屮	山							

HIGH FREQUENCY COMPOUNDS   **MEANING AND SOUND**

山寺 산사 a mountain temple   절 寺 사 sa

山水畫 산수화 a picture exhibiting the   물 水 수 su
           scenery of a landscape   그림 畫 화 hwa

山莊 산장 a villa in a mountain   장중할 莊 장 chang

山頂 산정 the top of a mountain   정수리 頂 정 chŏng

鑛山 광산 a mine   쇳돌 鑛 광 kwang

登山 등산 mountain climbing   오를 登 등 tŭng

火山 화산 a volcano   불 火 화 hwa

TYPICAL CONVERSATIONAL USAGE FOR READING AND TRANSLATION. EXERCISE:

1. 塵合泰山(진합태산) : 티끌모아 泰山이라 ; 아무리 작은 것이라도 자꾸 모이면 큰 것이 된다는 뜻. A mountain is made of many tiny things. (Drop by drop fills the tub.)

2. 泰山이 높다 하되 하늘 아래 메이로다. Even though the great mountains are high, they are still under the heavens.

3. 人山人海(인산인해) : 사람이 헤아릴 수 없이 많이 모인 상태.

This is the shape of a river or waterfall. The pictorial quality of the ideograph is sufficiently suggestive of flowing fluid, or water.

su
WATER
4 S.
Rad. 85

水 물 수

丿 丬 氺 水

HIGH FREQUENCY COMPOUNDS

水力電氣 수력전기 hydraulic power

水利 수리 utilization of water

水素爆彈 수소폭탄 a hydrogen bomb

水泳 수영 swimming

水筒 수통 a canteen; a water bottle

水平線 수평선 the horizon

MEANING AND SOUND

기운 氣 기 ki

이로울 利 리 ri

폭발할 爆 폭 p'ok

수영할 泳 영 yŏng

대통 筒 통 t'ong

평평할 平 평 p'yŏng

TYPICAL CONVERSATIONAL USAGE FOR READING AND TRANSLATION. EXERCISE:

1. 국에 덴 놈 찬물 보고 분다 : 어떤 일에 한번 겁을 먹으면 그와 비슷한 것만 보아도 조심한다는 말. One who has burned his lips with broth blows on cold water. (Once bitten, twice shy)

2. 山戰水戰 다 겪었네 : 살면서 모든 世上經驗 다 겪어 보았다. I have fought in the mountain and have fought in the sea: which means I have experienced all the world in my life time.

3. 바다에 水平線, 사막에 地平線 모두 한일자같이 보인다.

This represents a bit of the earth, the vertical line being something that grows out thru the earth.
(*Genesis* 2 : 6) (*Job* 33 : 6)

土 흙 토

t'o
SOIL
EARTH
3 S.
Rad. 32

一 十 土

HIGH FREQUENCY COMPOUNDS

MEANING AND SOUND

土管 토관 an earthen pipe

土器 토기 earthenware

土産物 토산물 product of the district

土壤 토양 soil

土地所有權 토지소유권 landownership

土着 토착 aboriginality; indigenous

관 管 관 kwan

그릇 器 기 ki

낳을 産 산 san

흙 壤 양 yang

땅 地 지 chi

붙을 着 착 ch'ak

TYPICAL CONVERSATIONAL USAGE FOR READING AND TRANSLATION. EXERCISE:

1. 沙器 그릇이 나오기 前에는 거의 다 土器 그릇을 썼다.
   Before the appearance of porcelain ware almost everyone used earthenware.

2. 강화도의 土産物은 花紋席하고 감이다.
   Kanghwa Island's local products are the floral pattern mattress and persimmons.

3. 누가 土地所有權者인지 알아보세요.
   Would you find out who has the landownership?

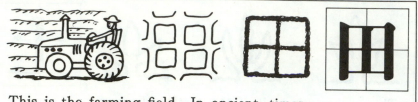

This is the farming field. In ancient times, it was a field partitioned into nine sections, in which one section's harvest was offered as the tax. It became adequate to show the drawing of a field of four plots 밭 전 of land, with irrigation ditches all around the edges.

chŏn
FIELD
5 S.
Rad. 102

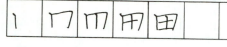

HIGH FREQUENCY COMPOUNDS

田畓 전답 paddy fields and dry fields

田園 전원 fields and gardens

田園文學 전원문학 pastoral literature

田園生活 전원생활 country life

鹽田 염전 a salt farm

油田 유전 an oil field

MEANING AND SOUND

논 畓 답 tap

동산 園 원 won

배울 學 학 hak

날 生 생 saeng

소금 鹽 염 yŏm

기름 油 유 yu

TYPICAL CONVERSATIONAL USAGE FOR READING AND TRANSLATION. EXERCISE:

1. 門前沃畓 (문전옥답) : 바로 집 앞에 있는 토지 ; 좋은 논과 밭을 말한다. The land right in front of one's house. (fertile fields)

2. 내가 은퇴하면 번잡한 都市보다 경치 좋은 田園에서 여생을 보내겠다. When I retire, I will spend the rest of my life in the beautiful countryside rather than in the crowded city.

3. 仁川의 朱安에는 1970 年까지 鹽田이 있었다.
   Chuan in Inchŏn had saltfarms until 1970.

You can see ⊞ representing "field" or "land," and 辰 or 辰 a "plough." To plough the land is symbolical of agriculture.

nong
AGRICULTURE
13 S.

農 농사 농

丶	冂	帀	曲	曲	曲	芇	芇	芇	農	農	農

HIGH FREQUENCY COMPOUNDS	MEANING AND SOUND
農事 농사 farming	일 事 사 sa
農業 농업 agriculture	업 業 업 ŏp
農業協同組合 농업협동조합 an Agricul-	화할 協 협 hyŏp
tural Cooperative Federation	한가지 同 동 tong
農作物 농작물 the crops; farm produce	지을 作 작 chak
農場 농장 a farm	마당 場 장 chang
農村 농촌 a farm village	마을 村 촌 ch'on

TYPICAL CONVERSATIONAL USAGE FOR READING AND TRANSLATION. EXERCISE:

1. 논과 밭에 農作物이 잘 되어 收穫이 많은 해를 豊年이라 한다. It is called a bumper year when the harvests from the fields are bountiful.

2. 경작이 시작될 때 다른 기술도 뒤따른다. 따라서 農民은 人間文明의 創始者이다. When tillage begins, other arts follow. The farmers therefore are the founders of human civilization. (D. Webster)

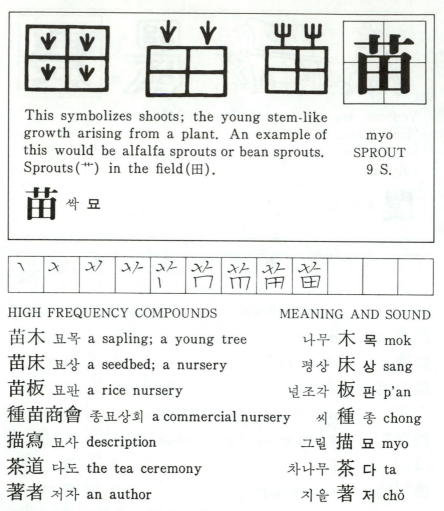

This symbolizes shoots; the young stem-like growth arising from a plant. An example of this would be alfalfa sprouts or bean sprouts. Sprouts (艹) in the field (田).

myo
SPROUT
9 S.

苗 싹 묘

HIGH FREQUENCY COMPOUNDS

苗木 묘목 a sapling; a young tree

苗床 묘상 a seedbed; a nursery

苗板 묘판 a rice nursery

種苗商會 종묘상회 a commercial nursery

描寫 묘사 description

茶道 다도 the tea ceremony

著者 저자 an author

MEANING AND SOUND

나무 木 목 mok

평상 床 상 sang

널조각 板 판 p'an

씨 種 종 chong

그릴 描 묘 myo

차나무 茶 다 ta

지을 著 저 chŏ

TYPICAL CONVERSATIONAL USAGE FOR READING AND TRANSLATION. EXERCISE:

1. 볶은 콩에 싹이 날까 : 아주 希望이 없음을 뜻하는 말.
   No bud will burst from a roasted bean. (All hope is lost.)

2. 모내기라는 말은 苗板에서 모를 뽑아서 옮겨 심는 일을 말한다.
   When young rice plants are transplanted from the seedbed to the ricepaddy it is called *monaegi*.

3. 서울, 東大門 앞에는 種苗商會가 많다. There are many commercial nurseries in front of the East Gate in Seoul.

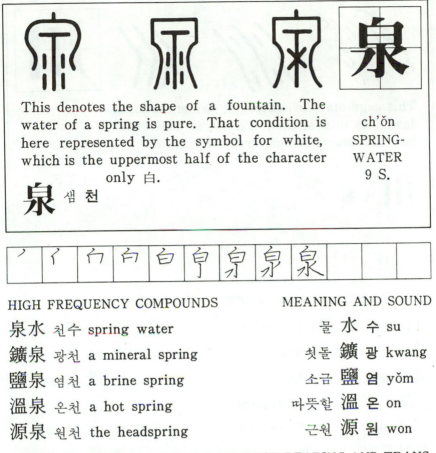

This denotes the shape of a fountain. The water of a spring is pure. That condition is here represented by the symbol for white, which is the uppermost half of the character only 白.

ch'ŏn
SPRING-
WATER
9 S.

泉 샘 천

HIGH FREQUENCY COMPOUNDS

泉水 천수 spring water

鑛泉 광천 a mineral spring

鹽泉 염천 a brine spring

溫泉 온천 a hot spring

源泉 원천 the headspring

MEANING AND SOUND

물 水 수 su

쇳돌 鑛 광 kwang

소금 鹽 염 yŏm

따뜻할 溫 온 on

근원 源 원 won

TYPICAL CONVERSATIONAL USAGE FOR READING AND TRANSLATION. EXERCISE:

1. 목마른 사람이 우물 판다 : 자기가 급하고 요긴해야 서둘러서 일을 시작한다는 말. A thirsty fellow digs a well. (Anyone in want should work out a plan to satisfy his desire.)

2. 溫泉에서 沐浴하면 皮膚病이 치료된다. If you bathe in a hot spring, it is a treatment for skin disease.

3. 〔♨〕 이것은 溫泉의 표시인데 韓國에도 많이 있다. This is a symbol of a hot spring. There are many hot springs in Korea too.

4. 콜로라도 江의 源泉이 어디인지 아느냐?

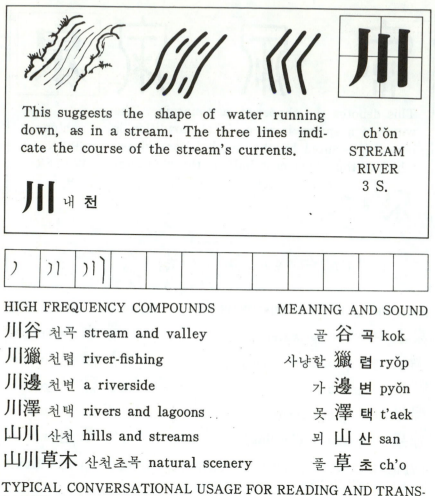

This suggests the shape of water running down, as in a stream. The three lines indicate the course of the stream's currents.

ch'ŏn
STREAM
RIVER
3 S.

川 내 천

))1)1|

HIGH FREQUENCY COMPOUNDS

川谷 천곡 stream and valley

川獵 천렵 river-fishing

川邊 천변 a riverside

川澤 천택 rivers and lagoons

山川 산천 hills and streams

山川草木 산천초목 natural scenery

MEANING AND SOUND

골 谷 곡 kok

사냥할 獵 렵 ryŏp

가 邊 변 pyŏn

못 澤 택 t'aek

뫼 山 산 san

풀 草 초 ch'o

TYPICAL CONVERSATIONAL USAGE FOR READING AND TRANSLATION. EXERCISE:

1. 소경이 開川 나무란다 : 제 잘못은 모르고 남만 탓한다는 말.
   The blind man blames the ditch. (It is useless to complain.)

2. 高山大川(고산대천) : 높은 山과 큰 江.
   High mountains and large rivers.

3. 川流不息(천류불식) : 냇물이 쉬지 않고 흐름.
   Continuous flow.

4. 山川依舊(산천의구) : 自然은 옛 모습대로 변함이 없음.
   Nature's appearance has never changed.

This depicts a picture of an islet, sandbank or delta in the middle of a river.

chu
REGION
STATE
6 S.

州 고을 주

HIGH FREQUENCY COMPOUNDS

州郡 주군 provinces and counties

州立 주립 established by the state

州兵 주병 a national guardsman

州知事 주지사 the governer of a state

MEANING AND SOUND

고을 郡 군 kun

설 立 립 rip

군사 兵 병 pyŏng

알 知 지 chi

TYPICAL CONVERSATIONAL USAGE FOR READING AND TRANSLATION. EXERCISE:

1. 美國은 州마다 州 政府가 있다.
   In America, each state has its own government.

2. 州立大學은 여기서 百 마일 떨어져 있다.
   The state college is hundred miles from here.

3. 州兵들은 夏期休暇 때 두 週間 特別訓練을 받는다.
   The National Guard received special training for two weeks during the summer vacation season.

4. 州知事는 어제 新聞에 새로운 敎育政策을 發表했다.
   The governor announced a new educational policy in yesterday's newspaper.

This picture represents a stone. The stone is located near a cliff. This is made use of as a radical.

sŏk
STONE
5 S.
Rad. 112

石 돌 석

HIGH FREQUENCY COMPOUNDS

石器時代 석기시대 the Stone Age

石鹽 석염 rock salt

石油 석유 petroleum

石炭 석탄 coal

石灰巖 석회암 limestone

金石文 금석문 inscription on bronze
and stone

化石 화석 fossilization; petrifaction

MEANING AND SOUND

대신할 代 대 tae

소금 鹽 염 yŏm

기름 油 유 yu

숯 炭 탄 t'an

재 灰 회 hoe

쇠 金 금 kŭm

글 文 문 mun

화할 化 화 hwa

TYPICAL CONVERSATIONAL USAGE FOR READING AND TRANSLATION. EXERCISE:

1. 성내어 돌부리 차면 내 발부리 아프다 : 쓸데없이 성을 내면 자기에게만 해롭다는 말. Kick a stone in anger, and you will hurt your own foot. (Quarreling does not pay.)

2. 내가 기둥으로 세운 이 돌이 하나님의 집이 될 것이요······ (創世記 28 : 22) This stone which I have set as a pillar shall be God's house······ (*Gen.* 28 : 22)

This is the sign of rising flames or fire, as it evolved from a pictograph of a campfire. Like Heraclitus of ancient Greece, Eastern thought has long compared life's vicissitudes with the flame: from fire come ashes, and from ashes comes life anew.

hwa
FIRE
4 S.
Rad. 86

火 불 화

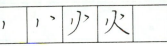

HIGH FREQUENCY COMPOUNDS

火傷 화상 a burn; a scald

火星 화성 Mars

火藥 화약 gunpowder

火葬 화장 cremation

火災 화재 fire accident

火災保險 화재보험 fire insurance

MEANING AND SOUND

다칠 傷 상 sang

별 星 성 sŏng

약 藥 약 yak

장사지낼 葬 장 chang

재앙 災 재 chae

보호할 保 보 po

TYPICAL CONVERSATIONAL USAGE FOR READING AND TRANSLATION. EXERCISE:

1. 火災는 담뱃불이나 漏電, 난로 사용의 不注意 등으로 생긴다. Fire accidents occur from cigarettes, short circuit or from careless usage of kerosene stoves.

2. 防火練習은 一年에 두 차례씩 실시하는데 다음주 火曜日에 있을 豫定이다. Fire drills are conducted twice a year and one is scheduled for next Tuesday.

3. 明若觀火 (명약관화) : 불을 보는 것처럼 밝음 ; 더 말할 나위 없이 明白함. As clear as daylight.

This is a picture of a four way street. The ideograph is a crossroad. So, quite naturally, it has come to mean "walking" or "to go."

haeng
WALKING
TO GO
6 S.

行 갈 **행**
　 항렬 **항**

HIGH FREQUENCY COMPOUNDS

行軍 행군 march

行方不明 행방불명 missing; lost

行商 행상 peddling; an itinerant

行人 행인 pedestrian; a wayfarer

行政 행정 administration

流行 유행 fashion; popularity

MEANING AND SOUND

군사 軍 군 kun

밝을 明 명 myŏng

장사 商 상 sang

사람 人 인 in

다스릴 政 정 chŏng

흐를 流 류 ryu

TYPICAL CONVERSATIONAL USAGE FOR READING AND TRANSLATION. EXERCISE:

1. 야간 行軍은 어두운 밤길이라 아주 어렵다. Night marches are very difficult because the way is not visible.

2. 行人은 차길을 건널 때 注意해야 하며 車도 行人을 살펴야 한다. When pedestrians cross a road they must be cautious and vehicles likewise must watch out for pedestrians.

3. 行政區域은 市街地圖에도 잘 나와 있다. Administrative districts are well defined even on the city map.

4. 田先生은 새해부터 우리 학교의 行政職을 맡게 되었다.

People are walking down the crossroad.
So there are foot prints (圭) along the street.
It appears to be a crossroad.

ka
STREET
12 S.

街 거리 **가**

| ノ | ィ | 彳 | 行 | 往 | 往 | 往 | 街 | | | |

HIGH FREQUENCY COMPOUNDS　　　　**MEANING AND SOUND**

街道 가도 a highway　　　　　　　　길 **道** 도 to

街頭演說 가두연설 a soapbox oratory;　머리 **頭** 두 tu

　　　　　a wayside speech　　　　펼 **演** 연 yŏn

街路燈 가로등 a road lamp　　　　　길 **路** 로 ro

街路樹 가로수 a roadside tree　　　나무 **樹** 수 su

商街 상가 business section　　　　장사 **商** 상 sang

**TYPICAL CONVERSATIONAL USAGE FOR READING AND TRANS-
LATION. EXERCISE:**

1. 선거 때가 되면 후보자들은 街頭演說에 열을 올린다. When
   election time rolls around, the candidates are enthusiastic
   in their speeches.

2. 어두운 밤중에도 街路燈이 켜 있어서 길 찾기에 便利하다.
   Even in the middle of a dark night, it is easy to find your
   way because the street lights are lit.

3. 街路樹는 여름에 시원한 그늘을 만들어 준다.
   The roadside trees make cool shade in summer.

This is a pictograph of a bird (至), bending its wings and darting downwards to the earth and reaching it. (至) is the modern form.

至 이를 지

chi
ARRIVE
REACH
6 S.
Rad. 133

一　乙　ス　玄　至　至

HIGH FREQUENCY COMPOUNDS

至今 지금 so far; up to now
至急郵便 지급우편 express mail

至大 지대 the greatest possible
至德 지덕 perfect virtue
至善 지선 the highest good
至誠 지성 devotion; sincerity

MEANING AND SOUND

이제 今 금 kŭm
급할 急 급 kŭp
우편 郵 우 u
큰 大 대 tae
큰 德 덕 tŏk
착할 善 선 sŏn
정성 誠 성 sŏng

TYPICAL CONVERSATIONAL USAGE FOR READING AND TRANS-LATION. EXERCISE:

1. 至今까지 그분한테서 答狀을 받지 못했어요.
   So far, I have had no reply from him yet.

2. 至急郵便物은 값이 비싸지만 속히 배달되는 특수 우편물이다.
   Express mail is expensive, but delivered quickly.

3. 至誠이면 感天 : 하늘은 스스로 돕는 자를 돕는다.
   Sincerity moves heaven.
   (Heaven helps those who help themselves.)

The water (水) flows down to the low land. The river must have a bridge. This character is the combination of (氵) and (工). (氵) is the transformation of (水) and (工) is shape of I beam. It represents a river.

kang
RIVER
6 S.

江 물 강

丶 氵 氵 汀 江

HIGH FREQUENCY COMPOUNDS

江南 강남 the south of river

江邊 강변 riverside; riverbank

江山 강산 rivers and mountains

江幅 강폭 the width of a river

江風 강풍 a river breeze

江湖 강호 rivers and lakes; scenery

MEANING AND SOUND

남쪽 南 남 nam

가 邊 변 pyŏn

메 山 산 san

폭 幅 폭 p'ok

바람 風 풍 p'ung

호수 湖 호 ho

TYPICAL CONVERSATIONAL USAGE FOR READING AND TRANSLATION. EXERCISE:

1. 世界에서 第一 긴 江이 무슨 江인가?
   Which river is the longest river in the world?

2. 江山은 쉽게 변하나 人間의 本性은 변하기 어렵다.
   Rivers and mountains may be easily changed, but human nature is changed with difficulty.

3. 서울의 漢江에는 다리가 18개 있다.
   There are eighteen bridges on the Han river in Seoul.

4. 江湖之樂(강호지락) : 自然을 벗삼아 누리는 즐거움.

A Navy ship participates in the Team Spirit operation in Korea. This character is the combination of water (氵), people (𠂉) and the figure of the top view of a ship (毋). A sailor salutes on the deck of ship.

海 바다 해　It means sea.

(海→海)

hae
SEA
10 S.

HIGH FREQUENCY COMPOUNDS

MEANING AND SOUND

海軍 해군 Navy

海難 해난 disaster at sea; ship wreck

海物 해물 marine products

海外 해외 overseas; abroad

公海 공해 the open sea; international waters

領海 영해 territorial waters; a marine belt

군사 軍 군 kun

어려울 難 난 nan

만물 物 물 mul

바깥 外 외 oe

공변될 公 공 kong

거느릴 領 령 ryŏng

TYPICAL CONVERSATIONAL USAGE FOR READING AND TRANSLATION. EXERCISE:

1. 萬川歸海, 而海不盈 (만천귀해, 이해불영) : 모든 강물이 바다로 흘러가지만 바다를 채울 수 없다. (傳道書 1 : 7) All the rivers run into the sea, yet the sea is not full. (*Ecc.* 1 : 7)

2. 海岸線이 보입니까? Do you see the costline?

3. 나는 진해의 海軍士官學校를 1980년에 卒業했다. I graduated from the Korean Naval Academy which is in Chinhae in 1980.

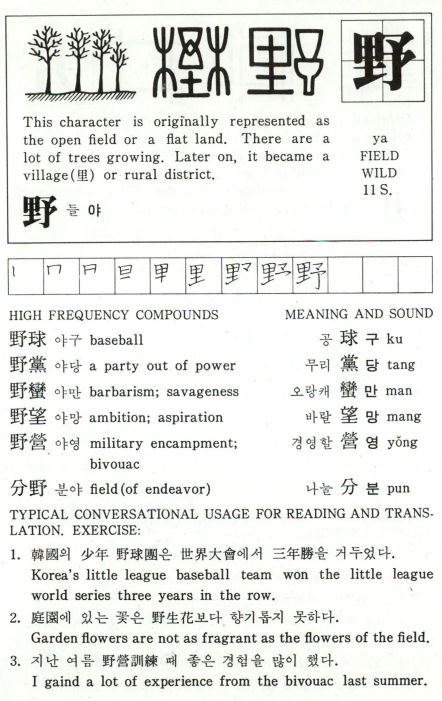

This character is originally represented as the open field or a flat land. There are a lot of trees growing. Later on, it became a village(里) or rural district.

ya
FIELD
WILD
11 S.

野 들 야

HIGH FREQUENCY COMPOUNDS

野球 야구 baseball

野黨 야당 a party out of power

野蠻 야만 barbarism; savageness

野望 야망 ambition; aspiration

野營 야영 military encampment; bivouac

分野 분야 field(of endeavor)

MEANING AND SOUND

공 球 구 ku

무리 黨 당 tang

오랑캐 蠻 만 man

바랄 望 망 mang

경영할 營 영 yŏng

나눌 分 분 pun

TYPICAL CONVERSATIONAL USAGE FOR READING AND TRANSLATION. EXERCISE:

1. 韓國의 少年 野球團은 世界大會에서 三年勝을 거두었다.
   Korea's little league baseball team won the little league world series three years in the row.

2. 庭園에 있는 꽃은 野生花보다 향기롭지 못하다.
   Garden flowers are not as fragrant as the flowers of the field.

3. 지난 여름 野營訓練 때 좋은 경험을 많이 했다.
   I gaind a lot of experience from the bivouac last summer.

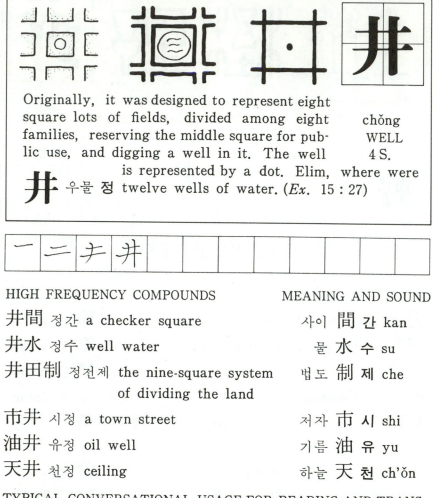

Originally, it was designed to represent eight square lots of fields, divided among eight families, reserving the middle square for public use, and digging a well in it. The well 井 우물 정 is represented by a dot. Elim, where were twelve wells of water. (*Ex.* 15 : 27)

chŏng
WELL
4 S.

HIGH FREQUENCY COMPOUNDS

井間 정간 a checker square

井水 정수 well water

井田制 정전제 the nine-square system of dividing the land

市井 시정 a town street

油井 유정 oil well

天井 천정 ceiling

MEANING AND SOUND

사이 間 간 kan

물 水 수 su

법도 制 제 che

저자 市 시 shi

기름 油 유 yu

하늘 天 천 ch'ŏn

TYPICAL CONVERSATIONAL USAGE FOR READING AND TRANSLATION. EXERCISE:

1. 臨渴掘井 (임갈굴정) : 목이 말라야 우물을 판다.
   One who is thirsty, makes a fountain.
2. 井底之蛙 (정저지와) : 우물 안 개구리.
   A frog in the well. (He did not know the ouside world.)
3. 甘井先渴 (감정선갈) : 맛있는 우물은 다른 우물보다 먼저 마른다. The well that has tasty water runs dry before the other wells because people drink only from that well.

The boy raced on a hurdle track. (阝) originally means a mound but looks like a flag.
This character represents a ground.

ryuk; yuk
LAND
11 S.

陸 뭍 륙

了	阝	阝一	阝十	阝土	阝圭	阝圭	阝圭	陸	

HIGH FREQUENCY COMPOUNDS

陸橋 육교 a footbridge; a overpass

陸軍 육군 Army; the land forces

陸路 육로 land route

大陸 대륙 continent; mainland

離陸 이륙 take-off; leaving the ground

着陸 착륙 landing

MEANING AND SOUND

다리 橋 교 kyo

군사 軍 군 kun

길 路 로 ro

큰 大 대 tae

떠날 離 리 ri

붙을 着 착 ch'ak

TYPICAL CONVERSATIONAL USAGE FOR READING AND TRANS-
LATION. EXERCISE:

1. 저 陸橋 앞에 무슨 商店이 있읍니까?
   What kind of store is in front of that overpass.

2. 나는 高等學校를 卒業하자마자 美陸軍에 入隊했다. I joined
   the U.S. Army as soon as I graduated from high school.

3. 美大陸은 언제 누가 發見했어요?
   Who and when discovered America?

4. 안개가 많이 끼면 航空機의 離着陸이 어렵다. If it is very
   foggy it is difficult for aircraft to land and take off.

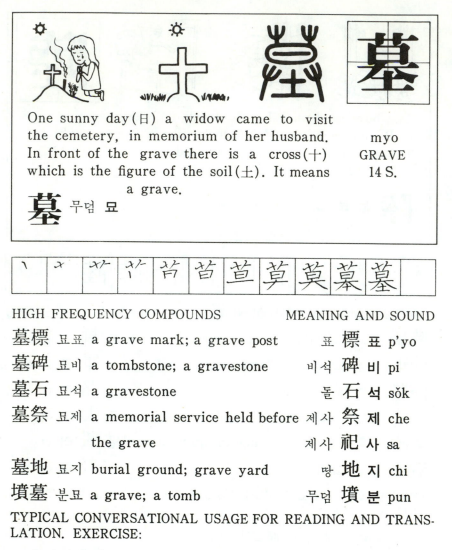

One sunny day(日) a widow came to visit the cemetery, in memorium of her husband. In front of the grave there is a cross(十) which is the figure of the soil(土). It means a grave.

myo
GRAVE
14 S.

墓 무덤 묘

HIGH FREQUENCY COMPOUNDS

MEANING AND SOUND

墓標 묘표 a grave mark; a grave post

墓碑 묘비 a tombstone; a gravestone

墓石 묘석 a gravestone

墓祭 묘제 a memorial service held before the grave

墓地 묘지 burial ground; grave yard

墳墓 분묘 a grave; a tomb

표 標 표 p'yo

비석 碑 비 pi

돌 石 석 sŏk

제사 祭 제 che

제사 祀 사 sa

땅 地 지 chi

무덤 墳 분 pun

TYPICAL CONVERSATIONAL USAGE FOR READING AND TRANSLATION. EXERCISE:

1. 무덤에서 울리는 슬픈 소리에 귀를 기울이라.
   Hark from the tombs a doleful sound. (*Issac Watts*)
2. 埋葬된자는 잃어진 것이 아니라 먼저 간 것이다.
   The buried are not lost, but gone before. (*Ebnezer Elliott*)
3. 墓碑는 風雨에 마멸되어 읽어 볼 수가 없다. I can not read the tombstone because it has been eroded away.
4. 顯忠日에는 墓地에 가는 사람들이 많습니다.

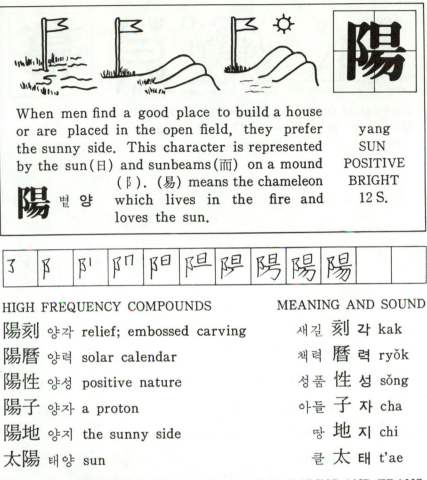

When men find a good place to build a house or are placed in the open field, they prefer the sunny side. This character is represented by the sun (日) and sunbeams (禹) on a mound (阝). (易) means the chameleon which lives in the fire and loves the sun.

陽 볕 양

yang
SUN
POSITIVE
BRIGHT
12 S.

HIGH FREQUENCY COMPOUNDS

陽刻 양각 relief; embossed carving

陽曆 양력 solar calendar

陽性 양성 positive nature

陽子 양자 a proton

陽地 양지 the sunny side

太陽 태양 sun

MEANING AND SOUND

새길 刻 각 kak

책력 曆 력 ryŏk

성품 性 성 sŏng

아들 子 자 cha

땅 地 지 chi

클 太 태 t'ae

TYPICAL CONVERSATIONAL USAGE FOR READING AND TRANSLATION. EXERCISE:

1. 憤을 내어도 罪를 짓지 말며 해가 지도록 憤을 품지 말라. (에베소書 4 : 26) When you are angry, do not commit on sin; do not remain angry until sundown. (*Ephesian* 4 : 26)

2. 해와 달이 캄캄해질 것이다. (요엘書 3 : 15)
The sun and moon will grow dark. (*Joel* 3 : 15)

3. 陰曆은 農業에 陽曆보다 便利하다. In agriculture the lunar calendar is more convenient than the solar calendar.

4. 陰地轉陽地變 (음지전 양지변) : 음지가 양지로 변한다.

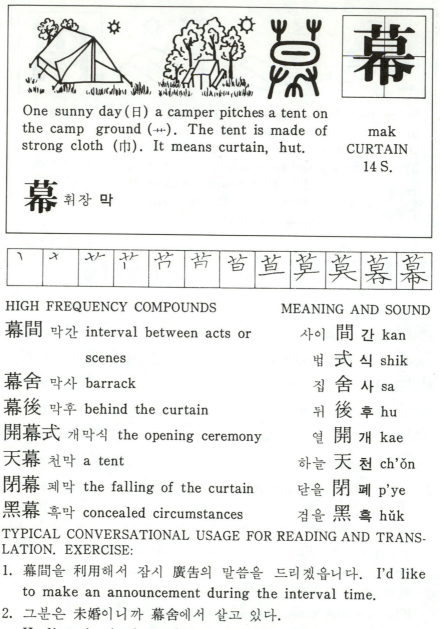

One sunny day (日) a camper pitches a tent on the camp ground (艹). The tent is made of strong cloth (巾). It means curtain, hut.

mak
CURTAIN
14 S.

幕 휘장 막

HIGH FREQUENCY COMPOUNDS

幕間 막간 interval between acts or scenes

幕舍 막사 barrack

幕後 막후 behind the curtain

開幕式 개막식 the opening ceremony

天幕 천막 a tent

閉幕 폐막 the falling of the curtain

黑幕 흑막 concealed circumstances

MEANING AND SOUND

사이 間 간 kan

법 式 식 shik

집 舍 사 sa

뒤 後 후 hu

열 開 개 kae

하늘 天 천 ch'ŏn

닫을 閉 폐 p'ye

검을 黑 흑 hŭk

TYPICAL CONVERSATIONAL USAGE FOR READING AND TRANSLATION. EXERCISE:

1. 幕間을 利用해서 잠시 廣告의 말씀을 드리겠읍니다. I'd like to make an announcement during the interval time.

2. 그분은 未婚이니까 幕舍에서 살고 있다.
He lives in the barrack because he is single.

3. 여름 放學에 캠핑가려고 天幕을 하나 샀다.
I bought a tent in order to go camping this summer.

3. 樹木　수목　Trees

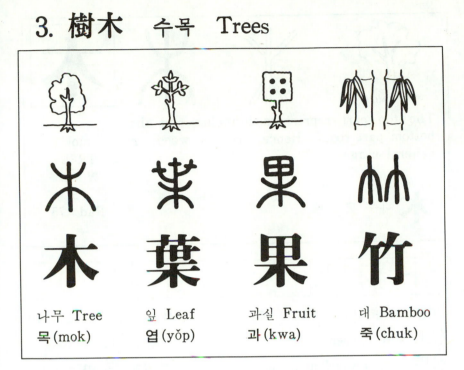

나무 Tree	잎 Leaf	과실 Fruit	대 Bamboo
목 (mok)	엽 (yŏp)	과 (kwa)	죽 (chuk)

하나님이 가라사대 땅은 풀과 씨 맺는 菜蔬와 各其 種類대로 씨 가진 열매 맺는 果木을 내라 하시매 그대로 되어 땅이 풀과 各其 種類대로 씨 맺는 菜蔬와 各其 種類대로 씨 가진 열매 맺는 나무를 내니 하나님의 보시기에 좋았더라. 저녁이 되며 아침이 되니 이는 세째날이니라. (創世記 1 : 11~13)

God said: Let the earth produce vegetation, various kinds of seed-bearing herbs and fruit-bearing trees with their respective seeds in the fruit upon the earth; and it was so. The earth produced vegetation, various kinds of seed-bearing herbs and fruit-bearing trees with their respective seeds in the fruit, and God saw that it was good. There was evening and there was morning, a third day.
(*Genesis* 1 : 11~13)

義人은 棕櫚나무같이 蕃盛하며 레바논의 柏香木같이 發育하리로다. (詩篇, *Psalms* 92 : 12)

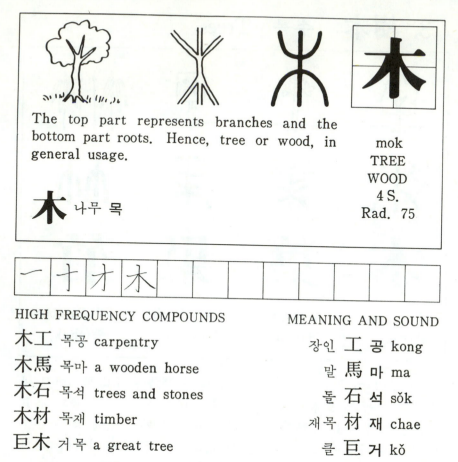

The top part represents branches and the bottom part roots. Hence, tree or wood, in general usage.

mok
TREE
WOOD
4 S.
Rad. 75

木 나무 목

一 十 才 木

HIGH FREQUENCY COMPOUNDS

木工 목공 carpentry

木馬 목마 a wooden horse

木石 목석 trees and stones

木材 목재 timber

巨木 거목 a great tree

MEANING AND SOUND

장인 工 공 kong

말 馬 마 ma

돌 石 석 sŏk

재목 材 재 chae

클 巨 거 kŏ

TYPICAL CONVERSATIONAL USAGE FOR READING AND TRANSLATION. EXERCISE:

1. 나무가 쓰러지면 그늘이 사라진다.
   When the tree falls, there is no shade.

2. 원수는 외나무다리에서 만난다 : 남에게 악한 일을 하면 그 벌을 받을 때가 반드시 온다는 말. Meeting an enemy on a single log-bridge.

3. 열 번 찍어 안 넘어지는 나무 없다. Ten strokes, and any tree will fall. (repetition and continuity)

4. 예수님은 어릴 때 父親의 木手일을 도와 드렸다. When Jesus was a child, he helped his father with his carpentry business.

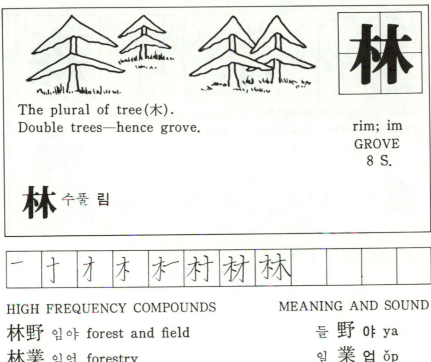

The plural of tree(木).
Double trees—hence grove.

rim; im
GROVE
8 S.

林 수풀 림

一 十 才 木 术 村 材 林

HIGH FREQUENCY COMPOUNDS

林野 임야 forest and field
林業 임업 forestry
山林 산림 mountain and forest
松林 송림 a pine tree forest
竹林 죽림 bamboo forest

MEANING AND SOUND

들 野 야 ya
일 業 업 ŏp
뫼 山 산 san
소나무 松 송 song
대나무 竹 죽 chuk

TYPICAL CONVERSATIONAL USAGE FOR READING AND TRANSLATION. EXERCISE:

1. 十年樹木, 百年樹人 (십년수목, 백년수인) : 나무는 10년 기르면 大木이 되지만, 사람에겐 100년 동안의 教育이 必要하다는 뜻. Ten years to cultivate trees, but a hundred to groom people; a long term plan for fostering talent; the difficulty of nurturing talent.
2. 林業은 제지나 建築과의 연관이 많다. Forestry has a lot of relations with construction and paper manufacture.
3. 松林 가까이 살면 長壽한다는 말이 있다. They say that if you live close to a pine forest you will live long life.

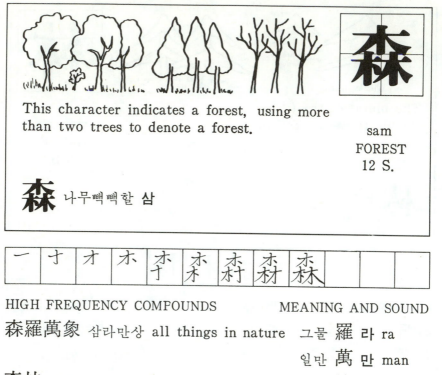

This character indicates a forest, using more than two trees to denote a forest.

sam
FOREST
12 S.

森 나무빽빽할 삼

| 一 | 十 | 才 | 木 | 杢 | 柔 | 森 | 森 | 森 | | |

HIGH FREQUENCY COMPOUNDS   MEANING AND SOUND

森羅萬象 삼라만상 all things in nature   그물 羅 라 ra

                                     일만 萬 만 man

森林 삼림 a forest; a wood   수풀 林 림 rim

森森 삼삼 woody; bosky   형상 象 상 sang

森嚴 삼엄 solemnity; graveness   엄할 嚴 엄 ŏm

TYPICAL CONVERSATIONAL USAGE FOR READING AND TRANSLATION. EXERCISE:

1. 밤이 되면 森羅萬象은 고요히 잠이 든다. When night falls, all things of nature go to sleep silently.

2. 이 부근의 집들은 森林 속에 숨겨져 있는 것들이 많다. Among the houses in this area there are many that are hidden in the woods.

3. 國賓이 親善訪問 오면 警備가 森嚴하다. When guests of the state come to visit, security is very tight.

4. 종려나무 잎은 勝利의 象徵이다. The palm leaves are the symbol of victory.

This character is formed from grass (艹), a generation (世), and a tree (木); leaves are upon the tree (now 葉). It means leaves.

yŏp
LEAF
13 S.

葉 잎사귀 엽

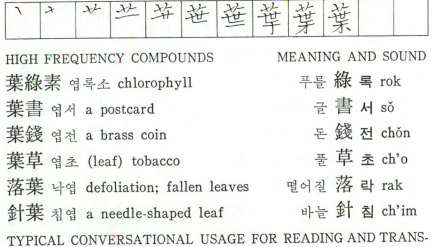

| 丶 | 丷 | 艹 | 艹 | 荜 | 荜 | 荜 | 葷 | 葦 | 葉 | | |

HIGH FREQUENCY COMPOUNDS

葉綠素 엽록소 chlorophyll

葉書 엽서 a postcard

葉錢 엽전 a brass coin

葉草 엽초 (leaf) tobacco

落葉 낙엽 defoliation; fallen leaves

針葉 침엽 a needle-shaped leaf

MEANING AND SOUND

푸를 綠 록 rok

글 書 서 sŏ

돈 錢 전 chŏn

풀 草 초 ch'o

떨어질 落 락 rak

바늘 針 침 ch'im

TYPICAL CONVERSATIONAL USAGE FOR READING AND TRANSLATION. EXERCISE:

1. 빨갛게 물든 나뭇잎이 떨어진다.
   The deep red leaves fall down from the tree.
2. 지난 주말에 동생한테 葉書 한 장 보냈읍니다.
   Last weekend, I sent a postcard to my younger brother.
3. 植物이 파란 것은 葉綠素가 있기 때문이다. The plants are green because they have chlorophyll in them.
4. 이 地域은 針葉樹林으로 有名하다.
   This area is famous for its coniferous forests.

Just as today man rides cars, and not long ago mounted horses, so man in ancient times climbed trees. Zaccheus and a sycamore tree. (*Luke* 19 : 1~4)

乘 탈 승
곱할 승

sŭng
TO RIDE
TO MOUNT
9 S.

(乘→乘)

HIGH FREQUENCY COMPOUNDS

乘客 승객 a passenger

乘馬 승마 horse riding

乘務員 승무원 a crewman

乘車券 승차권 a railroad ticket

便乘 편승 getting a lift; a hitchhike

合乘 합승 a shared ride; riding together

MEANING AND SOUND

손 客 객 kaek

말 馬 마 ma

힘쓸 務 무 mu

수레 車 차 ch'a

편할 便 편 p'yŏn

합할 合 합 hap

TYPICAL CONVERSATIONAL USAGE FOR READING AND TRANSLATION. EXERCISE:

1. 京仁間 電鐵의 乘客들 중에는 大學生들이 많다. Among the passengers on the Seoul-Inch'ŏn electric train there are many college students.

2. 말을 타고 근무하는 警察들을 騎馬隊라고 한다. Policemen who work while riding horses are called mounted policemen.

3. 乘勝長驅(승승장구) : 싸움에 이긴 氣勢를 타고 거리낌없이 휘몰아치는 일. Making long march flushed with victories.

4. 乘夜逃走(승야도주) : 밤을 이용하여 도망함. A flight at night.

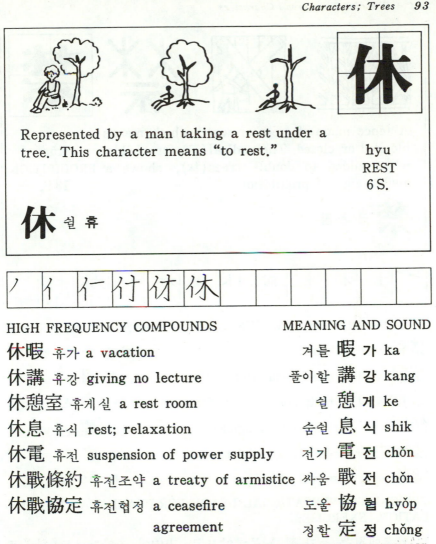

Represented by a man taking a rest under a tree. This character means "to rest."

hyu
REST
6 S.

休 쉴 휴

ノ イ 仁 什 休 休

HIGH FREQUENCY COMPOUNDS

MEANING AND SOUND

休暇 휴가 a vacation

休講 휴강 giving no lecture

休憩室 휴게실 a rest room

休息 휴식 rest; relaxation

休電 휴전 suspension of power supply

休戰條約 휴전조약 a treaty of armistice

休戰協定 휴전협정 a ceasefire
                                agreement

겨를 暇 가 ka

풀이할 講 강 kang

쉴 憩 게 ke

숨쉴 息 식 shik

전기 電 전 chŏn

싸움 戰 전 chŏn

도울 協 협 hyŏp

정할 定 정 chŏng

TYPICAL CONVERSATIONAL USAGE FOR READING AND TRANSLATION. EXERCISE:

1. 大學生들의 데모로 인하여 오늘도 休講되었다. Demonstration of the students made the cancellation of all classes.

2. 잠자는 것은 일어나기 위함이며, 休息하는 것은 일하기 위함이다. (도꾸토미 소호오) We sleep to get up, and we rest to work.

3. 저는 年休동안 母國을 訪問할 豫定입니다. I have a plan to visit my home country during the annual leave.

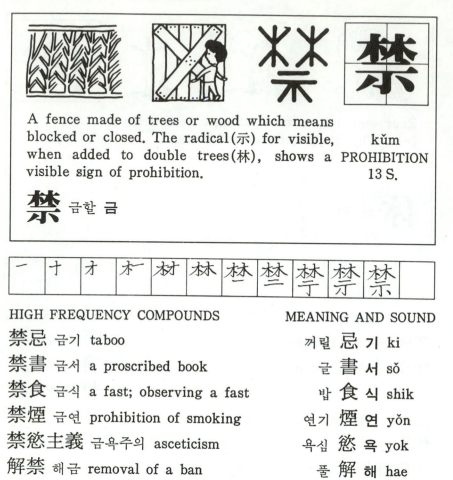

A fence made of trees or wood which means blocked or closed. The radical(示) for visible, when added to double trees(林), shows a visible sign of prohibition.

kŭm

PROHIBITION

13 S.

禁 금할 금

HIGH FREQUENCY COMPOUNDS

MEANING AND SOUND

禁忌 금기 taboo

꺼릴 忌 기 ki

禁書 금서 a proscribed book

글 書 서 sŏ

禁食 금식 a fast; observing a fast

밥 食 식 shik

禁煙 금연 prohibition of smoking

연기 煙 연 yŏn

禁慾主義 금욕주의 asceticism

욕심 慾 욕 yok

解禁 해금 removal of a ban

풀 解 해 hae

TYPICAL CONVERSATIONAL USAGE FOR READING AND TRANSLATION. EXERCISE:

1. 인도에서는 소가 禁忌 동물이므로 市內에 돌아다녀도 함부로 잡지 못한다. Because cows are sacred in India, even if they wander around downtown one can't capture at will.

2. 예수님은 曠野에서 四十日 동안 禁食 기도를 하셨다.
   Jesus fasted and prayed for fourty days in the wilderness.

3. 駐車禁止(주차금지) : 차를 세워 두지 마시오. No parking.

4. 본 寺院 境內에서의 사냥을 禁함.
   Shooting is prohibited within the precincts of the temple.

Fruit trees(木) grow in the backyard. When it's harvest time, a left hand holds the branch while the right hand picks off a fruit. It means generally "to take up," "to adopt," and "to collect."

ch'ae
TO PICK
11 S.

採 캘 채

一 十 才 扩 扩 扙 採 採 採 採

HIGH FREQUENCY COMPONDS	MEANING AND SOUND
採鑛 채광 mining	쇳돌 鑛 광 kwang
採光窓 채광창 a skylight; a dormer	창문 窓 창 ch'ang
採掘 채굴 digging; mining	팔 掘 굴 kul
採用 채용 acceptance; adoption	쓸 用 용 yong
採點 채점 grading; marking	점 點 점 chǒm
採集 채집 collecting	모을 集 집 chip
採擇 채택 choice; selection	가릴 擇 택 t'aek

TYPICAL CONVERSATIONAL USAGE FOR READING AND TRANS-LATION. EXERCISE:

1. 곤충 採集은 우리 둘째 아이의 趣味이다.
   Insect collecting is my second son's hobby.

2. 나는 펜팔을 통해서 우표 모으기를 始作했다.
   I started to collect stamps through pen pals.

3. 한국의 公務員 採用 시험 제도는 고려 때부터 있었다.
   Korea's civil service examinations started from the Koryǒ dynasty.

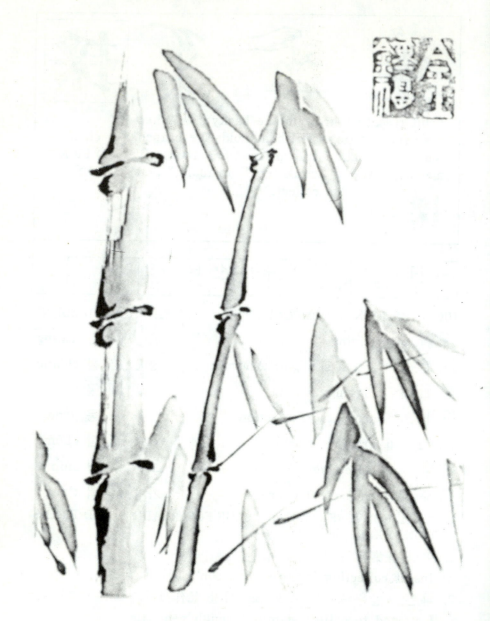

Bamboos
A black-and-white painting by
Rev. Jong-bok Kim, author's brother

This character was represented by the leaves of bamboo. This is made use of as a radical.

chuk
BAMBOO
6 S.
Rad. 118

竹 대 죽

ノ	╱	仁	仁	竹	竹				

HIGH FREQUENCY COMPOUNDS

竹器 죽기 bamboo ware

竹林 죽림 a bamboo thicket

竹馬 죽마 a bamboo horse

竹夫人 죽부인 a Dutch wife

竹細工 죽세공 bamboo work

竹筍 죽순 bamboo shoots[sprouts]

竹槍 죽창 bamboo spear

MEANING AND SOUND

그릇 器 기 ki

수풀 林 림 rim

말 馬 마 ma

계집벼슬 夫 부 pu

장인 工 공 kong

죽순 筍 순 sun

창 槍 창 ch'ang

TYPICAL CONVERSATIONAL USAGE FOR READING AND TRANSLATION. EXERCISE:

1. 竹筍은 비가 온 후에 빨리 자란다.
   Bamboo shoots grow fast after rain.
2. 우리집 庭園에는 대나무가 많이 자라고 있다.
   Our garden has many bamboo trees growing.
3. 竹馬之友(죽마지우) : 죽마를 타고 놀던 벗 ; 어릴 때부터 같이 놀며 자란 벗. 竹馬故友(죽마고우).
   A childhood friend; the friendship of bamboo horse.

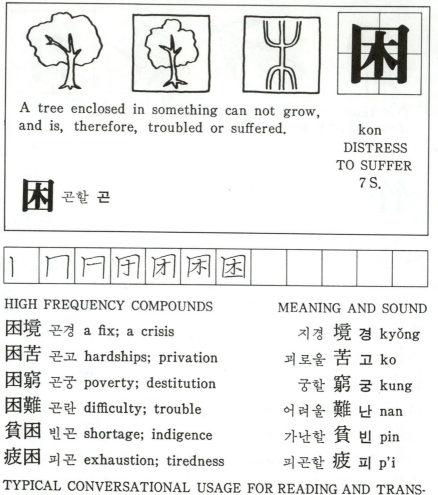

A tree enclosed in something can not grow, and is, therefore, troubled or suffered.

困 곤할 곤

kon
DISTRESS
TO SUFFER
7 S.

HIGH FREQUENCY COMPOUNDS

困境 곤경 a fix; a crisis

困苦 곤고 hardships; privation

困窮 곤궁 poverty; destitution

困難 곤란 difficulty; trouble

貧困 빈곤 shortage; indigence

疲困 피곤 exhaustion; tiredness

MEANING AND SOUND

지경 境 경 kyŏng

괴로울 苦 고 ko

궁할 窮 궁 kung

어려울 難 난 nan

가난할 貧 빈 pin

피곤할 疲 피 p'i

TYPICAL CONVERSATIONAL USAGE FOR READING AND TRANSLATION. EXERCISE:

1. 困境에 빠졌을 때에 主를 찾으라. 그가 너에게 慰勞와 所望의 빛을 주시리라. When you fall on hard times, call to God, then he will comfort you and give you a light of hope.

2. 가난은 너를 賢明하게도 만들고 슬프게도 만든다.
   Poverty makes you sad as well as wise. (*B. Brecht*)

3. 富裕했다가 가난해지는 것보다 가난했다가 부유해지는 것이 더 좋다. Riches come better after poverty than poverty after riches. (*John Ray*)

The figure of a flower tree(木) which looks like a flame(火) expresses the meaning, flower bloom like a burning flame, glory and prosperity.

yǒng
HONOUR
GLORY
14 S.

榮 영화 영　　　（榮→栄）

′	′′	′火′	′′火′′	〝〝	〝〝	〝〝	〝〝	榮		

HIGH FREQUENCY COMPOUNDS	MEANING AND SOUND
榮光 영광 glory	빛 光 광 kwang
榮譽 영예 honor	기릴 譽 예 ye
榮位 영위 a high position; an eminent position	자리 位 위 wi
榮轉 영전 a promotional transfer	구를 轉 전 chŏn
繁榮 번영 prosperity; welfare	번성할 繁 번 pŏn
尊榮 존영 nobility and glory	높을 尊 존 chon

TYPICAL CONVERSATIONAL USAGE FOR READING AND TRANSLATION. EXERCISE:

1. 榮枯盛衰(영고성쇠) : Rise and fall, prosperity and decline.
2. 富貴榮華(부귀영화) : Riches, honour and splendour.
3. 꽃은 갓난 아기도 理解할 수 있는 言語이다. (*Arthur Coxe*)
   Flowers are words which even a babe may understand.
4. 事業의 成功과 會社의 繁榮을 祈願합니다.
   I pray for your successful business and prosperity of your company.

4. 鳥魚類　조어류　Birds and Fish

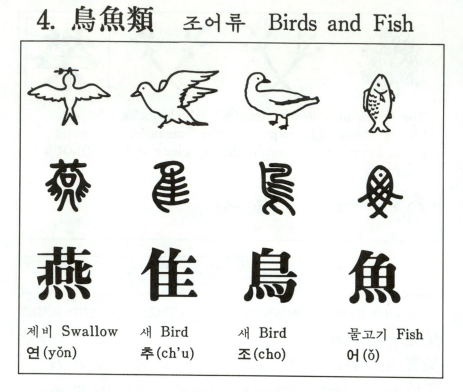

제비 Swallow	새 Bird	새 Bird	물고기 Fish
연(yŏn)	추(ch'u)	조(cho)	어(ŏ)

　하나님이 가라사대 물들은 生物로 蕃盛케 하라 땅 위 하늘의 穹蒼에는 새가 날으라 하시고 하나님이 큰 물고기와 물에서 蕃盛하여 움직이는 모든 生物을 그 種類대로, 날개 있는 모든 새를 그 種類대로 創造하시니 하나님의 보시기에 좋았더라. 하나님이 그들에게 福을 주어 가라사대 生育하고 蕃盛하여 여러 바다 물에 充滿하라 새들도 땅에 蕃盛하라 하시니라. 저녁이 되며 아침이 되니 이는 다섯째 날이니라. (創世記, *Gen.* 1 : 20~23)

　主의 손으로 만든 모든 것을 다스리게 하시고 萬物을 그 발 아래 두셨으니 곧 모든 牛羊과 들짐승이며 空中의 새와 바다의 魚族과 海路에 다니는 것이니이다. (詩篇 8 : 6~8)

You have put him charge of everything you made; everything is put under his authority: all sheep and oxen, and wild animals too, the birds and fish, and all the life in the sea. (*Psalms* 8 : 6~8)

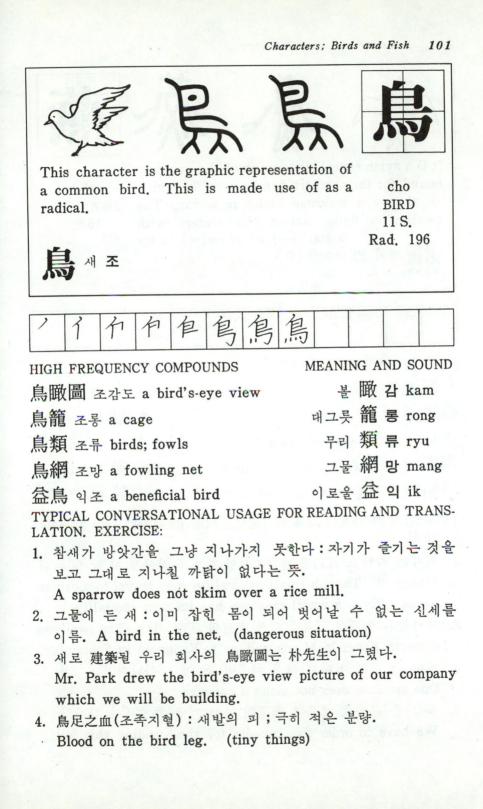

This character is the graphic representation of a common bird. This is made use of as a radical.

cho
BIRD
11 S.
Rad. 196

鳥 새 조

ノ 亻 亇 阝 阜 鸟 鳥 鳥

HIGH FREQUENCY COMPOUNDS

MEANING AND SOUND

鳥瞰圖 조감도 a bird's-eye view

볼 瞰 감 kam

鳥籠 조롱 a cage

대그릇 籠 롱 rong

鳥類 조류 birds; fowls

무리 類 류 ryu

鳥網 조망 a fowling net

그물 網 망 mang

益鳥 익조 a beneficial bird

이로울 益 익 ik

TYPICAL CONVERSATIONAL USAGE FOR READING AND TRANSLATION. EXERCISE:

1. 참새가 방앗간을 그냥 지나가지 못한다 : 자기가 즐기는 것을 보고 그대로 지나칠 까닭이 없다는 뜻.
A sparrow does not skim over a rice mill.

2. 그물에 든 새 : 이미 잡힌 몸이 되어 벗어날 수 없는 신세를 이름. A bird in the net. (dangerous situation)

3. 새로 建築될 우리 회사의 鳥瞰圖는 朴先生이 그렸다.
Mr. Park drew the bird's-eye view picture of our company which we will be building.

4. 鳥足之血(조족지혈) : 새발의 피 ; 극히 적은 분량.
Blood on the bird leg.　(tiny things)

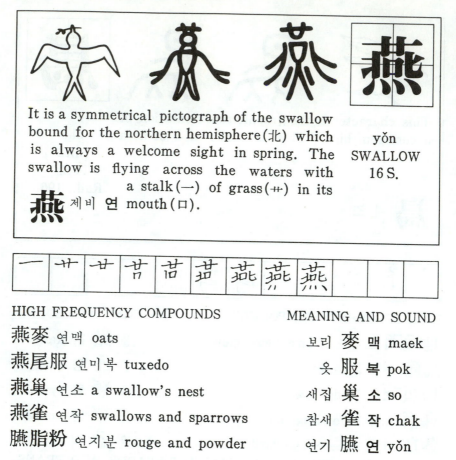

It is a symmetrical pictograph of the swallow bound for the northern hemisphere (北) which is always a welcome sight in spring. The swallow is flying across the waters with a stalk (一) of grass (卄) in its mouth (口).

燕 제비 연 mouth (口).

yŏn
SWALLOW
16 S.

HIGH FREQUENCY COMPOUNDS

燕麥 연맥 oats

燕尾服 연미복 tuxedo

燕巢 연소 a swallow's nest

燕雀 연작 swallows and sparrows

臙脂粉 연지분 rouge and powder

MEANING AND SOUND

보리 麥 맥 maek

옷 服 복 pok

새집 巢 소 so

참새 雀 작 chak

연기 臙 연 yŏn

TYPICAL CONVERSATIONAL USAGE FOR READING AND TRANSLATION.

1. 제비는 작아도 江南을 간다 : 모양은 비록 작아도 저 할 일은 다 한다는 말. Though small, a swallow may travel to southern China. (Even a small creature has its own speciality.)

2. 제비들은 韓國에 三月에 와서 九月에 江南 간다. The swallows come to Korea in March and go to Kangnam in September.

3. 제비 한 마리 왔다고 해서 여름이 온 것은 아니다. One swallow does not make a summer.

4. 올 가을 結婚式 때문에 燕尾服 다섯 벌을 注文해야 한다. We have to order five tuxedos for the wedding this fall.

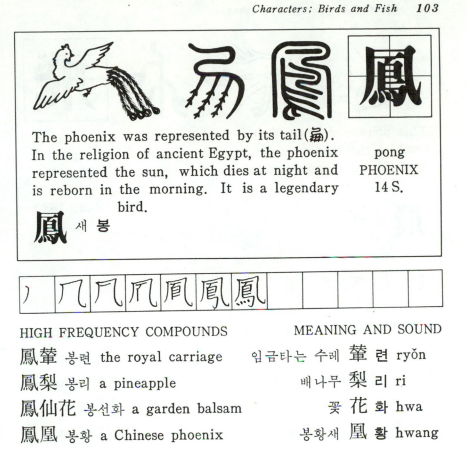

The phoenix was represented by its tail (扁).
In the religion of ancient Egypt, the phoenix
represented the sun, which dies at night and
is reborn in the morning. It is a legendary
bird.

pong
PHOENIX
14 S.

鳳 새 봉

HIGH FREQUENCY COMPOUNDS

MEANING AND SOUND

鳳輦 봉련 the royal carriage   임금타는 수레 輦 련 ryŏn

鳳梨 봉리 a pineapple   배나무 梨 리 ri

鳳仙花 봉선화 a garden balsam   꽃 花 화 hwa

鳳凰 봉황 a Chinese phoenix   봉황새 凰 황 hwang

TYPICAL CONVERSATIONAL USAGE FOR READING AND TRANS-LATION. EXERCISE:

1. 龍尾鳳湯 (용미봉탕) : 맛이 아주 좋은 飮食을 가리키는 말.
   Food that tastes very good.

2. 韓國에서는 제일 큰 高校 野球試合으로 鳳凰大旗 쟁탈전이 해
   마다 전국적으로 실시된다. In Korea the high school baseball
   game called the Phoenix Flag competition is carried out
   throughout the entire country every year.

3. '울 밑에 선 鳳仙花'는 韓國歌曲의 하나로서 有名하게 많이
   불리는 노래이다. "The garden balsam grown under the
   fence" is sung as one of the Korea's famous folk songs.

4. 그 女子의 옷에는 鳳凰새 수가 놓아져 있다.

This picture shows a flying duck. It resembles the modern space shuttle. This is made use of as a radical.

飛 날 비

pi
TO FLY
9 S.
Rad. 183

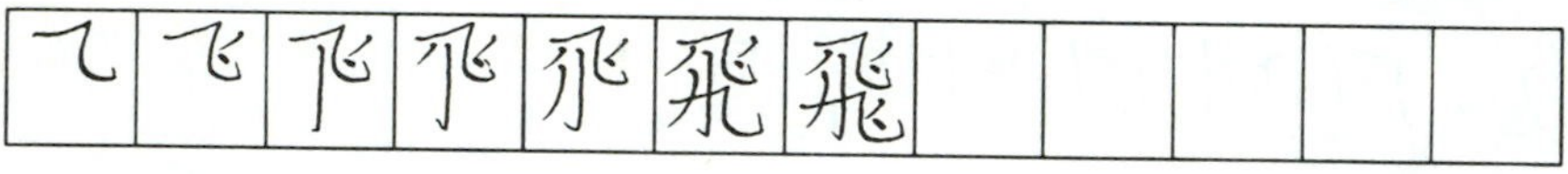

HIGH FREQUENCY COMPOUNDS

飛躍 비약 a flying jump

飛行機 비행기 an airplane

飛行士 비행사 a pilot

飛行場 비행장 an airfield

飛行中隊 비행중대 a squadron (air force)

雄飛 웅비 a great leap

MEANING AND SOUND

뛸 躍 약 yak

갈 行 행 haeng

틀 機 기 ki

선비 士 사 sa

마당 場 장 chang

가운데 中 중 chung

떼 隊 대 tae

수컷 雄 웅 ung

TYPICAL CONVERSATIONAL USAGE FOR READING AND TRANSLATION. EXERCISE:

1. 韓國의 言語學者 최 현배 선생은 飛行機를 '날틀'이라고 이름지어 불렀다. The Korean philologist Ch'oe Hyŏn-bae called the airplane *nalt'ŭl* (flying machine).

2. 烏飛梨落 (오비이락) : 까마귀 날자 배 떨어진다 ; 무슨 일을 시작하자마자 일이 생긴다는 말이다. The crow flies and at once a pear falls. (coincidental situation)

This character indicates clearly three birds in a nest on a tree.

SO
NEST
11 S.

巢 새집 소

| 〈 | 〈〈〈 | 巛 | 𡿧 | 𢗘 | 𡿺 | 𡿸 | 單 | 巣 | 巢 | | |

HIGH FREQUENCY COMPOUNDS   MEANING AND SOUND

巢窟 소굴 a den; a haunt   움 窟 굴 kul

巢蜜 소밀 virgin honey   꿀 蜜 밀 mil

巢父 소보 ancient Chinese hermit, who   아비 父 부 pu

         lives in a tree   남자의 미칭 父 보 po

巢穴 소혈 a nesting hole   구멍 穴 혈 hyŏl

歸巢 귀소 homing   돌아올 歸 귀 kwi

鳥巢 조소 a bird's nest   새 鳥 조 cho

TYPICAL CONVERSATIONAL USAGE FOR READING AND TRANS-
LATION. EXERCISE:

1. 여우도 窟이 있고 새들도 깃들일 곳이 있으되 人子는 머리 둘 곳도 없노라. The fox has a den, and birds have nests but the Son of man has no place to lay his head.

2. 巢父許由 問答하던 箕山潁水가 예 아니냐? Isn't this the famous place where So Po and Hŏ Yu had their conversation?

3. 中國의 巢父는 기독교 신비주의자이며 柱上聖者라고 하는 시 메온과 같은 점이 많다.

These are the long feathers of the wings of birds. The modern character still retains the outline of its original form.

u
FEATHERS
6 S.
Rad. 124

羽 깃 우

HIGH FREQUENCY COMPOUNDS

羽冠 우관 a crest

羽毛 우모 a feather

羽扇 우선 the fan made of feather

羽衣 우의 a robe of feather

右翼 우익 the right wing

MEANING AND SOUND

갓 冠 관 kwan

털 毛 모 mo

부채 扇 선 sŏn

옷 衣 의 ŭi

날개 翼 익 ik

TYPICAL CONVERSATIONAL USAGE FOR READING AND TRANSLATION. EXERCISE:

1. 나는 새도 깃을 쳐야 날아간다 : 무슨 일이든지 그 순서를 밟아 나가야만 목적을 달성할 수 있다는 말. Birds take off after gaining strength in their feathers. (Preparation goes before the execution of any business.)

2. 정당 정치에서 左翼계라고 하면 共産主義 계통을 나타낸다. When we say left wing in party politics, it represents the communistic parties.

3. 生活 필수품 중에 먼지떨이, 넥타이 같은 것은 羽毛로 만들어 졌다. Among the items in daily use made of feathers are feather dusters, neckties, etc.

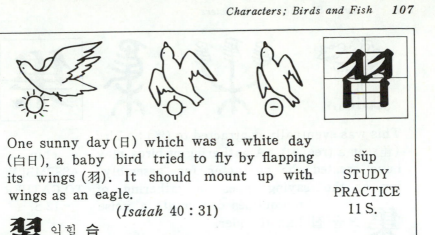

One sunny day(日) which was a white day (白日), a baby bird tried to fly by flapping its wings (羽). It should mount up with wings as an eagle.
(*Isaiah* 40 : 31)

sŭp
STUDY
PRACTICE
11 S.

習 익힐 習

| フ | ヲ | ヲ | 羽 | 羽 | 羽 | 習 | 習 | | | |

HIGH FREQUENCY COMPOUNDS

習慣 습관 a habit; a custom

習得 습득 acquirement; learning

習字 습자 calligraphy; penmanship

講習會 강습회 an institute;a short course

練習 연습 practice; drill

學習 학습 study; learning

MEANING AND SOUND

익숙할 慣 관 kwan

얻을 得 득 tŭk

글자 字 자 cha

익힐 講 강 kang

익힐 練 련 ryŏn

배울 學 학 hak

TYPICAL CONVERSATIONAL USAGE FOR READING AND TRANSLATION. EXERCISE:

1. 練習은 教師 중 가장 좋은 教師다.
   Practice is the best of all instructors. (*P. Syrus*)

2. 肉體의 練習은 약간의 유익이 있으나 경건은 범사에 유익하니라. For physical training is of a little benefit, but godliness is profitable for all things. (1 *Tim.* 4 : 8)

3. 慣習은 人間生活의 위대한 案內者이다.
   Custom is the great guide of human life.

4. 習慣은 제 2의 天性이다. Habit is second nature.

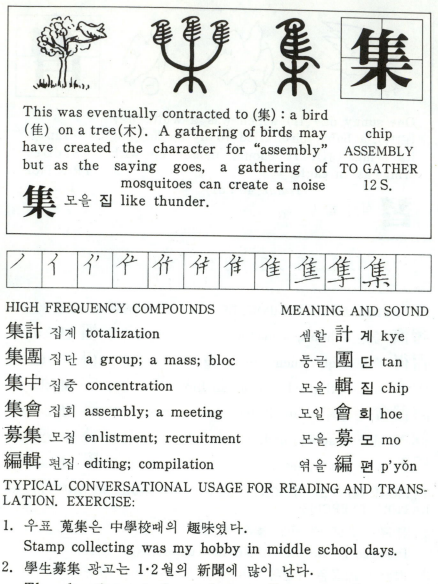

This was eventually contracted to (集) : a bird
(隹) on a tree(木). A gathering of birds may   chip
have created the character for "assembly"   ASSEMBLY
but as the saying goes, a gathering of   TO GATHER
mosquitoes can create a noise   12 S.
集 모을 집 like thunder.

丿 亻 亻 亻 竹 什 住 隹 隹 隼 集

HIGH FREQUENCY COMPOUNDS

集計 집계 totalization

集團 집단 a group; a mass; bloc

集中 집중 concentration

集會 집회 assembly; a meeting

募集 모집 enlistment; recruitment

編輯 편집 editing; compilation

MEANING AND SOUND

셈할 計 계 kye

둥글 團 단 tan

모을 輯 집 chip

모일 會 회 hoe

모을 募 모 mo

엮을 編 편 p'yŏn

TYPICAL CONVERSATIONAL USAGE FOR READING AND TRANS-LATION. EXERCISE:

1. 우표 蒐集은 中學校때의 趣味였다.
   Stamp collecting was my hobby in middle school days.

2. 學生募集 광고는 1·2월의 新聞에 많이 난다.
   The advertisements for student enrollments are in a lot of
   the January and Februrary newspapers.

3. 그는 月刊雜誌 編輯長으로 30년 일했기 때문에 編輯에는 귀
   신이다. He is an expert at editing, because he worked for
   30 years as editor in chief of a monthly magazine.

This character, indicating a bird(隹) sitting on a man's hand(又), means one or single; and is used as a counting unit for boats, vessels, ships and an odd one of a pair.

ch'ŏk
SINGLE
ONE
10 S.

隻 외짝 척

ノ	イ	亻	仆	件	隹	隻	隻			

HIGH FREQUENCY COMPOUNDS

MEANING AND SOUND

隻騎 척기 only one mounted soldier

隻手 척수 one arm

隻身 척신 singleness; celibacy

隻眼 척안 a one-eyed person

隻愛 척애 unrequited love

말탈 騎 기 ki

손 手 수 su

몸 身 신 shin

눈 眼 안 an

사랑 愛 애 ae

TYPICAL CONVERSATIONAL USAGE FOR READING AND TRANSLATION. EXERCISE:

1. 그는 不幸하게도 韓國戰爭때 隻手가 되었다.
   Unfortunately, his arm was lost during the Korean war.

2. 이스라엘의 指導者 한 사람은 隻眼이었다.
   One of the Israel's leaders had only one eye.

3. 돛단배 한 隻이 水平線 너머로 사라졌다.
   One sailboat disappeared beyond the horizon.

4. 隻愛를 現代人들은 짝사랑이라고 말한다.
   Modern people call ch'ŏk-ae *tchaksarang*.

5. 隻分隻厘(척분척리) : A very small sum of money.

This character indicates a pair of birds(雔) sitting on a man's hand(又). It means a pair or a couple.

ssang
PAIR
18 S.

雙 둘 쌍

| ノ | イ | 什 | 仹 | 隹 | 雔 | 雔 | 雙 | 雙 | | | |

HIGH FREQUENCY COMPOUNDS

雙童 쌍동(이) twins

雙方 쌍방 both parties

雙墳 쌍분 twin graves

雙手 쌍수 both hands

雙眼鏡 쌍안경 a binocular

雙窓 쌍창 a double-leaf window

MEANING AND SOUND

아이 童 동 tong

모 方 방 pang

봉분 墳 분 pun

손 手 수 su

눈 眼 안 an

창 窓 창 ch'ang

TYPICAL CONVERSATIONAL USAGE FOR READING AND TRANSLATION. EXERCISE:

1. 우리 班의 雙童이는 늘 같은 옷을 입는다.
   The twins in our class wear the same clothes everyday.

2. 우리는 종종 바닷가에 나가서 물개와 고래의 擧動을 雙眼鏡으로 구경한다. We often go to the beach and watch the movement of whales and seals through binoculars.

3. 지난週에 싸운 사람들이 雙方 모두 和解를 해서 기쁘다.
   I am glad that the people, who fought last week, apologize to each other.

This character is made up of "move" (辶), and "a bird"(隹). When birds "move," they always fly forward, never backward. So the character means "advance and entry." An orderly movement encouraged by the proverb: he who sows not in advance loses ground.

chin
ADVANCE
ENTRY
12 S.

進 나아갈 진

| ノ | イ | 亻 | 亣 | 隹 | 隹 | 谁 | 進 | | | |

HIGH FREQUENCY COMPOUNDS

進擊 진격 an advance; an attack

進路 진로 a course; a route

進步 진보 progress; advance

進學 진학 entrance into a school of higher grade

進化 진화 evolution

推進 추진 propulsion; pushing forward

MEANING AND SOUND

칠 擊 격 kyŏk

길 路 로 ro

걸음 步 보 po

배울 學 학 hak

화할 化 화 hwa

밀 推 추 ch'u

TYPICAL CONVERSATIONAL USAGE FOR READING AND TRANS-LATION. EXERCISE:

1. 金社長이 그 學生에게 獎學金을 대주어 그의 進學길이 열렸다. President Kim offered a scholarship to the student, opening the door to his higher education.

2. 進化論者들을 다윈의 후예들이라고도 칭한다. Evolutionists are what we call descendants of Charles Darwin.

3. 進退兩難(진퇴양난) : 앞으로 나아갈 수도 뒤로 물러설 수도 없이 꼼짝할 수 없는 窮地에 빠짐. A dilemma.

This character represents a bird flying up toward the sky disappearing from sight, as if becoming nonexistent. It is used to express a negative meaning.

pul, pu
NOT
NEGATIVE
4 S.

不 아닐 불
부

一 フ 不 不

HIGH FREQUENCY COMPOUNDS

不可能 불가능 impossibility

不潔 불결 uncleanliness

不景氣 불경기 hard times; depression; slackness; a slump

不公平 불공평 unfairness

不規則 불규칙 irregularity

不當 부당 injustice

不自由 부자유 lack of freedom

MEANING AND SOUND

능할 能 능 nŭng

깨끗할 潔 결 kyŏl

기운 氣 기 ki

평평할 平 평 p'yŏng

법 規 규 kyu

마땅 當 당 tang

말미암을 由 유 yu

TYPICAL CONVERSATIONAL USAGE FOR READING AND TRANSLATION. EXERCISE:

1. 燈下不明(등하불명) : 등잔 밑이 어둡다 ; 가까운 데서 생긴 일을 도리어 먼 데서 일어난 일보다 잘 모른다는 뜻. It gets dark under the lamp. (Even though things occur near you, you do not know them as well as if you were far away.)

2. 不景氣에는 耐乏生活을 해야 한다.
   At the time of a depression, we must practice austerities.

In another appropriate combination of radicals, this character for island is composed of (山) for mountain and (鳥) for bird. Islands are open rocky or mountainous and are the resting places for birds crossing the sea.

to
ISLAND
10 S.

島 섬 도

| ′ | ′ | ⼴ | ⼾ | ⼽ | ⼾ | ⼾ | 鳥 | 鳥 | 島 | 島 | |

HIGH FREQUENCY COMPOUNDS	MEANING AND SOUND
島民 도민 the islanders	백성 民 민 min
島嶼 도서 islands	섬 嶼 서 sŏ
群島 군도 a group of islands	무리 群 군 kun
無人島 무인도 an uninhabited island	없을 無 무 mu
半島 반도 a peninsula	반 半 반 pan
列島 열도 a chain of islands	벌일 列 렬 ryŏl

TYPICAL CONVERSATIONAL USAGE FOR READING AND TRANSLATION. EXERCISE:

1. 韓國의 영토는 아시아 大陸의 東部, 中國本土 동쪽의 韓半島 와 그 부속 島嶼로 이루어졌다. The Korean territory is in the eastern area of the Asian continent, also to the east of the Chinese mainland. It is made up of a peninsula and many islands.

2. 韓半島 동쪽에는 列島로 構成된 日本이 위치해 있다. Japan, which is located to the east of the Korean peninsula, comprises a chain of islands.

It represents the fish. A shape of fish defined clearly. Gradually, it had been modified in simpler form. A fish is the symbol of Christianity. "Come! Follow Me and I will make you fishers of men." (*Matthew* 4 : 19)

ŏ
FISH
11 S.
Rad. 195

魚 물고기 어

HIGH FREQUENCY COMPOUNDS

魚群 어군 a school of fish

魚網 어망 a fishing net

漁夫 어부 a fisherman

漁船 어선 a fishing boat

漁村 어촌 a fishing village

MEANING AND SOUND

무리 群 군 kun

그물 網 망 mang

고기잡을 漁 어 ŏ

배 船 선 sŏn

마을 村 촌 ch'on

TYPICAL CONVERSATIONAL USAGE FOR READING AND TRANSLATION. EXERCISE:

1. 도마 위에 오른 고기 : 어찌할 수 없이 된 運命을 비유한 말. A fish on the chopping block. (It can not be helped; beyond hope.)

2. 고래 싸움에 새우 등 터진다 : 남의 싸움에 아무 관계가 없는 사람이 공연히 해를 입게 된다는 뜻. In a fight between whales, the back of a shrimp bursts. (Third person gets hurt.)

3. 緣木求魚(연목구어) : 나무에 올라가서 물고기를 구한다 ; 도저히 不可能한 일을 굳이 하려 함. Seeking a fish in a tree.

4. 一魚濁水(일어탁수) : 한 마리의 고기가 물을 흐린다. A tiny fish pollutes the whole stream of water.

5. 動物 동물 Animals

馬	牛	羊	熊
말 Horse	소 Ox, Cow	양 Sheep	곰 Bear
마 (ma)	우 (u)	양 (yang)	웅 (ung)

여호와 하나님이 흙으로 各種 들짐승과 空中의 各種 새를 지
으시고 아담이 어떻게 이름을 짓나 보시려고 그것들을 그에게로
이끌어 이르시니 아담이 各 生物을 일컫는 바가 곧 그 이름이라.
아담이 모든 六畜과 空中의 새와 들의 모든 짐승에게 이름을 주
니라 (創世記 2 : 19~20).

Out of the ground the Lord God had formed all the beasts
of the field and all the birds of the air and He brought
them to Adam to see … So Adam gave names to all the
domestic animals, to all the birds of the air and to all the
wild beasts. (*Genesis 2 : 19~20*)

血肉있는 모든 生物을 너는 各其 암수 한 雙씩 方舟로 이끌어
들여 너와 함께 生命을 保存케 하되 새가 그 種類대로 六畜이 그
種類대로 땅에 기는 모든 것이 그 種類대로 各其 둘씩 네게로 나
오리니 그 生命을 保存케 하라. (創世記, *Genesis 6 : 19~20*)

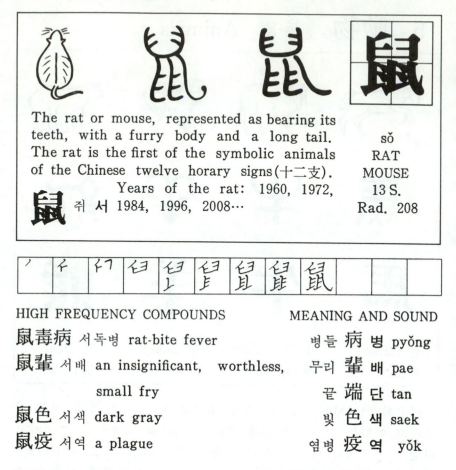

The rat or mouse, represented as bearing its teeth, with a furry body and a long tail. The rat is the first of the symbolic animals of the Chinese twelve horary signs (十二支).
Years of the rat: 1960, 1972, 1984, 1996, 2008···

鼠 쥐 서

sŏ
RAT
MOUSE
13 S.
Rad. 208

HIGH FREQUENCY COMPOUNDS

鼠毒病 서독병 rat-bite fever

鼠輩 서배 an insignificant, worthless, small fry

鼠色 서색 dark gray

鼠疫 서역 a plague

MEANING AND SOUND

병들 病 병 pyŏng

무리 輩 배 pae

끝 端 단 tan

빛 色 색 saek

염병 疫 역 yŏk

TYPICAL CONVERSATIONAL USAGE FOR READING AND TRANSLATION. EXERCISE:

1. 독 안에 든 쥐 : 아무래도 벗어날 수 없는 處地. A rat, bottled up in a jar. (a man who cannot escape from danger)

2. 다람쥐 체바퀴 돌 듯한다 : 한없이 反復하나 決末이 없다는 뜻. Like a chipmunk running round the wheel of sieve. (Running in circles, getting nowhere)

3. 낮말은 새가 듣고 밤말은 쥐가 듣는다. Birds listen to day-talk, and rats to night-talk. (Be careful of what you say.)

4. 首鼠兩端(수서양단) : 머뭇거리며 進退·去就를 결정짓지 못하고 관망하는 상태. Hesitating or waving between two extremities.

This character represents an ox. The ox is
the second of the symbolical animals.
Years of the ox by the Chinese zodiac signs:
1961, 1973, 1985, 1997···

u
OX
4 S.
Rad. 93

牛 소 우

HIGH FREQUENCY COMPOUNDS	MEANING AND SOUND
牛乳 우유 cow's milk	젖 乳 유 yu
牛肉 우육 beef	고기 肉 육 yuk
韓牛 한우 a Korean cow	나라 韓 한 han
牛皮 우피 a cowhide	가죽 皮 피 p'i

TYPICAL CONVERSATIONAL USAGE FOR READING AND TRANS-
LATION. EXERCISE:

1. 못된 송아지 엉덩이에 뿔 난다 : 사람이 변변치 못하면 말썽만
   피운다는 말. A naughty calf grows a horn on its buttocks.
   (An ill-bred boy behaves rudely.)

2. 쥐구멍으로 소 몰라고 한다 : 不可能한 일을 하라고 한다는 말.
   Trying to drive an ox through a rathole.

3. 누운 소 타기 : 매우 간단하고 쉬운 일이라는 말.
   As easy as riding a lying-down cow.

4. 소 잃고 외양간 고친다 : 이미 일이 실패된 뒤에 손질한다.
   Repair the cowshed after the cow is lost.

5. 牛耳讀經(우이독경) : 쇠귀에 경 읽기 ; 아무리 가르치고 일러주
   어도 알아듣지 못함. Reading to the deaf.

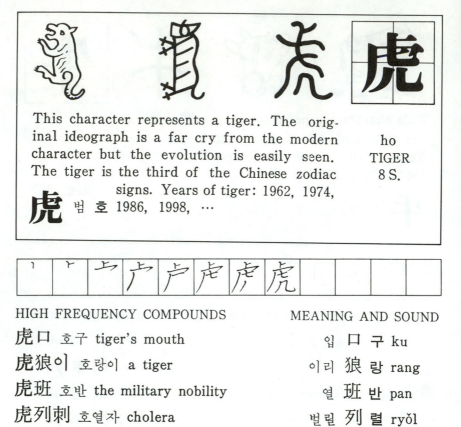

This character represents a tiger. The original ideograph is a far cry from the modern character but the evolution is easily seen. The tiger is the third of the Chinese zodiac signs. Years of tiger: 1962, 1974, 1986, 1998, ⋯

虎 범 호

ho
TIGER
8 S.

ㅣ　ㅏ　ㅗ　广　广　卢　虍　虏　虎

HIGH FREQUENCY COMPOUNDS

虎口 호구 tiger's mouth

虎狼이 호랑이 a tiger

虎班 호반 the military nobility

虎列刺 호열자 cholera

虎皮 호피 a tiger skin

MEANING AND SOUND

입 口 구 ku

이리 狼 랑 rang

열 班 반 pan

벌릴 列 렬 ryŏl

가죽 皮 피 p'i

TYPICAL CONVERSATIONAL USAGE FOR READING AND TRANSLATION. EXERCISE:

1. 虎視耽耽(호시탐탐) : Watches for an opportunity.

2. 하루 강아지 범 무서운 줄 모른다. A day-old puppy doesn't know enough to fear the tiger. (Know yourself...)

3. 사람은 죽으면 이름을 남기고 범은 죽으면 가죽을 남긴다. Though a man dies, he leaves his name; though a tiger dies, he leaves his skin.

4. 무는 호랑이 뿔이 없다 : 일을 兼全하기가 쉽지 않다는 말. A biting tiger has no horns. (Nothing is perfect in this world.)

This character is a pictograph of the squatting rabbit or hare, with its tail perked up. The rabbit, a symbol of fecundity, is the fourth of the Chinese twelve zodiac signs.
Years of the rabbit: 1951, 1963, 1975, 1987, 1999...

t'o
RABBIT
HARE
8 S.

兔 토끼 **토**

HIGH FREQUENCY COMPOUNDS	MEANING AND SOUND
兔舍 토사 a hutch; a rabbit box	집 舍 사 sa
兔脣 토순 a harelip; cleft palate	입술 脣 순 sun
兔眼 토안 lagophthalmos	눈 眼 안 an
白兔 백토 a white rabbit	흰 白 백 paek

TYPICAL CONVERSATIONAL USAGE FOR READING AND TRANSLATION. EXERCISE:

1. 兔營三窟(토영삼굴) : 토끼가 위험을 피하려고 구멍 셋을 만든 다는 뜻으로, 자신의 安全을 위하여 미리 몇 가지 계책을 짜 놓음을 가리키는 말이다. Rabbit makes three holes to escape danger. (countermeasures for self-safety)

2. 韓國에는 별주부전 혹은 토끼전이라는 재미있는 이야기가 전해지고 있다. There is an interesting story that has been passed down in Korea called the story of the rabbit or the story of the turtle.

3. 이솝의 寓話 가운데에는 토끼와 거북이가 경주하는 이야기가 있다. Among Aesop's Fables there is a story of a race between a hare and a tortoise.

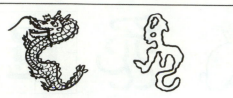 

A large lizard in ancient times(?), or a legendary creature which combined the qualities of a sea horse, lizard, snake and bison. Years of dragon:1952, 1964, 1976, 1988, 2000···
The fifth in the cycle of twelve
龍 용 룡 symbolic animals.

yong;
ryong
DRAGON
16 S.
Rad. 212

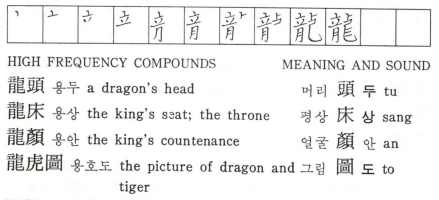

HIGH FREQUENCY COMPOUNDS

龍頭 용두 a dragon's head

龍床 용상 the king's seat; the throne

龍顏 용안 the king's countenance

龍虎圖 용호도 the picture of dragon and
tiger

MEANING AND SOUND

머리 頭 두 tu

평상 床 상 sang

얼굴 顏 안 an

그림 圖 도 to

TYPICAL CONVERSATIONAL USAGE FOR READING AND TRANSLATION. EXERCISE:

1. 開川에서 龍 난다 : 미천한 집안에서 훌륭한 사람이 나온다는 말. A dragon rises from a ditch. (This means the son of a humble family rises to glory.)

2. 한국의 民畫나 자수에는 호랑이와 龍이 싸우는 그림이 있는데 이를 龍虎圖라고 한다. In Koean folk art or embroidery, you will see a tiger fighting with a dragon. These are called "dragon and tiger illustrations."

3. 龍頭蛇尾(용두사미) : 용의 머리와 뱀의 꼬리 ; 처음은 왕성하나 끝이 不振함. Dragon's head and snake's tail. (bright beginning, dull finish)

This character is a striking image of the horse. The horse represents the seventh animal of the twelve zodiac signs. Years of the horse: 1954, 1966, 1978, 1990, 2002...

ma
HORSE
10 S.
Rad. 187

馬 말 마

HIGH FREQUENCY COMPOUNDS

馬力 마력 horsepower

馬兵 마병 a cavalryman

馬夫 마부 a coachman; a wagoner

馬草 마초 fodder; forage

MEANING AND SOUND

힘 力 력 ryŏk

군사 兵 병 pyŏng

사내 夫 부 pu

풀 草 초 ch'o

TYPICAL CONVERSATIONAL USAGE FOR READING AND TRANSLATION. EXERCISE:

1, 늙은 말이 콩 더 달라고 한다 : 사람은 늙어갈수록 慾心이 많아진다는 말. An old horse wants more beans. (When a man grows old, he looks for more reward and honor)

2. 메뚜기 등에 당나귀 짐 : 지나치게 버거운 일을 맡김. A load of an ass on the back of a grasshopper. (The overloading of responsibility)

3. 走馬看山(주마간산) : 달리는 말 위에서 山川을 구경함; 여가가 없이 횤획 지나쳐 봄을 이름. Taking a cursory view.

4. 天高馬肥(천고마비) : 하늘이 높고 말이 살찐다는 뜻으로, 가을이 썩 좋은 절기임을 일컫는 말. Sky high and horses fat. (suitable weather in autumn)

These symbols are sketches of a sheep's head with horns. The sheep is the eighth symbolic animal of the twelve zodiac signs. Years of the sheep: 1955, 1967, 1979, 1991...

yang
SHEEP
GOAT
LAMB
6 S.
Rad. 123

羊 양 양

丶　丷　丷　芦　羊　羊

HIGH FREQUENCY COMPOUNDS

羊毛 양모 wool

羊皮 양피 sheepskin; woolfell

山羊 산양 a goat

洋裝 양장 western style of dress

養子 양자 an adopted child

養育 양육 bringing up; nurture

MEANING AND SOUND

털 毛 모 mo

가죽 皮 피 p'i

뫼 山 산 san

꾸밀 裝 장 chang

기를 養 양 yang

기를 育 육 yuk

TYPICAL CONVERSATIONAL USAGE FOR READING AND TRANS-LATION. EXERCISE:

1. 한나라 蔡倫이 종이를 發明하기 전에 西洋에서는 羊皮紙를 사용했다. Before Ts'ai Lun of the Han dynasty invented paper, parchment was used in the western world.

2. 子息이 없는 사람들이 남의 아이를 데려다 기르는 것을 入養이라고 부른다. When people who have no children take the children of others to raise as their own, it is called adoption.

3. 九折羊腸(구절양장) : 양의 창자처럼 산길 같은 것이 꼬불꼬불하고 험함을 일컫는 말. Meanders; a winding path.

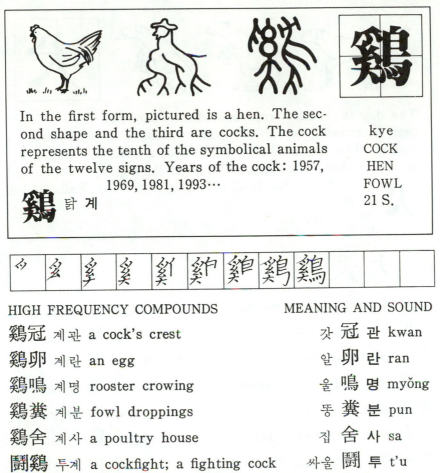

In the first form, pictured is a hen. The second shape and the third are cocks. The cock represents the tenth of the symbolical animals of the twelve signs. Years of the cock: 1957, 1969, 1981, 1993···

鷄 닭 계

kye
COCK
HEN
FOWL
21 S.

HIGH FREQUENCY COMPOUNDS

鷄冠 계관 a cock's crest

鷄卵 계란 an egg

鷄鳴 계명 rooster crowing

鷄糞 계분 fowl droppings

鷄舍 계사 a poultry house

鬪鷄 투계 a cockfight; a fighting cock

MEANING AND SOUND

갓 冠 관 kwan

알 卵 란 ran

울 鳴 명 myŏng

똥 糞 분 pun

집 舍 사 sa

싸울 鬪 투 t'u

TYPICAL CONVERSATIONAL USAGE FOR READING AND TRANSLATION. EXERCISE:

1. 꿩 대신 닭 : 적당한 것이 없을 때 비슷한 것으로 대신함을 말함. Use a chicken instead of a pheasant.
   (If you cannot get what you want, use what you can get.)

2. 닭 잡아먹고 오리발 내어 놓는다. After eating a chicken, produce a duck's leg. (fooling people with dubious evidence)

3. 村鷄官廳(촌계관청) : 촌닭 관청에 온 것 같다 ; 시골 사람이 번화한 都市에 오거나 經驗이 없는 일을 당하여 넋이 빠져 있는 모습. The feeling of one in unfamiliar surroundings.

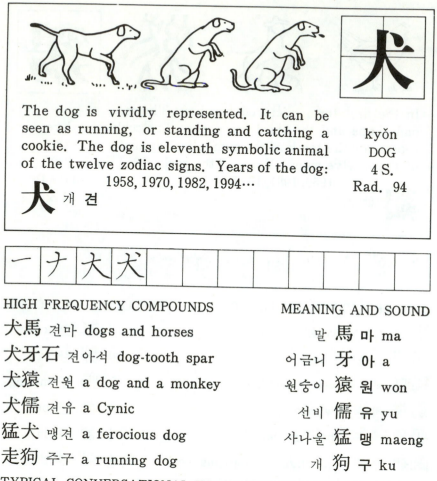

The dog is vividly represented. It can be seen as running, or standing and catching a cookie. The dog is eleventh symbolic animal of the twelve zodiac signs. Years of the dog: 1958, 1970, 1982, 1994…

犬 개 견

kyǒn
DOG
4 S.
Rad. 94

一 ナ 大 犬

HIGH FREQUENCY COMPOUNDS

犬馬 견마 dogs and horses

犬牙石 견아석 dog-tooth spar

犬猿 견원 a dog and a monkey

犬儒 견유 a Cynic

猛犬 맹견 a ferocious dog

走狗 주구 a running dog

MEANING AND SOUND

말 馬 마 ma

어금니 牙 아 a

원숭이 猿 원 won

선비 儒 유 yu

사나울 猛 맹 maeng

개 狗 구 ku

TYPICAL CONVERSATIONAL USAGE FOR READING AND TRANSLATION. EXERCISE:

1. 도둑놈 개에게 물린 꼴이다. As dumb as a thief who is bitten by a dog. (A thief bitten by a dog dares not cry out in pain lest the noise wake the master of the house.)

2. 산 개가 죽은 사자보다 낫다. (傳道書 9 : 4) A living dog is better than a dead lion. (*Ecclesiastes* 9 : 4)

3. 犬馬之勞 (견마지로) : 임금이나 나라에 충성을 다하는 勞力 ; 자기의 勞力을 謙遜하게 일컫는 말. One's humble service to the king.

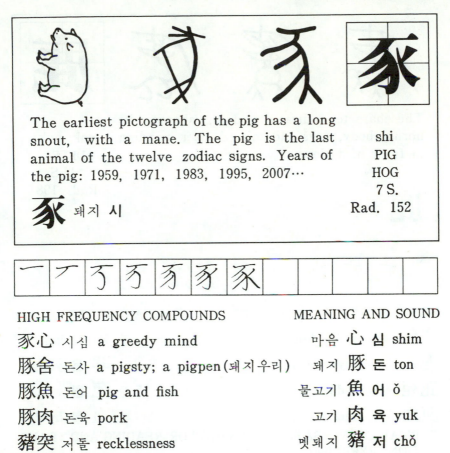

The earliest pictograph of the pig has a long snout, with a mane. The pig is the last animal of the twelve zodiac signs. Years of the pig: 1959, 1971, 1983, 1995, 2007···

豕 돼지 시

shi
PIG
HOG
7 S.
Rad. 152

HIGH FREQUENCY COMPOUNDS

豕心 시심 a greedy mind

豚舍 돈사 a pigsty; a pigpen (돼지우리)

豚魚 돈어 pig and fish

豚肉 돈육 pork

豬突 저돌 recklessness

MEANING AND SOUND

마음 心 심 shim

돼지 豚 돈 ton

물고기 魚 어 ŏ

고기 肉 육 yuk

멧돼지 豬 저 chŏ

TYPICAL CONVERSATIONAL USAGE FOR READING AND TRANSLATION. EXERCISE:

1. 돼지 우리에 주석 자물쇠 : 체격에 맞지 않는 지나친 치장. A pigsty, decorated with a bronze lock. (unbalance)

2. 멧돝 잡으러 갔다가 집돝까지 잃는다 : 먼 데 있는 것을 탐하다가 가까운 데 있는 것을 잃는다는 말. While chasing after a wild boar, lose a hog. (Greed brings only loss.)

3. 너희 眞珠를 돼지 앞에 던지지 말라. (마태복음 7 : 6) Do not throw your pearls before the hogs. (*Matthew* 7 : 6)

4. 굶주린 돼지같이 혼자 먹지 말고, 나누어 먹어라. You don't eat alone like a greedy pig, you should share.

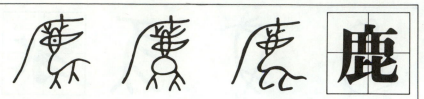

The character indicates a deer, showing its horns, body, legs and tail. A deer standing in front of a slope.

rok; nok
DEER
11 S.
Rad. 198

鹿 사슴 록

HIGH FREQUENCY COMPOUNDS

鹿角 녹각 deer's horns

鹿茸 녹용 a young antler

鹿苑 녹원 a deer farm

鹿血 녹혈 deer's blood

MEANING AND SOUND

뿔 角 각 kak

무성할 茸 용 yong

동산 苑 원 won

피 血 혈 hyŏl

TYPICAL CONVERSATIONAL USAGE FOR READING AND TRANSLATION. EXERCISE:

1. 사슴잡는 사냥꾼에겐 토끼가 보이지 않는다 : 큰 것을 바라보는 사람은 사소한 것은 거들떠보지도 않는다는 말. The deer hunter does not look at the hare.

2. 주 여호와는 나의 힘이시라 나의 발을 사슴과 같게 하사 나로 나의 높은 곳에 다니게 하시리로다. (하박국 3 : 19) The Lord God is my strength; He makes my feet like hinds' feet, He makes me tread upon my high places. (*Habakkuk* 3 : 19)

3. 옛날부터 노루(사슴) 뿔은 효험이 많은 名藥으로 알려져 왔다. From the ancient times deer horns have been known as an effective medicine.

4. 漢藥房에 가서 鹿茸 한 劑 지어다가 둘째애한테 달여 먹이자.

象

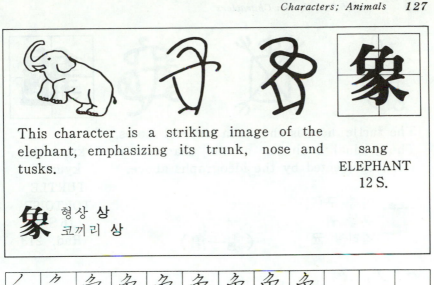

This character is a striking image of the elephant, emphasizing its trunk, nose and tusks.

sang
ELEPHANT
12 S.

象 형상 **상**
코끼리 **상**

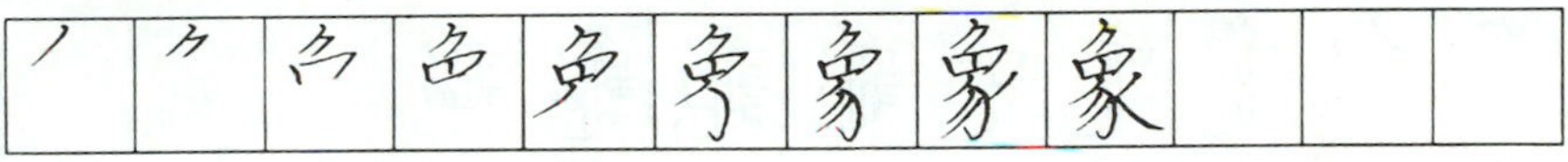

HIGH FREQUENCY COMPOUNDS	MEANING AND SOUND
象牙 상아 ivory	어금니 牙 **아** a
象牙塔 상아탑 a tower of ivory	탑 塔 **탑** t'ap
象徵 상징 a symbol; an emblem	부를 徵 **징** ching
象徵主義 상징주의 symbolism	주인 主 **주** chu
象形文 상형문 a hieroglyph	형상 形 **형** hyŏng
想像 상상 imagination; guess	생각 想 **상** sang

TYPICAL CONVERSATIONAL USAGE FOR READING AND TRANSLATION. EXERCISE:

1. 盲人摸象(맹인모상) : 장님 코끼리 만지기 ; 일부분만 보고 전체인 것처럼 말함. A blind man feeling an elephant; forming an opinion from limited data.
2. 象牙海岸을 아이버리코스트라고 하며 아프리카의 西海岸에 위치하고 있다. Sang-a hae-an is called the Ivory Coast and is located on the western coast of Africa.
3. 象徵主義는 문학과 예술에 나타난 思潮의 하나이다. Symbolism is one of the trends of thought appearing in art and literature.

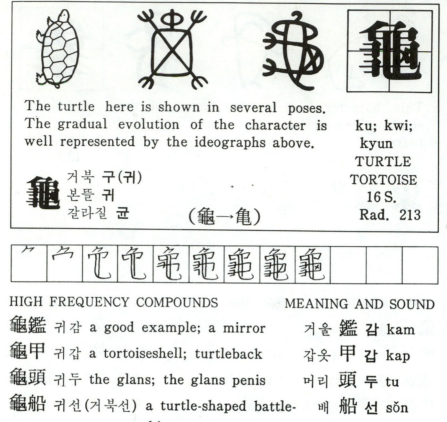

The turtle here is shown in several poses. The gradual evolution of the character is well represented by the ideographs above.

ku; kwi;
kyun
TURTLE
TORTOISE
16 S.
Rad. 213

거북 구(귀)
본뜰 귀
갈라질 균

(龜→亀)

HIGH FREQUENCY COMPOUNDS

MEANING AND SOUND

龜鑑 귀감 a good example; a mirror

거울 鑑 감 kam

龜甲 귀갑 a tortoiseshell; turtleback

갑옷 甲 갑 kap

龜頭 귀두 the glans; the glans penis

머리 頭 두 tu

龜船 귀선(거북선) a turtle-shaped battle-ship

배 船 선 sŏn

龜裂 균열 cracking

찢을 裂 렬 ryŏl

TYPICAL CONVERSATIONAL USAGE FOR READING AND TRANSLATION. EXERCISE:

1. 자라 보고 놀란 놈이 솥뚜껑 보고도 놀란다 : 어떤 것에 한번 놀란 사람은 비슷한 것만 보아도 놀란다는 말. Frightened at a turtle, startled at the lid of a kettle. (The lid of a kettle resembles a turtle.)

2. 거북선은 임진왜란 때 李舜臣 將軍이 제작한 世界 最初의 鐵甲 船이다. 노가 양쪽에 여러 개 있고 銃 구멍이 주위에 있으며 위는 철판으로 덮여 튼튼하였으므로 攻擊과 守備에 뛰어나 놀라운 海上戰鬪의 記錄을 남기었다. (西紀 1592 년)

6. 蟲類 충류 Insects and Reptiles

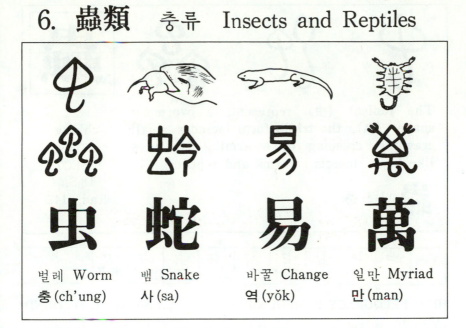

벌레 Worm	뱀 Snake	바꿀 Change	일만 Myriad
충 (ch'ung)	사 (sa)	역 (yŏk)	만 (man)

땅에 작고도 가장 지혜로운 것 넷이 있나니 곧 힘이 없는 種類로되 먹을 것을 여름에 豫備하는 개미와 약한 種類로되 집을 바위 사이에 짓는 사반과 임군이 없으되 다 떼를 지어 나아가는 메뚜기와 손에 잡힐 만하여도 王宮에 있는 도마뱀이니라. (箴言30:24~28)

There are four things that are small on the earth, but they are exceedingly wise: The ants are a people not strong, yet they provide their food in the summer; the rabbits are but a feeble folk, yet they make their homes in the rocks; the locusts have no king, yet all of them march in rank; the lizard you can take with your hands, yet it is found in king's palaces. (*Proverbs* 30 : 24~28)

헤롯이 榮光을 하나님께로 돌리지 아니하는 고로 主의 使者가 곧 치니 蟲이 먹어 죽으니라. (使徒行傳 12 : 23)

But instantly an angel of the Lord struck him, because he not ascribe the glory to God. He was eaten by worms, and died. (*Acts* 12 : 23)

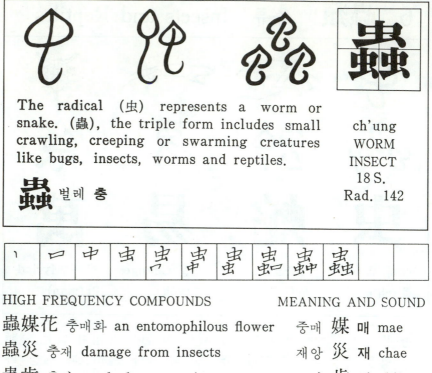

The radical (虫) represents a worm or snake. (蟲), the triple form includes small crawling, creeping or swarming creatures like bugs, insects, worms and reptiles.

ch'ung
WORM
INSECT
18 S.
Rad. 142

蟲 벌레 충

HIGH FREQUENCY COMPOUNDS

MEANING AND SOUND

蟲媒花 충매화 an entomophilous flower   중매 媒 매 mae

蟲災 충재 damage from insects   재앙 災 재 chae

蟲齒 충치 tooth decay; caries   이 齒 치 ch'i

驅蟲 구충 extermination of insects   몰아낼 驅 구 ku

寄生蟲 기생충 parasitic worms; vermin   부칠 寄 기 ki

害蟲 해충 destructive insects   해칠 害 해 hae

TYPICAL CONVERSATIONAL USAGE FOR READING AND TRANSLATION. EXERCISE:

1. 蛔蟲은 人體內에서 영양분을 빨아먹는 벌레이다. Roundworms are worms that get their nutrients from the human body.

2. 昨年農事는 害蟲으로 인하여 凶作이 되었다. Due to destructive insects, there was a bad harvest last year.

3. 韓國에서는 國民學校 어린이들에게 일년에 봄 가을 두 번씩 단체로 驅蟲藥을 먹인다. In Korea, the elementary school boys are given a vermifuge as a group twice a year, once in spring and once in fall.

During the summer night, many fireflies fly around the residence area. (火) represents the illuminant light by the firefly (虫, insects). It means a firefly.

hyŏng
FIREFLY
16 S.

螢 반딧불 형   (螢→蛍)

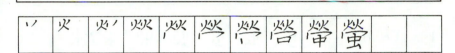

HIGH FREQUENCY COMPOUNDS   MEANING AND SOUND

螢光 형광 fluorescent light   빛 光 광 kwang

螢石 형석 fluorite; fluorspar   돌 石 석 sŏk

螢雪 형설 diligent study   눈 雪 설 sŏl

螢火 형화 the light of glowworm   불 火 화 hwa

TYPICAL CONVERSATIONAL USAGE FOR READING AND TRANSLATION. EXERCISE:

1. 螢光燈은 白熱電燈보다 밝다. The fluorescent light bulb is brighter than the electric light bulb.

2. 韓國의 선비들은 여름에 반딧불을 밝히고 공부하였다고 한다. They say that the classic scholars studied by the firefly's light in Korea.

3. 螢雪之功(형설지공) : 고생을 하면서 공부하여 얻은 보람. (中國 晉나라 車胤이 반딧불로 글을 읽고 孫康이 눈빛으로 글을 읽었다는 故事에서 온 말.) The fruits of diligent study.

4. 촛불은 自己 몸을 태우고 남을 밝힌다. The candle-light burns itself but gives light to others.

5. 螢雪의 功이 헛되지 않아 그는 錦衣還鄕하였다.

There is a snake devouring a field mouse. The snake or the serpent is the sixth animal of the Chinese twelve zodiac signs. Years of the snake: 1953, 1965, 1977, 1989, 2001···

sa
SNAKE
11 S

蛇 뱀 사

| 丨 | 冂 | 口 | 中 | 虫 | 虫 | 虫` | 虫` | 虫⼁ | 虴⼂ | 蛇 |

HIGH FREQUENCY COMPOUNDS

蛇蝎 사갈 snakes and scorpions

蛇足 사족 serpent's feet; redundancy

蛇行 사행 meandering

毒蛇 독사 a venomous serpent

白蛇 백사 a white snake

生蛇湯 생사탕 a snake decoction

花蛇 화사 a floral snake

MEANING AND SOUND

전갈 蝎 갈 kal

발 足 족 chok

갈 行 행 haeng

독할 毒 독 tok

흰 白 백 paek

날 生 생 saeng

꽃 花 화 hwa

TYPICAL CONVERSATIONAL USAGE FOR READING AND TRANSLATION EXERCISE:

1. 蛇蝎視 (사갈시) : 뱀이나 전갈을 보듯 함 ; 惡毒한 것으로 보고 끔찍이 싫어함. To abominate a person like a serpent.

2. 뱀의 머리는 될지언정 龍의 꼬리는 되지 마라.
   Better be the head of a snake than the tail of a dragon.

3. 여호와 하나님의 지으신 들짐승 中에 뱀이 가장 奸巧하더라.
   (創世記 3 : 1) The Serpent was more crafty than any beast of the field which the Lord God had made. (*Genesis* 3 : 1)

It represents a lizard, probably the chameleon, a primitive reptile. At the top is the
head and at the bottom are the feet of the
reptile. This character signifies change or
transformation like the color
change of a lizard.

易 바꿀 역
　 쉬울 이

yŏk; i
TO CHANGE
8 S.

| 丨 | 冂 | 冃 | 日 | 尸 | 昮 | 易 | 易 | | | |

HIGH FREQUENCY COMPOUNDS

易經 역경 the Book of Changes

易學 역학 the science of divination

貿易 무역 trade

容易 용이 ease; simplicity

MEANING AND SOUND

경서 經 경 kyŏng

배울 學 학 hak

무역할 貿 무 mu

얼굴 容 용 yong

TYPICAL CONVERSATIONAL USAGE FOR READING AND TRANSLATION. EXERCISE:

1. 韓國의 太極旗는 易學의 원리에 근거하고 있다. The Korean
   national flag is based on the principle of the science of
   divination.

2. 先進國의 保護貿易主義는 開發途上國의 輸出에 커다란 타격을
   준다. The advanced countries' protectionism gives great
   blows to the exportation of the developing countries.

3. 車線을 바꿀 때 먼저 信號를 주고 천천히 돌리세요.
   When you change lanes, you have to give a signal first and
   turn slowly.

4. 1弗 바꿀 수 있읍니까?
   Do you have change for a dollar?

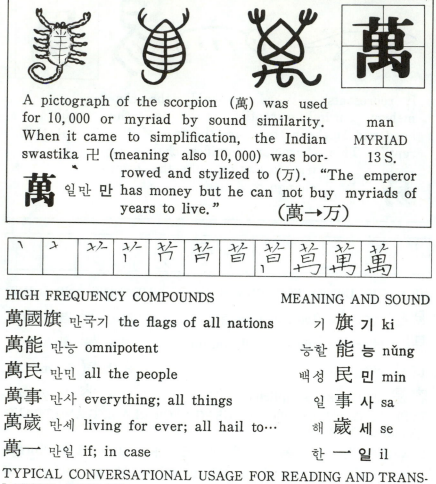

A pictograph of the scorpion (萬) was used for 10,000 or myriad by sound similarity. When it came to simplification, the Indian swastika 卍 (meaning also 10,000) was borrowed and stylized to (万). "The emperor has money but he can not buy myriads of years to live."

man
MYRIAD
13 S.

萬 일만 만

(萬→万)

HIGH FREQUENCY COMPOUNDS

			MEANING AND SOUND
萬國旗	만국기	the flags of all nations	기 旗 기 ki
萬能	만능	omnipotent	능할 能 능 nǔng
萬民	만민	all the people	백성 民 민 min
萬事	만사	everything; all things	일 事 사 sa
萬歲	만세	living for ever; all hail to…	해 歲 세 se
萬一	만일	if; in case	한 一 일 il

TYPICAL CONVERSATIONAL USAGE FOR READING AND TRANSLATION. EXERCISE:

1. 萬象更新(만상갱신) : 온갖 물건이 다시 고쳐지고 새롭게 됨.
   Everything in the universe is changed, is new.

2. 三十年 만에 故國에 와 보니 모든 것이 새롭게 변하였구나 !
   Visiting my homeland after 30 years' absence, I am surprised that everything has been so newly changed!

3. 우리 學校는 봄 가을 運動會 때마다 萬國旗로 장식한다. Our school is decorated with the flags of all the nations at every spring and fall athletic meeting.

CHARACTERS WITH THE INSECT RADICAL (虫) I

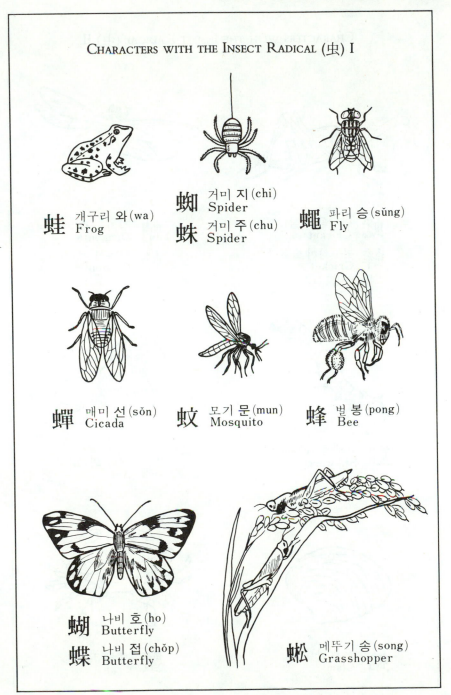

蛙 개구리 와(wa)
Frog

蜘 거미 지(chi)
Spider
蛛 거미 주(chu)
Spider

蠅 파리 승(sǔng)
Fly

蟬 매미 선(sǒn)
Cicada

蚊 모기 문(mun)
Mosquito

蜂 벌 봉(pong)
Bee

蝴 나비 호(ho)
Butterfly
蝶 나비 접(chŏp)
Butterfly

蜙 메뚜기 송(song)
Grasshopper

CHARACTERS WITH THE INSECT RADICAL (虫) II

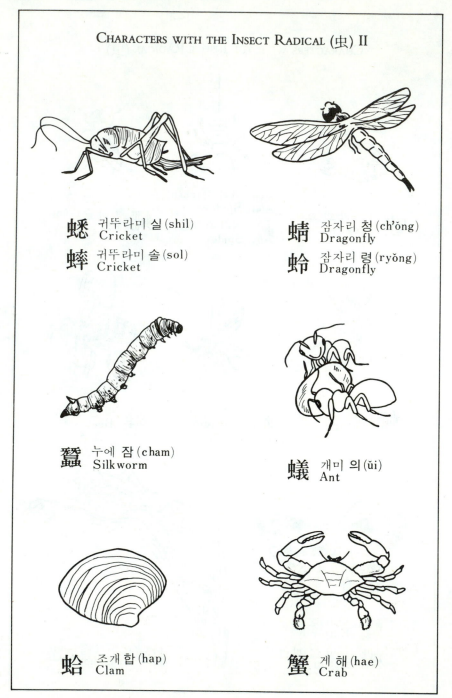

蟋 귀뚜라미 실 (shil)
Cricket

蟀 귀뚜라미 솔 (sol)
Cricket

蜻 잠자리 청 (ch'ŏng)
Dragonfly

蛉 잠자리 령 (ryŏng)
Dragonfly

蠶 누에 잠 (cham)
Silkworm

蟻 개미 의 (ŭi)
Ant

蛤 조개 합 (hap)
Clam

蟹 게 해 (hae)
Crab

7. 人間 인간 Mankind

사람 Man	오줌 Urine	똥 Excrement	꼬리 Tail
인 (in)	뇨 (nyo)	시 (shi)	미 (mi)

하나님이 自己形像 곧 하나님의 形像대로 사람을 創造하시되 男子와 女子를 創造하시고 하나님이 그들에게 福을 주시며 그들에게 이르시되 生育하고 蕃盛하여 땅에 充滿하라. 땅을 征服하라 바다의 고기와 空中의 새와 땅에 움직이는 모든 生物을 다스리라 하시니라. (創世記 1 : 27~28)

So God created man in His image; in the image of God He created him; male and female He created them. God blessed them; God said to them: Be fruitful; multiply; fill the earth and subdue it; bear rule over the fish of the sea; over the birds of the air and over every living, moving creature on the earth. (*Genesis* 1 : 27~28)

世上의 王들과 모든 百姓과 方伯과 땅의 모든 士師며 靑年 男子와 處女와 老人과 아이들아 다 여호와의 이름을 讚揚할지어다. 그 이름이 홀로 높으시며 그 榮光이 天地에 뛰어나심이로다. (詩篇. *Psalms* 148 : 11~13)

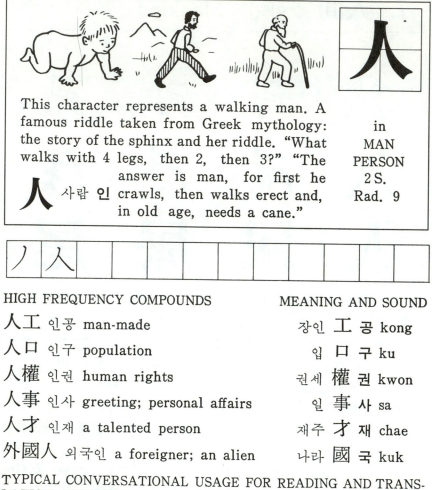

This character represents a walking man. A famous riddle taken from Greek mythology: the story of the sphinx and her riddle. "What walks with 4 legs, then 2, then 3?" "The answer is man, for first he crawls, then walks erect and, in old age, needs a cane."

人 사람 인

in
MAN
PERSON
2 S.
Rad. 9

ノ 人

HIGH FREQUENCY COMPOUNDS

人工 인공 man-made

人口 인구 population

人權 인권 human rights

人事 인사 greeting; personal affairs

人才 인재 a talented person

外國人 외국인 a foreigner; an alien

MEANING AND SOUND

장인 工 공 kong

입 口 구 ku

권세 權 권 kwon

일 事 사 sa

재주 才 재 chae

나라 國 국 kuk

TYPICAL CONVERSATIONAL USAGE FOR READING AND TRANSLATION. EXERCISE:

1. 人生朝露(인생조로) : 인생이 아침 이슬과 같이 덧없다는 말. Man's life is like the morning dew.

2. 人間은 굴뚝에서 나가는 연기와 같고, 풀과 같다고 聖經은 말한다. Bible says that man is like smoke from a chimney and like grass.

3. 人間은 萬物의 영장이므로, 모든 自然과 萬物을 다스린다. The human race, as the lord of all creation, rules over all of nature, and over all things.

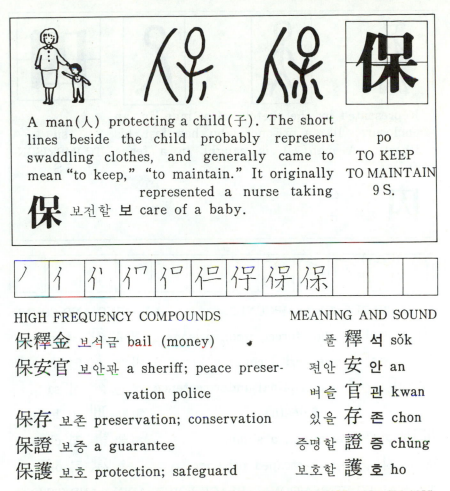

A man(人) protecting a child(子). The short lines beside the child probably represent swaddling clothes, and generally came to mean "to keep," "to maintain." It originally represented a nurse taking care of a baby.

保 보전할 보

po
TO KEEP
TO MAINTAIN
9 S.

HIGH FREQUENCY COMPOUNDS

保釋金 보석금 bail (money)

保安官 보안관 a sheriff; peace preservation police

保存 보존 preservation; conservation

保證 보증 a guarantee

保護 보호 protection; safeguard

MEANING AND SOUND

풀 釋 석 sŏk

편안 安 안 an

벼슬 官 관 kwan

있을 存 존 chon

증명할 證 증 chŭng

보호할 護 호 ho

TYPICAL CONVERSATIONAL USAGE FOR READING AND TRANSLATION. EXERCISE:

1. 여기는 保護席이므로 老弱者가 앉아야 합니다. The aged and handicapped must sit here as these seats are reserved for them.

2. 서부 영화에는 언제나 保安官이 등장한다. In Western movies, the sheriff always makes an appearance.

3. 서울에 있는 南大門은 國寶 제 1 호로 지정되어 貴重하게 保存 되고 있다. The South Gate, which is in Seoul, is designated as national treasure No. 1 and is being very well preserved.

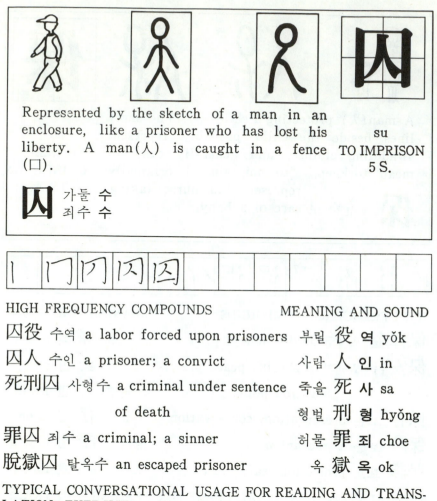

Represented by the sketch of a man in an enclosure, like a prisoner who has lost his liberty. A man(人) is caught in a fence (口).

su

TO IMPRISON

5 S.

囚   가둘 수
     죄수 수

HIGH FREQUENCY COMPOUNDS   MEANING AND SOUND

囚役 수역 a labor forced upon prisoners   부릴 役 역 yŏk

囚人 수인 a prisoner; a convict   사람 人 인 in

死刑囚 사형수 a criminal under sentence   죽을 死 사 sa
                       of death   형벌 刑 형 hyŏng

罪囚 죄수 a criminal; a sinner   허물 罪 죄 choe

脫獄囚 탈옥수 an escaped prisoner   옥 獄 옥 ok

TYPICAL CONVERSATIONAL USAGE FOR READING AND TRANSLATION. EXERCISE:

1. 美國에는 罪囚들이 많은데, 矯導所의 시설이 不足하여 刑量을 줄이며 석방시키는 형편이다. In America, there are lots of criminals but they are lacking prison facilities, so they shorten sentences and free criminals.

2. 使徒 바울은 福音을 전파하다가 로마 獄에 갇혔었다. St. Paul was jailed in Rome for preaching the gospel.

3. 그는 미친 사람으로 看做되어 자기 방에 갇혀 버렸다. Supposed to be mad, he was imprisoned in his own room.

This character is a man running and 𝗎 under the first and second pictures, indicates foot prints.

chu
TO RUN
7 S.

走 달릴 주

一 十 土 ㄠ 圭 赱 走

HIGH FREQUENCY COMPOUNDS   MEANING AND SOUND

走廣跳 주광도 the broad jump(멀리뛰기)   넓을 廣 광 kwang

走路 주로 a track; a course   길 路 로 ro

走馬燈 주마등 a revolving lantern;   등불 燈 등 tŭng

         kaleidoscopic change   뛸 跳 도 to

走者 주자 a runner   놈 者 자 cha

走電性 주전성 electrotaxis   성품 性 성 sŏng

逃走 도주 flight; an escape   달아날 逃 도 to

滑走路 활주로 a runway   미끄러질 滑 활 hwal

TYPICAL CONVERSATIONAL USAGE FOR READING AND TRANS-LATION. EXERCISE:

1. 滑走路를 달리던 旅客機 한 대가 짙은 안개 때문에 脫線하였다.
   A passenger liner which was taxiing down the runway over-ran the end of it due to thick fog.

2. 金鍾鎰은 서울 아시아 경기대회의 走廣跳 종목에서 금메달을 땄다. Kim Chong-il won the gold medal for the broad jump at the Seoul Asian Games.

This character comprises several radicals indicating the defence of his clan or tribe by arrows(矢). It may be said to mean guardian.

chok
TRIBE
CLAN
11 S.

族 겨레 족

| 丶 | 亠 | 亠 | 方 | 方 | 方 | 方 | 族 | | | |

HIGH FREQUENCY COMPOUNDS

族閥主義 족벌주의 nepotism

族譜 족보 a genealogy; a table of descent

族長 족장 a patriarch

族親 족친 relatives

同族 동족 the same race; consan-
　　　　guinity

民族 민족 a race; a people; a tribe

MEANING AND SOUND

문벌 閥 벌 pŏl

계보 譜 보 po

긴 長 장 chang

친할 親 친 ch'in

한가지 同 동 tong

백성 民 민 min

TYPICAL CONVERSATIONAL USAGE FOR READING AND TRANSLATION. EXERCISE:

1. 이스라엘에는 十二지파에 열두 族長이 있었다. There were twelve leaders of the twelve tribes of Israel.
2. 우리 家門에도 族譜가 있다. Our family has a record of our family tree, too.
3. 몰몬교는 族譜를 重要視한다. The Mormon church places great emphasis on the family tree.
4. 韓國人은 白衣民族이다. Koreans are the white-clad people.

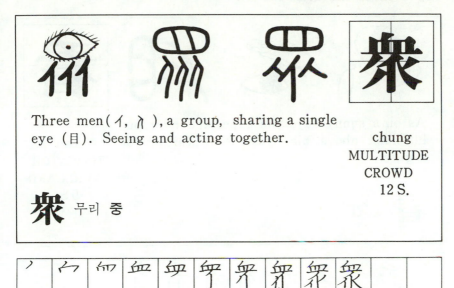

Three men (亻, 人), a group, sharing a single eye (目). Seeing and acting together.

chung
MULTITUDE
CROWD
12 S.

衆 무리 중

丿 冂 血 血 血 宇 罙 罙 衆 衆

HIGH FREQUENCY COMPOUNDS

公衆 공중 the public; public

公衆道德 공중도덕 public morality

群衆 군중 a multitude; a crowd

群衆心理 군중심리 mob psychology

大衆 대중 a crowd of people; the masses

聽衆 청중 an audience; an attendance

MEANING AND SOUND

공변될 公 공 kong

큰 德 덕 tŏk

무리 群 군 kun

다스릴 理 리 ri

큰 大 대 tae

들을 聽 청 ch'ŏng

TYPICAL CONVERSATIONAL USAGE FOR READING AND TRANS-LATION. EXERCISE:

1. 오늘의 講演者는 聽衆들한테 우뢰 같은 갈채를 받았다. Today's speaker received a thunderous applause from the audience.

2. 衆寡不敵(중과부적) : 수효의 적은 것은 많은 것을 對敵할 수 없다는 뜻. Those of a lesser number can not compete with those of a greater number.

3. 衆口鑠金(중구삭금) : 뭇사람의 말은 쇠같이 굳은 물건도 녹인다는 말로 여러 사람의 意見의 말은 무섭다는 뜻. The power of popular criticism is terrible.

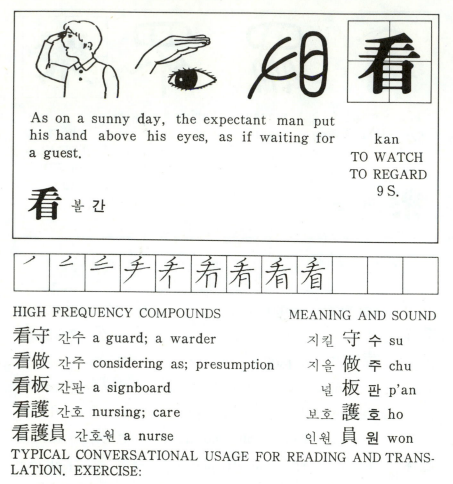

As on a sunny day, the expectant man put his hand above his eyes, as if waiting for a guest.

看 볼 간

kan
TO WATCH
TO REGARD
9 S.

HIGH FREQUENCY COMPOUNDS

MEANING AND SOUND

看守 간수 a guard; a warder   지킬 守 수 su

看做 간주 considering as; presumption   지을 做 주 chu

看板 간판 a signboard   널 板 판 p'an

看護 간호 nursing; care   보호 護 호 ho

看護員 간호원 a nurse   인원 員 원 won

TYPICAL CONVERSATIONAL USAGE FOR READING AND TRANSLATION. EXERCISE:

1. 看守들은 時間마다 번갈아 가며 交代로 근무한다. Prison guards work alternately switching off every hour.

2. 두 時까지 연락이 없으면 포기하는 것으로 看做하겠다. If there is no contact by two o'clock, I will assume that you give up.

3. 그는 看板이 좋아서 출세했다. He has risen in the world with his brilliant academic background.

4. 女子 看護員만 있는 줄 알았더니 男子 看護員도 환자를 잘 돌보고 있다. I thought that there were only female nurses but male nurses also take good care of the patients.

Probably, the man is a guest sheltered under a roof (宀). In the second form, a leg (𠯵) is added to show that he is a traveler. Instead later forms add (貝), shell money which symbolize the exchange of ceremonial gifts by guest and host.

pin
GUEST
14 S.

賓 손님 빈

HIGH FREQUENCY COMPOUNDS

國賓 국빈 a national guest

來賓 내빈 a guest; a visitor

迎賓館 영빈관 a guest house (as a hotel)

主賓席 주빈석 the seat of honor

貧富 빈부 wealth and poverty

殯所 빈소 a mortuary; a lying-in-state room

MEANING AND SOUND

나라 國 국 kuk

올 來 래 rae

집 館 관 kwan

자리 席 석 sŏk

가난할 貧 빈 pin

빈소 殯 빈 pin

곳 所 소 so

TYPICAL CONVERSATIONAL USAGE FOR READING AND TRANSLATION. EXERCISE:

1. 生鮮과 손님은 사흘이 지나면 상한다. Fish and guest in three days are stale. (*John Lyly*)

2. 첫날은 손님이지만, 둘째 날은 짐이요, 세째 날은 害蟲이다. The first day a man is a guest, the second a burden, the third a pest. (*Laboulaye*)

3. 그러므로 무엇이든지 남에게 待接을 받고자 하는 대로 너희도 남을 待接하라. 이것이 律法이요 先知者니라. (마태福音. 7 : 12)

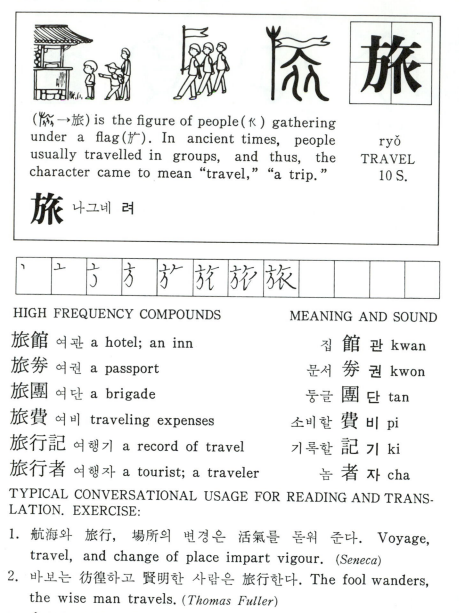

(旅→旅) is the figure of people(ᓚ) gathering under a flag(ᠵ). In ancient times, people usually travelled in groups, and thus, the character came to mean "travel," "a trip."

ryŏ
TRAVEL
10 S.

旅 나그네 려

HIGH FREQUENCY COMPOUNDS

旅館 여관 a hotel; an inn

旅券 여권 a passport

旅團 여단 a brigade

旅費 여비 traveling expenses

旅行記 여행기 a record of travel

旅行者 여행자 a tourist; a traveler

MEANING AND SOUND

집 館 관 kwan

문서 券 권 kwon

둥글 團 단 tan

소비할 費 비 pi

기록할 記 기 ki

놈 者 자 cha

TYPICAL CONVERSATIONAL USAGE FOR READING AND TRANSLATION. EXERCISE:

1. 航海와 旅行, 場所의 변경은 活氣를 돋워 준다. Voyage, travel, and change of place impart vigour. (*Seneca*)

2. 바보는 彷徨하고 賢明한 사람은 旅行한다. The fool wanders, the wise man travels. (*Thomas Fuller*)

3. 日本 觀光客이 第一 많아요. They are mostly Japanese tourists.

4. 外國을 旅行하려면 旅券과 免疫證을 가지고 가야 한다. When you take trip abroad you must carry your passport and shot records.

8. 身體 신체 The Human Body

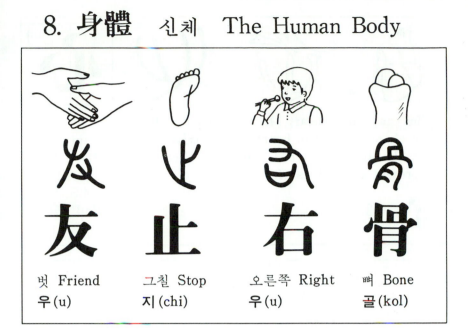

벗 Friend	그칠 Stop	오른쪽 Right	뼈 Bone
우 (u)	지 (chi)	우 (u)	골 (kol)

몸은 하나인데 많은 肢體가 있고 몸의 肢體가 많으나 한 몸임과 같이 그리스도도 그러하니라. 몸은 한 肢體뿐 아니요 여럿이니 만일 발이 이르되 나는 손이 아니니 몸에 붙지 아니하였다 할지라도 이로 因하여 몸에 붙지 아니한 것이 아니요, 만일 한 肢體가 苦痛을 받으면 모든 肢體도 함께 苦痛을 받고 한 肢體가 榮光을 얻으면 모든 肢體도 함께 즐거워하나니 너희는 그리스도의 몸이요 肢體의 各部分이라. (고린도前書 12 : 12, 15, 26)

For as the body is one and has many members, but all the members of that one body, being many, are one body, so also is Christ. If the foot should say, "Because I am not a hand, I am not of the body," is it therefore not of the body? And if one member suffers, all the members suffer with it; or if one member is honoured, all the members rejoice with it. (I *Corinthians* 12 : 12, 15, 26)

만일 네 발이 너를 犯罪케 하거든 찍어 버리라. 절뚝발이로 永生에 들어가는 것이 두 발을 가지고 地獄에 던지우는 것보다 나으리라. (마가福音, *Mark* 9 : 45)

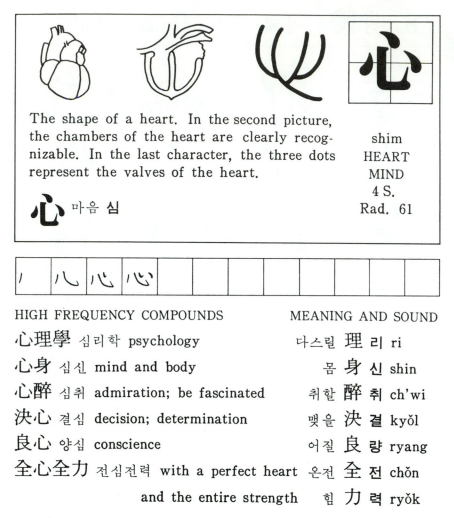

The shape of a heart. In the second picture, the chambers of the heart are clearly recognizable. In the last character, the three dots represent the valves of the heart.

心 마음 심

shim
HEART
MIND
4 S.
Rad. 61

HIGH FREQUENCY COMPOUNDS

MEANING AND SOUND

心理學 심리학 psychology
다스릴 理 리 ri

心身 심신 mind and body
몸 身 신 shin

心醉 심취 admiration; be fascinated
취할 醉 취 ch'wi

決心 결심 decision; determination
맺을 決 결 kyŏl

良心 양심 conscience
어질 良 량 ryang

全心全力 전심전력 with a perfect heart
온전 全 전 chŏn

and the entire strength
힘 力 력 ryŏk

TYPICAL CONVERSATIONAL USAGE FOR READING AND TRANSLATION. EXERCISE:

1. 하나님과 사람을 대하여 恒常 良心에 거리낌이 없기를 힘쓰노라. (使徒行傳 24 : 16) I always take pains to have a clear conscience toward God and toward man. (*Acts* 24 : 16)

2. 人面獸心 (인면수심) : 얼굴은 사람 꼴을 하고 있으나 마음은 짐승과 같다는 뜻 ; 이중 인격자를 말함. The face of a man but a heart of a beast. (double personality).

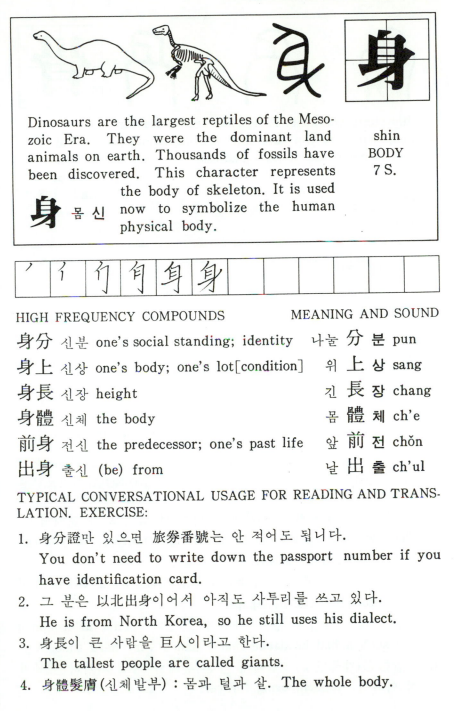

shin
BODY
7 S.

Dinosaurs are the largest reptiles of the Mesozoic Era. They were the dominant land animals on earth. Thousands of fossils have been discovered. This character represents the body of skeleton. It is used now to symbolize the human physical body.

身 몸 신

HIGH FREQUENCY COMPOUNDS   MEANING AND SOUND

身分 신분 one's social standing; identity   나눌 分 분 pun

身上 신상 one's body; one's lot[condition]   위 上 상 sang

身長 신장 height   긴 長 장 chang

身體 신체 the body   몸 體 체 ch'e

前身 전신 the predecessor; one's past life   앞 前 전 chŏn

出身 출신 (be) from   날 出 출 ch'ul

TYPICAL CONVERSATIONAL USAGE FOR READING AND TRANSLATION. EXERCISE:

1. 身分證만 있으면 旅券番號는 안 적어도 됩니다.
   You don't need to write down the passport number if you have identification card.

2. 그 분은 以北出身이어서 아직도 사투리를 쓰고 있다.
   He is from North Korea, so he still uses his dialect.

3. 身長이 큰 사람을 巨人이라고 한다.
   The tallest people are called giants.

4. 身體髮膚 (신체발부) : 몸과 털과 살. The whole body.

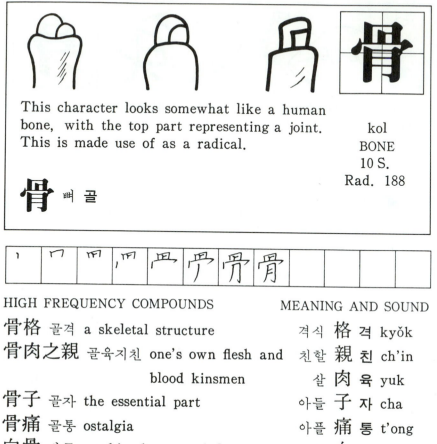

This character looks somewhat like a human bone, with the top part representing a joint. This is made use of as a radical.

kol
BONE
10 S.
Rad. 188

骨 뼈 골

ノ	冂	冋	冎	咼	骨	骨	骨			

HIGH FREQUENCY COMPOUNDS

骨格 골격 a skeletal structure

骨肉之親 골육지친 one's own flesh and blood kinsmen

骨子 골자 the essential part

骨痛 골통 ostalgia

白骨 백골 a white bone; a skeleton

MEANING AND SOUND

격식 格 격 kyŏk

친할 親 친 ch'in

살 肉 육 yuk

아들 子 자 cha

아플 痛 통 t'ong

흰 白 백 paek

TYPICAL CONVERSATIONAL USAGE FOR READING AND TRANSLATION. EXERCISE:

1. 저 이층집은 骨格이 튼튼하므로 한층 더 올려도 될 것이다. That two story building has a strong structure, so you can build up one more story.

2. 그 신문 社說의 骨子가 뭐야? What is the main contents of the editorial in the newspaper?

3. 오늘 午後는 골치가 몹시 아파서 혼났다. This afternoon I had such a bad headache that I had a very hard time.

4. 刻骨難忘(각골난망) : 남에게 입은 은혜가 뼈에 새겨져 잊혀지지 아니함. Remembering forever.

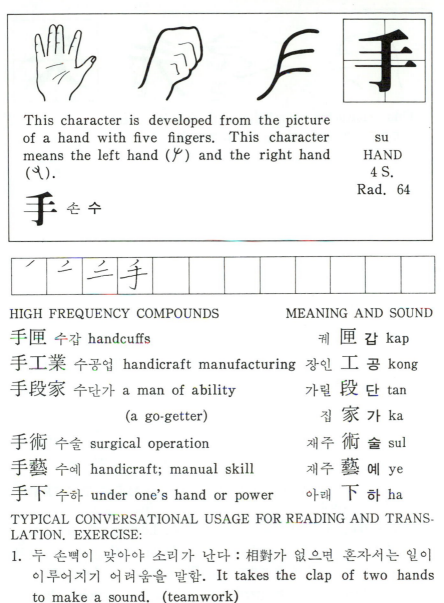

This character is developed from the picture of a hand with five fingers. This character means the left hand (у) and the right hand (х).

su
HAND
4 S.
Rad. 64

手 손 수

ノ 二 三 手

HIGH FREQUENCY COMPOUNDS

手匣 수갑 handcuffs

手工業 수공업 handicraft manufacturing

手段家 수단가 a man of ability

(a go-getter)

手術 수술 surgical operation

手藝 수예 handicraft; manual skill

手下 수하 under one's hand or power

MEANING AND SOUND

궤 匣 갑 kap

장인 工 공 kong

가릴 段 단 tan

집 家 가 ka

재주 術 술 sul

재주 藝 예 ye

아래 下 하 ha

TYPICAL CONVERSATIONAL USAGE FOR READING AND TRANSLATION. EXERCISE:

1. 두 손뼉이 맞아야 소리가 난다 : 相對가 없으면 혼자서는 일이 이루어지기 어려움을 말함. It takes the clap of two hands to make a sound. (teamwork)

2. 法은 멀고 주먹은 가깝다 : 事理를 따지기보다는 腕力이 먼저 힘을 쓴다는 뜻. The law is far, the fist is near.

3. 自手削髮 못한다 : 제손으로 자기의 머리를 깎을 수 없다 ; 어떤 일을 제 혼자 힘으로 처리하기 어렵다는 뜻.

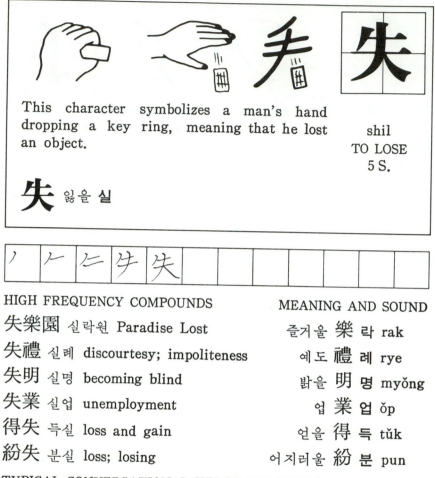

This character symbolizes a man's hand dropping a key ring, meaning that he lost an object.

shil
TO LOSE
5 S.

失 잃을 실

ノ ヒ ヒ 午 失

HIGH FREQUENCY COMPOUNDS

失樂園 실락원 Paradise Lost

失禮 실례 discourtesy; impoliteness

失明 실명 becoming blind

失業 실업 unemployment

得失 득실 loss and gain

紛失 분실 loss; losing

MEANING AND SOUND

즐거울 樂 락 rak

예도 禮 례 rye

밝을 明 명 myŏng

업 業 업 ŏp

얻을 得 득 tŭk

어지러울 紛 분 pun

TYPICAL CONVERSATIONAL USAGE FOR READING AND TRANSLATION. EXERCISE:

1. 失而復得(실이부득) : 잃었다가 되찾음. Lost and found again.
2. 失樂園은 존 밀턴의 敍事詩인데, 聖經의 창세기 에덴동산의 내용을 근거로 쓴 古典名作이다. *Paradise Lost*, John Milton's epic influenced by the garden of Eden, is a famous classic.
3. 身分證을 紛失했으니까 廣告를 내서 빨리 찾아야 하겠다. I have lost my I.D. card, so I have to put an ad so that I can find it quickly.
4. 그는 不幸하게도 韓國戰爭 때 失明하였다.

This character means "to receive," signified by one person handing a business card to another. (受) represents "two hands": one is offering an object, and the other is receiving it.

su

TO RECEIVE
TO ACCEPT
8 S.

受 받을 수

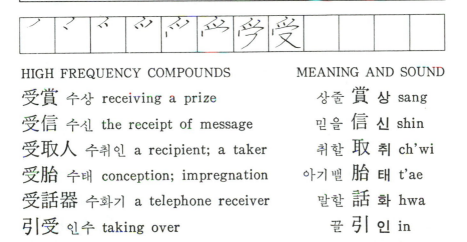

HIGH FREQUENCY COMPOUNDS	MEANING AND SOUND

受賞 수상 receiving a prize 　　　상줄 賞 상 sang

受信 수신 the receipt of message 　　믿을 信 신 shin

受取人 수취인 a recipient; a taker 　　취할 取 취 ch'wi

受胎 수태 conception; impregnation 　아기밸 胎 태 t'ae

受話器 수화기 a telephone receiver 　말할 話 화 hwa

引受 인수 taking over 　　　　끌 引 인 in

TYPICAL CONVERSATIONAL USAGE FOR READING AND TRANSLATION. EXERCISE:

1. 다음번의 노벨 平和賞 受賞者는 누구일까? I wonder who the recipient of the next Novel Peace Prize will be.

2. 우리 補給課의 무전기는 受信 狀態가 좋지 않다. We do not have good reception of the supply section's radio.

3. 시카고에서 온 소포의 受取人이 누군지 아세요? Do you know who the recipient of the package which came from Chicago is?

4. 작년에 教會 버스 한 대를 引受했다. We received a church bus last year.

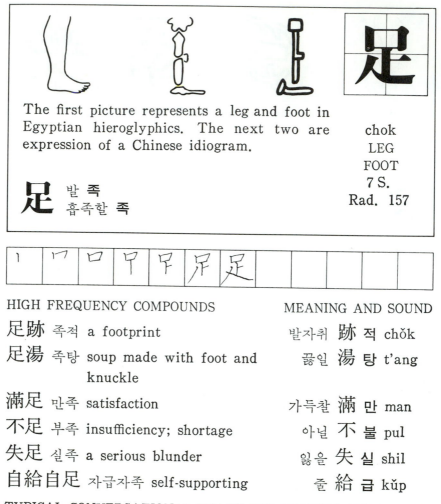

The first picture represents a leg and foot in Egyptian hieroglyphics. The next two are expression of a Chinese idiogram.

chok
LEG
FOOT
7 S.
Rad. 157

足 발 족
　　흡족할 족

HIGH FREQUENCY COMPOUNDS

MEANING AND SOUND

足跡 족적 a footprint ... 발자취 跡 적 chŏk

足湯 족탕 soup made with foot and knuckle ... 끓일 湯 탕 t'ang

滿足 만족 satisfaction ... 가득찰 滿 만 man

不足 부족 insufficiency; shortage ... 아닐 不 불 pul

失足 실족 a serious blunder ... 잃을 失 실 shil

自給自足 자급자족 self-supporting ... 줄 給 급 kŭp

TYPICAL CONVERSATIONAL USAGE FOR READING AND TRANSLATION. EXERCISE:

1. 우리 人事課에는 사무기기가 不足해요. We have a shortage of office equipment in the personnel section.

2. 韓國이 統一만 된다면 모든 부문에서 거의 다 自給自足할 수 있게 될 것이다. If Korea were only reunified, it would probably be self-supporting in almost all areas.

3. 階段에서 失足하면 負傷당하기 쉬우니 조심하세요. Please be careful, because if you fall down on the stairway you get hurt.

The first picture is a representation of a foot-print, meaning the foot stops there.

chi
TO STOP
TO CEASE
4 S.
Rad. 77

止 그칠 지

一 ㅏ 止 止

HIGH FREQUENCY COMPOUNDS

止熱 지열 one's temperature falls; lowering the temperature

止血 지혈 arrest of bleeding

禁止 금지 prohibition; taboo

防止 방지 prevention

中止 중지 stop; discontinuance

廢止 폐지 discontinuance; abolition

MEANING AND SOUND

더울 熱 열 yŏl

피 血 혈 hyŏl

금할 禁 금 kŭm

막을 防 방 pang

가운데 中 중 chung

폐할 廢 폐 p'ye

TYPICAL CONVERSATIONAL USAGE FOR READING AND TRANS-LATION. EXERCISE:

1. 出入禁止(출입금지) : 드나들지 마세요. Keep out!

2. 韓國의 夜間 通行禁止 制度는 수 년 전에 廢止되었다. The curfew had been abolished a few years ago in Korea.

3. 橋梁을 修理하는 동안 모든 通行을 中止시켜야 한다. You have to stop all traffic while fixing the bridge.

4. 그 競技는 비 때문에 中止되었다. The match was called off owing to the rain.

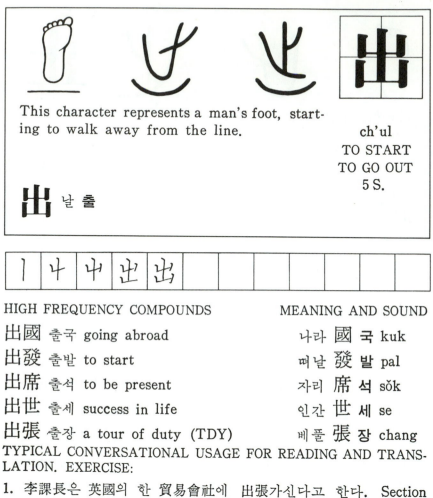

This character represents a man's foot, starting to walk away from the line.

ch'ul
TO START
TO GO OUT
5 S.

出 날 출

丨	屮	屮	出	出							

HIGH FREQUENCY COMPOUNDS

出國 출국 going abroad

出發 출발 to start

出席 출석 to be present

出世 출세 success in life

出張 출장 a tour of duty (TDY)

MEANING AND SOUND

나라 國 국 kuk

떠날 發 발 pal

자리 席 석 sŏk

인간 世 세 se

베풀 張 장 chang

TYPICAL CONVERSATIONAL USAGE FOR READING AND TRANSLATION. EXERCISE:

1. 李課長은 英國의 한 貿易會社에 出張가신다고 한다. Section chief Lee said that he would be going TDY to a trading company in England.

2. 美國에서 出國命令을 받은 北韓 外交官은 사정이 딱하게 됐다. The North Korean diplomat who received the order to depart the U.S. has been placed in an awkward situation.

3. 出世의 方法에는, 自身의 努力에 의한 것과 他人들의 어리석음에 의한 것 두 가지가 있을 뿐이다. There are only two ways of getting on in the world: by one's own industry, or by the stupidity of others. (*La Bruyère*)

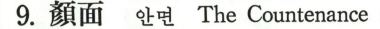

9. 顏面 안면 The Countenance

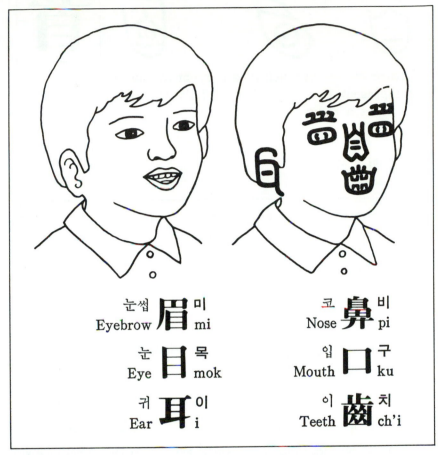

눈섭 Eyebrow	眉 미 mi		코 Nose	鼻 비 pi
눈 Eye	目 목 mok		입 Mouth	口 구 ku
귀 Ear	耳 이 i		이 Teeth	齒 치 ch'i

또 귀가 이르되 나는 눈이 아니니 몸에 붙지 않았다 할지라도 이로 因하여 몸에 붙지 아니한 것이 아니니 만일 온몸이 눈이면 듣는 곳은 어디며 온몸이 듣는 곳이면 넘새 맡는 곳은 어디뇨. 이제 肢體는 많으나 몸은 하나라. (고린도 前書 12 : 16∼17, 20)

Or if the ear should say, "Because I am not an eye, I do not belong to the body", it is nevertheless part of the body. If the entire body were an eye, where would the hearing, what of the smelling? As it is there are many members to form one body. (I *Cor.* 12 : 16∼17, 20)

Picture of an eye below an eyebrow, used to represent the entire head. This is made use of as a radical.

su
HEAD
9 S.
Rad. 185

首 머리 수

| ` | ゛ | ソ | ゾ | ゲ | 芐 | 肖 | 首 | 首 | | |

HIGH FREQUENCY COMPOUNDS

首都 수도 a capital

首相 수상 the prime minister

首席 수석 the top seat; the top of the class

首弟子 수제자 the best disciple

內閣首班 내각수반 the head of cabinet

元首 원수 a sovereign; head of state

MEANING AND SOUND

도읍 都 도 to

정승 相 상 sang

자리 席 석 sŏk

아우 弟 제 che

누각 閣 각 kak

으뜸 元 원 won

TYPICAL CONVERSATIONAL USAGE FOR READING AND TRANSLATION. EXERCISE:

1. 韓國의 首都 서울의 人口는 일천만으로 增加했다. The population of Seoul, the capital of Korea, has increased to ten million.

2. 금년도 서울대학교 首席合格의 영예는 나의 조카가 차지하였다. My nephew captured the honor of standing first on this year's Seoul National University entrance examination.

3. 예수님의 首弟子 베드로는 가야바 宮廷에서 닭이 울기 전에 세 번 주님을 모른다고 否認했다.

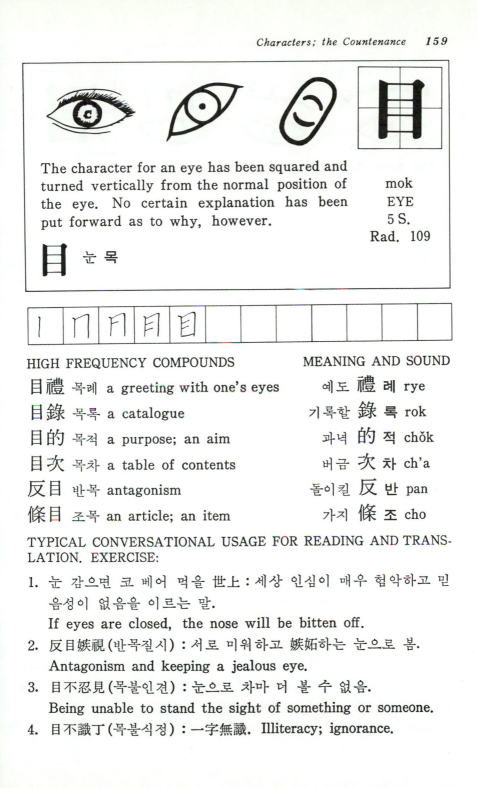

The character for an eye has been squared and turned vertically from the normal position of the eye. No certain explanation has been put forward as to why, however.

mok
EYE
5 S.
Rad. 109

目　눈 목

HIGH FREQUENCY COMPOUNDS

目禮 목례 a greeting with one's eyes

目錄 목록 a catalogue

目的 목적 a purpose; an aim

目次 목차 a table of contents

反目 반목 antagonism

條目 조목 an article; an item

MEANING AND SOUND

예도 禮 례 rye

기록할 錄 록 rok

과녁 的 적 chŏk

버금 次 차 ch'a

돌이킬 反 반 pan

가지 條 조 cho

TYPICAL CONVERSATIONAL USAGE FOR READING AND TRANSLATION. EXERCISE:

1. 눈 감으면 코 베어 먹을 世上 : 세상 인심이 매우 험악하고 믿음성이 없음을 이르는 말.
   If eyes are closed, the nose will be bitten off.

2. 反目嫉視 (반목질시) : 서로 미워하고 嫉妬하는 눈으로 봄.
   Antagonism and keeping a jealous eye.

3. 目不忍見 (목불인견) : 눈으로 차마 더 볼 수 없음.
   Being unable to stand the sight of something or someone.

4. 目不識丁 (목불식정) : 一字無識. Illiteracy; ignorance.

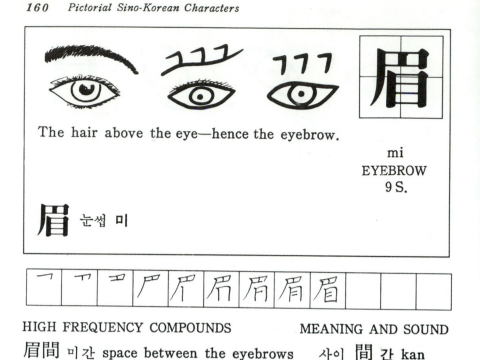

The hair above the eye—hence the eyebrow.

mi
EYEBROW
9 S.

眉 눈썹 미

| 一 | 刁 | ⼌ | 尹 | 尸 | 尽 | 屌 | 眉 | 眉 | | |

HIGH FREQUENCY COMPOUNDS   MEANING AND SOUND

眉間 미간 space between the eyebrows   사이 間 간 kan

眉目 미목 features; eyes and eyebrows   눈 目 목 mok

眉宇 미우 the brow; features   집 宇 우 u

眉月 미월 a crescent   달 月 월 wol

愁眉 수미 knitted eyebrows; a worried   근심 愁 수 su
look

TYPICAL CONVERSATIONAL USAGE FOR READING AND TRANS-
LATION. EXERCISE:

1. 眉間이 넓은 사람은 아량이 있다고 한다. Those who have wide
spaces between the eyebrows are said to be open-minded.

2. 李양은 눈하고 눈썹(眉目)이 참 아름다와요.
Miss Lee has very beautiful eyes and eyebrows.

3. 初生달은 中天에 떴고 실바람이 살랑거렸다. A crescent hung
in the middle of the sky and there was a breeze.

4. 眉目秀麗(미목수려): 얼굴이 빼어나게 아름다움.
Excellently good looks.

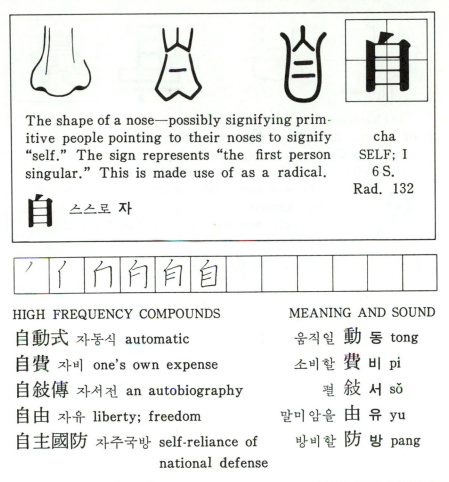

The shape of a nose—possibly signifying prim- itive people pointing to their noses to signify "self." The sign represents "the first person singular." This is made use of as a radical.

cha
SELF; I
6 S.
Rad. 132

自 스스로 **자**

HIGH FREQUENCY COMPOUNDS

自動式 자동식 automatic

自費 자비 one's own expense

自敍傳 자서전 an autobiography

自由 자유 liberty; freedom

自主國防 자주국방 self-reliance of national defense

MEANING AND SOUND

움직일 動 동 tong

소비할 費 비 pi

펼 敍 서 sŏ

말미암을 由 유 yu

방비할 防 방 pang

TYPICAL CONVERSATIONAL USAGE FOR READING AND TRANS- LATION. EXERCISE:

1. 엎어지면 코 닿을 데 : 매우 가까운 거리. The nose will touch it if one lies on the belly. (within a stone's throw)

2. 自由는 天賦人權 중의 하나이다.
   Freedom is one of the natural human rights.

3. 眞理를 알지니 眞理가 너희를 自由케 하리라. (요한福音 8 : 32)
   You will know the truth and the truth will set you free.

4. 自暴自棄(자포자기) : 마음에 不滿이 있어 行動을 되는대로 마 구 취하고 스스로 自身을 돌아보지 아니함. Self-abandonment

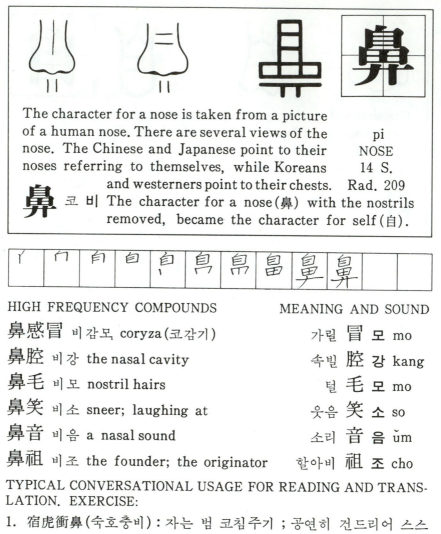

The character for a nose is taken from a picture of a human nose. There are several views of the nose. The Chinese and Japanese point to their noses referring to themselves, while Koreans and westerners point to their chests.

pi
NOSE
14 S.
Rad. 209

鼻 코 비 The character for a nose (鼻) with the nostrils removed, became the character for self (自).

HIGH FREQUENCY COMPOUNDS

鼻感冒 비감모, coryza (코감기)

鼻腔 비강 the nasal cavity

鼻毛 비모 nostril hairs

鼻笑 비소 sneer; laughing at

鼻音 비음 a nasal sound

鼻祖 비조 the founder; the originator

MEANING AND SOUND

가릴 冒 모 mo

속빌 腔 강 kang

털 毛 모 mo

웃음 笑 소 so

소리 音 음 ŭm

할아비 祖 조 cho

TYPICAL CONVERSATIONAL USAGE FOR READING AND TRANSLATION. EXERCISE:

1. 宿虎衝鼻 (숙호충비) : 자는 범 코침주기 ; 공연히 건드리어 스스로 危險을 산다는 뜻. Poking the nose of a sleeping tiger.

2. 眼鼻莫開 (안비막개) : 눈코 뜰 사이도 없다 ; 몹시 바쁘다는 뜻. I don't even have time to open my eyes and nose.

3. 翻亦破鼻 (번역파비) : 자빠져도 코가 깨진다 ; 일이 순조롭지 않으려니까 뜻밖에 큰 탈이 난다는 말. A luckless fellow has his nose broken even if he fell on his back.

4. 코가 쉰 댓 자나 빠졌다 : Be exhausted.

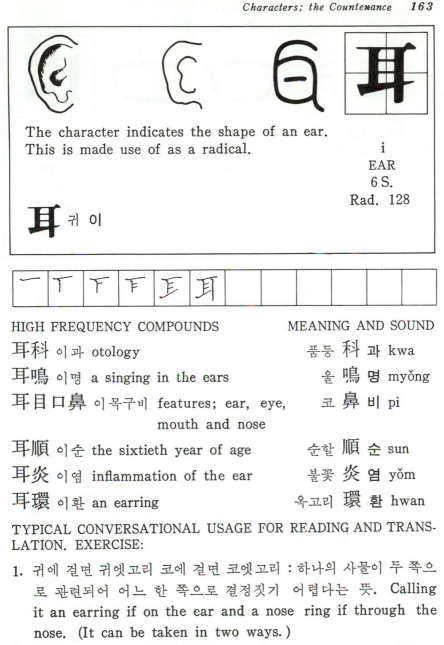

The character indicates the shape of an ear.
This is made use of as a radical.

i
EAR
6 S.
Rad. 128

耳 귀 이

一 丁 下 下 巨 耳

HIGH FREQUENCY COMPOUNDS	MEANING AND SOUND
耳科 이과 otology	품등 科 과 kwa
耳鳴 이명 a singing in the ears	울 鳴 명 myŏng
耳目口鼻 이목구비 features; ear, eye, mouth and nose	코 鼻 비 pi
耳順 이순 the sixtieth year of age	순할 順 순 sun
耳炎 이염 inflammation of the ear	불꽃 炎 염 yŏm
耳環 이환 an earring	옥고리 環 환 hwan

TYPICAL CONVERSATIONAL USAGE FOR READING AND TRANSLATION. EXERCISE:

1. 귀에 걸면 귀엣고리 코에 걸면 코엣고리 : 하나의 사물이 두 쪽으로 관련되어 어느 한 쪽으로 결정짓기 어렵다는 뜻. Calling it an earring if on the ear and a nose ring if through the nose. (It can be taken in two ways.)
2. 당나귀 귀 치레. The donkey makes up his ear. (when making a funny thing look funnier.)
3. 耳目一新 (이목일신) : 雰圍氣가 한껏 새로와짐.

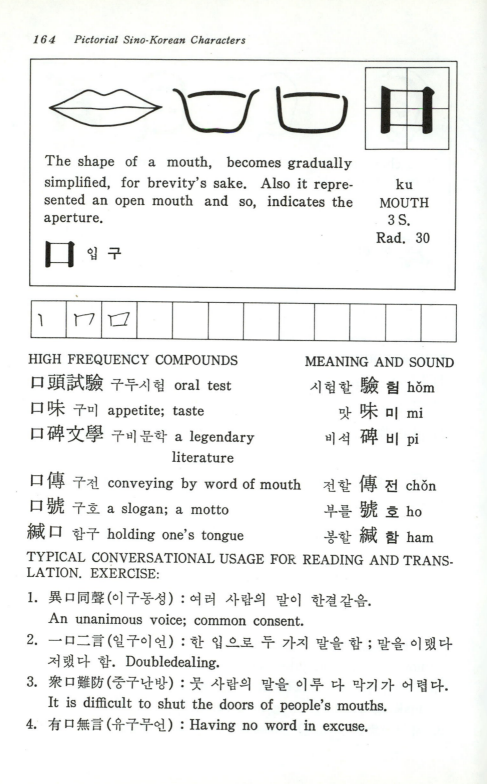

The shape of a mouth, becomes gradually simplified, for brevity's sake. Also it represented an open mouth and so, indicates the aperture.

ku
MOUTH
3 S.
Rad. 30

口 입 구

HIGH FREQUENCY COMPOUNDS

口頭試驗 구두시험 oral test

口味 구미 appetite; taste

口碑文學 구비문학 a legendary literature

口傳 구전 conveying by word of mouth

口號 구호 a slogan; a motto

緘口 함구 holding one's tongue

MEANING AND SOUND

시험할 驗 험 hŏm

맛 味 미 mi

비석 碑 비 pi

전할 傳 전 chŏn

부를 號 호 ho

봉할 緘 함 ham

TYPICAL CONVERSATIONAL USAGE FOR READING AND TRANSLATION. EXERCISE:

1. 異口同聲(이구동성) : 여러 사람의 말이 한결같음.
   An unanimous voice; common consent.

2. 一口二言(일구이언) : 한 입으로 두 가지 말을 함 ; 말을 이랬다 저랬다 함. Doubledealing.

3. 衆口難防(중구난방) : 뭇 사람의 말을 이루 다 막기가 어렵다.
   It is difficult to shut the doors of people's mouths.

4. 有口無言(유구무언) : Having no word in excuse.

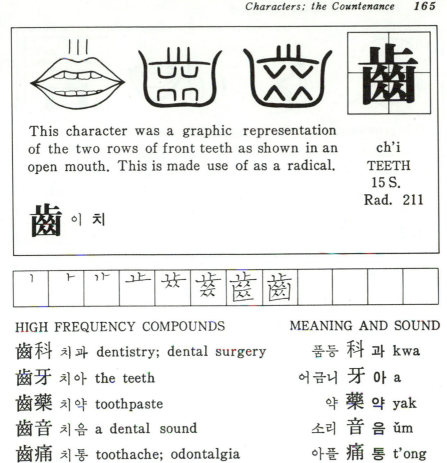

This character was a graphic representation of the two rows of front teeth as shown in an open mouth. This is made use of as a radical.

ch'i
TEETH
15 S.
Rad. 211

齒 이 치

| 丨 | 丨⼅ | ⼅⼖ | 上 | 步 | 齿 | 齿 | 齒 | | | |

HIGH FREQUENCY COMPOUNDS

齒科 치과 dentistry; dental surgery

齒牙 치아 the teeth

齒藥 치약 toothpaste

齒音 치음 a dental sound

齒痛 치통 toothache; odontalgia

年齒 연치 age; years

MEANING AND SOUND

품등 科 과 kwa

어금니 牙 아 a

약 藥 약 yak

소리 音 음 ŭm

아플 痛 통 t'ong

해 年 년 nyŏn

TYPICAL CONVERSATIONAL USAGE FOR READING AND TRANSLATION. EXERCISE:

1. 脣亡齒寒(순망치한) : 입술이 없어지면 이가 시리다 ; 서로 밀접한 사람 중에서 한 사람이 망하면 다른 사람에게도 영향이 있음을 이르는 말. If you lost your lips, your teeth will freeze. (which means coexistence).

2. 나는 요새 齒科醫師한테 두 주에 한 번씩 간다.
I visit the dentist's office once every two weeks.

3. '齒藥'과 '쥐약'의 발음을 혼동하지 않도록 하세요. You must discriminate between the pronunciations of *ch'iyak* and *chwiyak*.

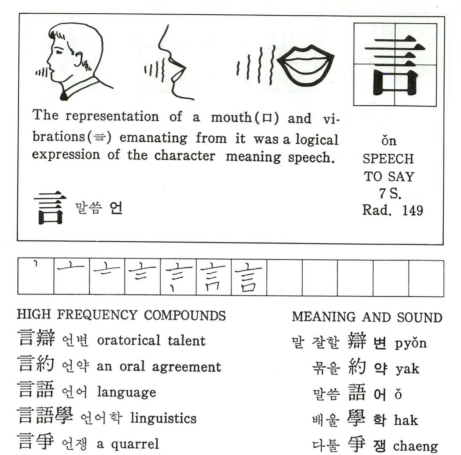

The representation of a mouth(口) and vibrations(≡) emanating from it was a logical expression of the character meaning speech.

言 말씀 언

ŏn
SPEECH
TO SAY
7 S.
Rad. 149

HIGH FREQUENCY COMPOUNDS

言辯 언변 oratorical talent

言約 언약 an oral agreement

言語 언어 language

言語學 언어학 linguistics

言爭 언쟁 a quarrel

MEANING AND SOUND

말 잘할 辯 변 pyŏn

묶을 約 약 yak

말씀 語 어 ŏ

배울 學 학 hak

다툴 爭 쟁 chaeng

TYPICAL CONVERSATIONAL USAGE FOR READING AND TRANSLATION. EXERCISE:

1. 言行一致(언행일치) : 하는 말과 행동이 같음.
   Words and deeds are at once.
2. 다른 하나의 言語를 배우는 것은 또 하나의 精神을 얻는 것이
   다. When you learn another language you also gain another
   spirit.
3. 甘言利說(감언이설) : 남의 脾胃에 맞도록 달콤한 말로 꾀어 대
   는 것. Honeyed words; flattery.
4. 발 없는 말(言)이 千里 간다 : 비밀로 한 말도 잘 퍼지니 말을
   삼가라는 뜻. Words without feet travel a thousand miles.

This character is the figure of a wispy beard.
It was originally drawn 乚 and finally (毛).
It means both human hair and animal fur.

mo
HAIR
FUR
4 S.
Rad. 82

毛 털 모

HIGH FREQUENCY COMPOUNDS

MEANING AND SOUND

毛細管 모세관 a capillary tube

가늘 細 세 se

대롱 管 관 kwan

毛織 모직 woolen fabric

짤 織 직 chik

毛皮 모피 skin; fur

가죽 皮 피 p'i

毛筆 모필 a writing brush (calligraphy)

붓 筆 필 p'il

不毛 불모 barrenness; sterility

아닐 不 불 pul

脫毛 탈모 loss of hair

벗을 脫 탈 t'al

TYPICAL CONVERSATIONAL USAGE FOR READING AND TRANS-
LATION. EXERCISE:

1. 九牛一毛 (구우일모) : 썩 많은 것 가운데서 매우 적은 것.
   One hair from nine oxen. (the slightest particle).
2. 중이 제 머리 못 깎는다. A monk can not shave his own head.
3. 不毛地를 開墾하여 農場으로 만들자.
   Let's develop the barren land into a farm.
4. 수염이 석 자라도 먹어야 양반. Even a three-foot long beard
   can not make you a gentleman unless you eat.

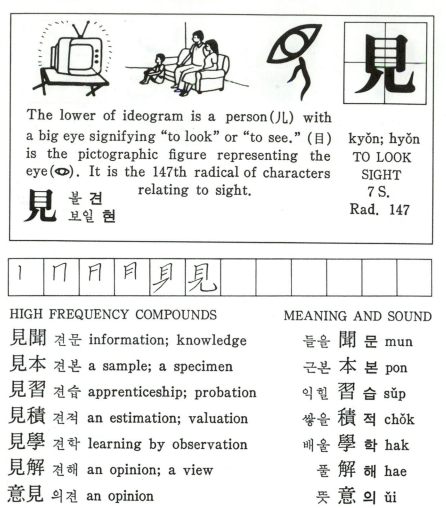

The lower of ideogram is a person(儿) with a big eye signifying "to look" or "to see." (目) is the pictographic figure representing the eye(◑). It is the 147th radical of characters relating to sight.

見 불 견
　　보일 현

kyŏn; hyŏn
TO LOOK
SIGHT
7 S.
Rad. 147

HIGH FREQUENCY COMPOUNDS

見聞 견문 information; knowledge

見本 견본 a sample; a specimen

見習 견습 apprenticeship; probation

見積 견적 an estimation; valuation

見學 견학 learning by observation

見解 견해 an opinion; a view

意見 의견 an opinion

MEANING AND SOUND

들을 聞 문 mun

근본 本 본 pon

익힐 習 습 sŭp

쌓을 積 적 chŏk

배울 學 학 hak

풀 解 해 hae

뜻 意 의 ŭi

TYPICAL CONVERSATIONAL USAGE FOR READING AND TRANSLATION. EXERCISE:

1. 見蚊拔劍(견문발검) : 모기 보고 칼 뺀다 : 시시한 일에 성을 낸다는 말. Like drawing one's sword on a mosquito.

2. 百聞不如一見(백문불여일견) : 백 번 듣는 것보다 한 번 보는 것이 낫다.　To see a thing once is better than hearing it a hundred times. (Seeing is believing.)

3. 先見知明(선견지명) : Farseeing intelligence; a long head.

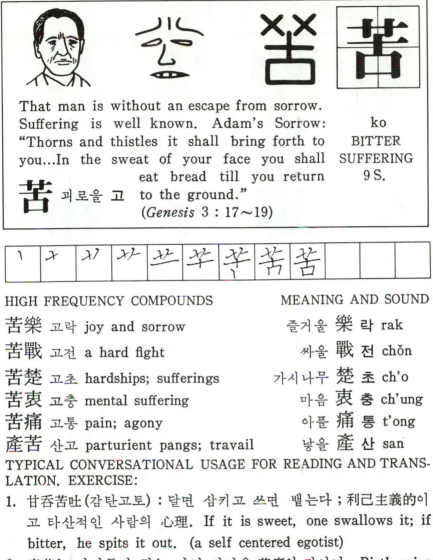

That man is without an escape from sorrow. Suffering is well known. Adam's Sorrow: "Thorns and thistles it shall bring forth to you...In the sweat of your face you shall eat bread till you return to the ground."
(*Genesis* 3 : 17～19)

苦 괴로울 고

ko
BITTER
SUFFERING
9 S.

HIGH FREQUENCY COMPOUNDS

苦樂 고락 joy and sorrow

苦戰 고전 a hard fight

苦楚 고초 hardships; sufferings

苦衷 고충 mental suffering

苦痛 고통 pain; agony

産苦 산고 parturient pangs; travail

MEANING AND SOUND

즐거울 樂 락 rak

싸울 戰 전 chŏn

가시나무 楚 초 ch'o

마음 衷 충 ch'ung

아플 痛 통 t'ong

낳을 産 산 san

TYPICAL CONVERSATIONAL USAGE FOR READING AND TRANSLATION. EXERCISE:

1. 甘呑苦吐 (감탄고토) : 달면 삼키고 쓰면 뱉는다 ; 利己主義的이고 타산적인 사람의 心理. If it is sweet, one swallows it; if bitter, he spits it out. (a self centered egotist)

2. 産苦는 여자들이 겪는 가장 어려운 苦痛일 것이다. Birth pains are the most painful thing that women go through.

3. 주님은 나같은 罪人을 대신하여 苦難을 받으셨네 ! The Lord received a trial for a sinner like me.

4. 苦盡甘來 (고진감래) : 고생이 끝나면 즐거움이 옴. Sweet after bitter; Pleasure follows pain.

10. 家族 가족 Family

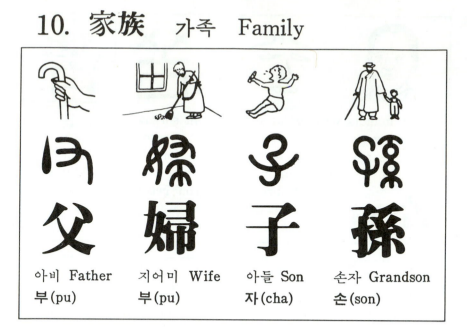

아비 Father	지어미 Wife	아들 Son	손자 Grandson
부(pu)	부(pu)	자(cha)	손(son)

子女들아 너희 父母를 主 안에서 順從하라. 이것이 옳으니라. 네 아버지와 어머니를 恭敬하라. 이것이 約束 있는 첫 誡命이니 이는 네가 잘 되고 땅에서 長壽하리라. 또 아비들아, 너희 子女를 怒엽게 하지 말고 오직 主의 敎養과 訓戒로 養育하라. (에베소書 6 : 1~4)

Children, obey your parents in the Lord, for this is right. "Honor your father and mother," which is the first commandment with promise: "that it may be well with you and you may live long on the earth." And you, fathers, do not provoke your children to wrath, but bring them up in the training admonition of the Lord. (*Ephesians* 6 : 1~4)

이러므로 사람이 父母를 떠나 그 아내와 合하여 그들이 한 肉體가 될지니 이 秘密이 크도다. 내가 그리스도와 敎會에 대하여 말하노라. (에베소書 5 : 31~32)

On this account a man shall leave his father and mother and shall be joined to his wife, and the two shall become one flesh. There is a great, hidden meaning in this, but I am speaking about Christ and the church. (*Ephesians* 5 : 31~32)

This ideograph suggests the Garden of Eden.
So God created man in his own image, in   ho
the image of God created he him; male(子)   GOOD
and female(女) created he them. (*G.* 1 : 27)   TO LIKE
     It was very "good." (*G.* 1 : 31)   6 S.

好 좋을 호 Two(女, 子) become one person(好) that
means "good." (*Genesis* 2 : 24)

HIGH FREQUENCY COMPOUNDS   MEANING AND SOUND

好感 호감 good feeling; good impression   느낄 感 감 kam

好景氣 호경기 a prosperous condition;   볕 景 경 kyŏng

          good times   기운 氣 기 ki

好奇心 호기심 curiosity   기이할 奇 기 ki

好事 호사 a happy event   일 事 사 sa

好評 호평 a favorable comment; a   평론할 評 평 p'yŏng
          favorable criticism

TYPICAL CONVERSATIONAL USAGE FOR READING AND TRANS-
LATION. EXERCISE:

1. 남에게 好感을 주는 人間性을 지니려면 많은 修養을 하여야
   한다. You have to cultivate your mind, if you intend to
   impress upon someone in a humanitarian way.

2. 담 너머에 있는 사과가 맛있어 보이게 마련이다. (好奇心)
   The apples on the other side of the wall are the sweetest.

3. 好事多魔(호사다마) : 좋은 일에 마귀의 妨害가 많다.
   Lights are usually followed by shadows.

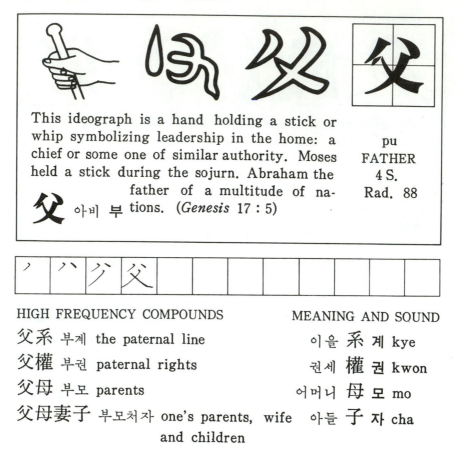

This ideograph is a hand holding a stick or whip symbolizing leadership in the home: a chief or some one of similar authority. Moses held a stick during the sojurn. Abraham the father of a multitude of nations. (*Genesis* 17 : 5)

父 아비 부

pu
FATHER
4 S.
Rad. 88

`丿  八  𠂆  父`

HIGH FREQUENCY COMPOUNDS

父系 부계 the paternal line

父權 부권 paternal rights

父母 부모 parents

父母妻子 부모처자 one's parents, wife and children

家父長制度 가부장제도 patriarchalism

MEANING AND SOUND

이을 系 계 kye

권세 權 권 kwon

어머니 母 모 mo

아들 子 자 cha

지을 制 제 che

TYPICAL CONVERSATIONAL USAGE FOR READING AND TRANSLATION. EXERCISE:

1. 어머니와 아버지를 父母라고 하는데 어릴 때 부모를 여의면 孤兒가 된다. Your mother and father are called parents, but when you are young and lose your parents you become an orphan.

2. 搖籃을 흔드는 손이 세계를 支配하는 손이다. The hand that rocks the cradle is the hand that rules the world. (*W.R. Wallace*)

3. 제 父親께서 저에게 한글을 가르쳐 주셨읍니다. My father taught me Han-gŭl.

4. 父傳子傳 (부전자전) : 대대로 아버지가 아들에게 전함. Like breeds like; like father, like son.

This character is a symbol for a mother or woman, two dots indicate the darker nipples of woman's breast when a woman becoming a mother, emphasizing the sacred duty of motherhood.

mo
MOTHER
WOMAN
5 S.

母 어미 모

<table>
<tr><td>乙</td><td>乙</td><td>母</td><td>母</td><td>母</td><td></td><td></td><td></td><td></td><td></td></tr>
</table>

HIGH FREQUENCY COMPOUNDS

MEANING AND SOUND

母校 모교 one's alma mater

학교 校 교 kyo

母國語 모국어 the native language

말씀 語 어 ŏ

母音 모음 a vowel

소리 音 음 ŭm

母胎 모태 the mother's womb

아이밸 胎 태 t'ae

祖母 조모 grandmother

할아비 祖 조 cho

航空母艦 항공모함 an aircraft carrier

빌 空 공 kong

TYPICAL CONVERSATIONAL USAGE FOR READING AND TRANSLATION. EXERCISE:

1. 금년부터 내 母校에 장학금을 희사하려고 決心했다.
   I have decided to contribute to my alma mater's scholarship fund from this year on.

2. 모세가 이스라엘의 지도자가 된 것은 어머니의 母國語 敎育과 기도의 힘이 컸기 때문이다. The powerful prayer of his mother and the teaching of the mother tongue resulted in Moses becoming the leader of the Israel.

3. 賢母良妻(현모양처): 어진 어머니면서 또한 착한 아내.

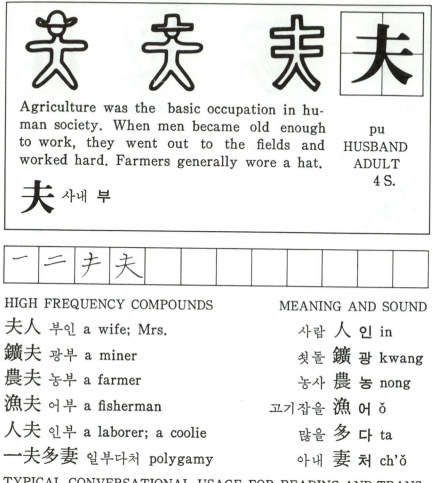

Agriculture was the basic occupation in human society. When men became old enough to work, they went out to the fields and worked hard. Farmers generally wore a hat.

pu
HUSBAND
ADULT
4 S.

夫 사내 부

HIGH FREQUENCY COMPOUNDS

夫人 부인 a wife; Mrs.

鑛夫 광부 a miner

農夫 농부 a farmer

漁夫 어부 a fisherman

人夫 인부 a laborer; a coolie

一夫多妻 일부다처 polygamy

MEANING AND SOUND

사람 人 인 in

쇳돌 鑛 광 kwang

농사 農 농 nong

고기잡을 漁 어 ŏ

많을 多 다 ta

아내 妻 처 ch'ŏ

TYPICAL CONVERSATIONAL USAGE FOR READING AND TRANSLATION. EXERCISE:

1. 60년대에 한국 鑛夫들이 雇用契約으로 서독 광산에 많이 갔었다. During the 1960's Korean mine workers were contractually employed and went to West Germany to work in mines.

2. 헤밍웨이의 《老人과 바다》에는 한 늙은 漁夫의 이야기가 感動的으로 그려져 있읍니다. 오랜 苦難과 辛酸을 꿋꿋이 견디어냈으나 끝내는 빈 배로 歸港할 수밖에 없었던 老人의 경험으로부터 空手來空手去라는 東洋的 諦觀을 느낄 수 있읍니다.

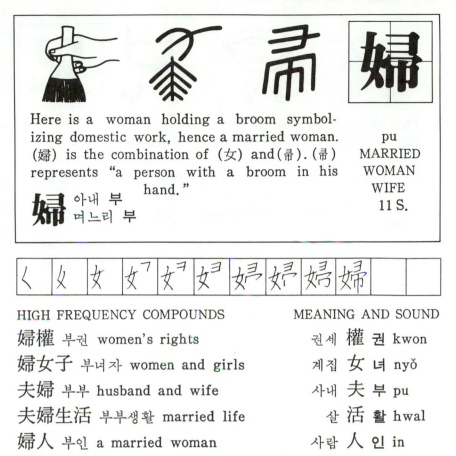

Here is a woman holding a broom symbolizing domestic work, hence a married woman. (婦) is the combination of (女) and (帚). (帚) represents "a person with a broom in his hand."

婦 아내 부
　며느리 부

pu
MARRIED
WOMAN
WIFE
11 S.

く　乆　女　女ᄀ　女ᄏ　女ᄏ　婦ᄏ　婦ᄏ　婦ᄏ　婦ᄏ

HIGH FREQUENCY COMPOUNDS

婦權 부권 women's rights

婦女子 부녀자 women and girls

夫婦 부부 husband and wife

夫婦生活 부부생활 married life

婦人 부인 a married woman

MEANING AND SOUND

권세 權 권 kwon

계집 女 녀 nyŏ

사내 夫 부 pu

살 活 활 hwal

사람 人 인 in

TYPICAL CONVERSATIONAL USAGE FOR READING AND TRANSLATION. EXERCISE:

1. 일반적으로 結婚한 여인을 婦人이라고 부른다.
   Generally married women are called *puin*.

2. 근래에 婦人들이 職場을 갖는 境遇가 늘어나면서, 婦權이 많이 伸張되고 있다. As the number of women who get jobs has increased, the power of the woman is increasing.

3. 아내가 귀여우면 처가집 말뚝 보고도 절을 한다 : 아내가 귀여우면 그의 周圍에 있는 보잘것없는 것 까지 고맙게 보인다는 말. If your wife is attractive, the door posts to her parents' home are also attractive.

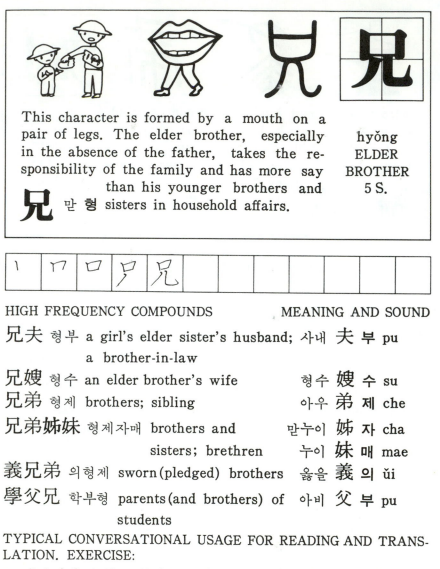

This character is formed by a mouth on a pair of legs. The elder brother, especially in the absence of the father, takes the responsibility of the family and has more say than his younger brothers and sisters in household affairs.

兄 만 형

hyŏng
ELDER
BROTHER
5 S.

HIGH FREQUENCY COMPOUNDS   MEANING AND SOUND

兄夫 형부 a girl's elder sister's husband; 사내 夫 부 pu
       a brother-in-law

兄嫂 형수 an elder brother's wife   형수 嫂 수 su

兄弟 형제 brothers; sibling   아우 弟 제 che

兄弟姉妹 형제자매 brothers and   맏누이 姉 자 cha
                sisters; brethren   누이 妹 매 mae

義兄弟 의형제 sworn(pledged) brothers   옳을 義 의 ŭi

學父兄 학부형 parents(and brothers) of   아비 父 부 pu
              students

TYPICAL CONVERSATIONAL USAGE FOR READING AND TRANSLATION. EXERCISE:

1. 教會에서 兄弟 姉妹라는 말을 많이 쓴다. Lots of churches use the words brothers and sisters.

2. 朴氏와 李氏는 작년에 義兄弟를 맺었다. Last year, Mr. Park and Mr. Lee had sworn to be brothers.

3. 다음 月曜日에 우리 學校에서 學父兄(母) 會議가 있다. Next Monday, the P. T. A. meeting will be held in our school.

This character is the combination of a rice-field (田) and power (力) which represents "the person who works in a ricefield." It signifies the male, man.

nam
MALE
7 S.

男 사내 남

HIGH FREQUENCY COMPOUNDS

男女 남녀 male and female

男女共學 남녀공학 coeducation

男妹 남매 one's own children; brother and sister

男便 남편 husband

美男子 미남자 a handsome man

長男 장남 eldest son

MEANING AND SOUND

계집 女 녀 nyŏ

함께 共 공 kong

누이 妹 매 mae

편할 便 편 p'yŏn

아름다울 美 미 mi

긴 長 장 chang

TYPICAL CONVERSATIONAL USAGE FOR READING AND TRANSLATION. EXERCISE:

1. 제 男便은 일주일 예정으로 日本에 출장을 갔어요.
   My husband went to Japan for one week of T.D.Y.

2. 男子는 法律을 만들고, 女子는 禮節을 만든다.
   Men make laws, women make manners. (*Guibert*)

3. 前에는 나의 長子의 名分을 빼앗고, 이제는 내 福을 빼앗았나이다. (창세기 27:36) Before he took my birthright and now he has stolen my blessing. (*Genesis* 27:36)

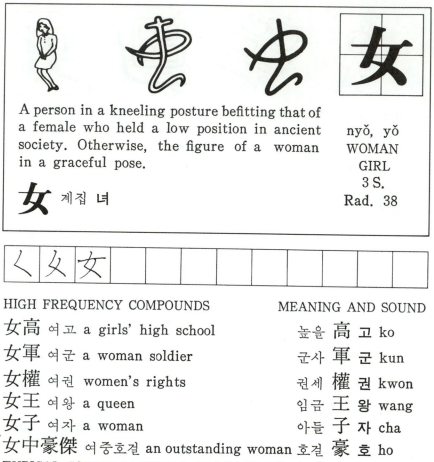

A person in a kneeling posture befitting that of a female who held a low position in ancient society. Otherwise, the figure of a woman in a graceful pose.

nyŏ, yŏ
WOMAN
GIRL
3 S.
Rad. 38

女 계집 녀

HIGH FREQUENCY COMPOUNDS

女高 여고 a girls' high school
女軍 여군 a woman soldier
女權 여권 women's rights
女王 여왕 a queen
女子 여자 a woman
女中豪傑 여중호걸 an outstanding woman

MEANING AND SOUND

높을 高 고 ko
군사 軍 군 kun
권세 權 권 kwon
임금 王 왕 wang
아들 子 자 cha
호걸 豪 호 ho

TYPICAL CONVERSATIONAL USAGE FOR READING AND TRANSLATION. EXERCISE:

1. 女高는 女子高等學校의 준말이다.
   Yŏgo is the contraction for the girls' high school.

2. 신라에는 眞聖女王, 眞德女王이 있었는데 그때까지 英國에는 아무 女王도 없었다. During the Shilla dynasty, Korea had Queen Chinsŏng and Queen Chindŏk but till then England still had not had a queen yet.

3. 女子 셋이 모이면 나무접시가 들논다 : 여자들이 모이면 말이 많고 떠들썩하다는 말. When three women get together, the wooden dishes swing back and forth.

A pregnant woman has a baby (子) in the uterus. It means pregnancy.

ing
PREGNANT
5 S.

孕 아이밸 **잉**

HIGH FREQUENCY COMPOUNDS	MEANING AND SOUND
孕母 잉모 a pregnant woman	어미 母 모 mo
孕婦 잉부 a pregnant woman	며느리 婦 부 pu
孕胎 잉태 conception; pregnancy	아이밸 胎 태 t'ae

TYPICAL CONVERSATIONAL USAGE FOR READING AND TRANSLATION. EXERCISE:

1. 다윗의 子孫 요셉아 네 아내 마리아 데려오기를 무서워 말라.
   저에게 孕胎된 자는 聖靈으로 된 것이라. (마태복음 1 : 20)
   Joseph, son of David, be not afraid to take Mary as your
   wife, for what is conceived in her is from the Holy Spirit.
   (*Matthew* 1 : 20)

2. 보라 ! 처녀가 孕胎하여 아들을 낳을 것이요 그 이름은 임마누
   엘이라 하리라. 飜譯하면 하나님이 우리와 함께 계시다 함이라.
   (마태복음 1 : 23) Behold! The virgin will be with child and
   shall bear a son, and they will name Him Immanuel, which
   means, God with us. (*Matthew* 1 : 23)

3. 밴 아이 아들 아니면 딸이지. A child who has been conceived
   in either a daughter or a son.

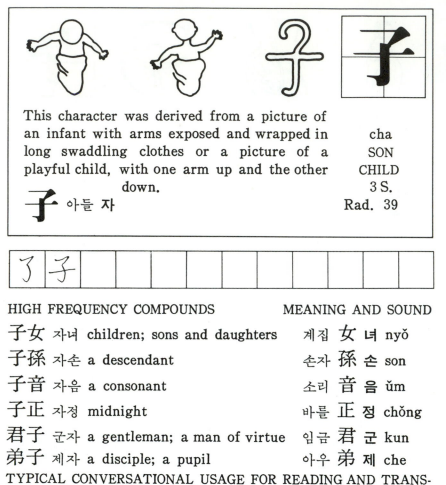

This character was derived from a picture of an infant with arms exposed and wrapped in long swaddling clothes or a picture of a playful child, with one arm up and the other down.

cha
SON
CHILD
3 S.
Rad. 39

子 아들 자

HIGH FREQUENCY COMPOUNDS

子女 자녀 children; sons and daughters
子孫 자손 a descendant
子音 자음 a consonant
子正 자정 midnight
君子 군자 a gentleman; a man of virtue
弟子 제자 a disciple; a pupil

MEANING AND SOUND

계집 女 녀 nyŏ
손자 孫 손 son
소리 音 음 ŭm
바를 正 정 chŏng
임금 君 군 kun
아우 弟 제 che

TYPICAL CONVERSATIONAL USAGE FOR READING AND TRANSLATION. EXERCISE:

1. 子息은 여호와의 주신 基業이요 胎의 열매는 그의 賞給이로다. 젊은 자의 子息은 壯士의 手中의 화살 같으니 이것이 그 箭筒에 가득한 자는 福되도다. (시편 127 : 3~5)
Children are a heritage from the Lord. The fruit of the womb is his reward. Like arrows in the hand of a warrior so are the children of one's youth. (*Psalms* 127 : 3~4)

2. 예수님에게는 열두 弟子가 있었는데 그 중에 유다는 스승 예수를 배반하였다. One of Jesus Christ's twelve disciples, Juda, betrayed the teacher Jesus.

A descendant (子) who continues the thread (系) of posterity. The first picture signifies a child playing with thread.

son
GRANDSON
DESCENDANT
10 S.

孫 손자 손

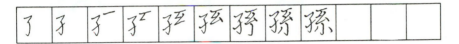

HIGH FREQUENCY COMPOUNDS	MEANING AND SOUND
孫女 손녀 a granddaughter	계집 **女** 녀 nyŏ
孫婦 손부 one's granddaughter-in-law	며느리 **婦** 부 pu
孫婿 손서 one's grandson-in-law	사위 **婿** 서 sŏ
孫子 손자 a grandson	아들 **子** 자 cha
後孫 후손 descendants	뒤 **後** 후 hu

TYPICAL CONVERSATIONAL USAGE FOR READING AND TRANS-LATION. EXERCISE:

1. 여호와의 仁慈하심은 自己를 경외하는 자에게 영원부터 영원까지 이르며 그의 義는 子孫의 子孫에게 미치리라. (시편 103 : 17)
   But the steadfast love of the Lord is from everlasting to everlasting upon those who fear him, and his righteousness to children's children. (*Psalms* 103 : 17)

2. 우리 가족은 大家族이라서 孫子 孫女도 많아요.
   Our family is a big one, so there are many grandchildren.

3. 우리 사위는 領事로 나가 있으니까 外國生活에 익숙하지!
   Our son-in-law has gone to work as the consulate general, so he became accustomed to foreign life.

11. 飲食 음식 Foods

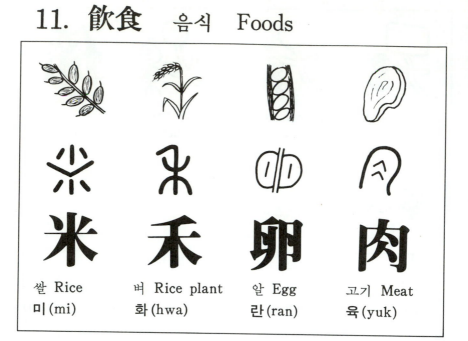

쌀 Rice	벼 Rice plant	알 Egg	고기 Meat
미 (mi)	화 (hwa)	란 (ran)	육 (yuk)

그런 즉 너희가 먹든지 마시든지 무엇을 하든지 다 하나님의 榮光을 爲하여 하라. (고린도 前書 10 : 31)

So, whether you eat or drink or whatever you do, do it all to the glory of God. (I *Corinthians* 10 : 31)

하나님의 나라는 먹는 것과 마시는 것이 아니요 오직 聖靈 안에서 義와 平康과 喜樂이라. (로마書 14 : 17)

For the kingdom of God does not consist in eating and drinking, but in righteousness and peace and joy in the Holy Spirit (*Romans* 14 : 17)

너나 네 子孫들이 會幕에 들어갈 때에는 葡萄酒나 毒酒를 마시지 말아서 너희 死亡을 免하라. 이는 너희 代代로 永永한 規例라. (레위기 10 : 9)

Do not drink wine or intoxicating drink, you, nor your sons with you, when you go into the tabernacle of meeting, lest you die. It shall be a statute forever throughout your generations. (*Leviticus* 10 : 9)

Pictured is a table on which bowls are over-flowing with food. The detached upper portion occurring in some forms, is probably a lifted lid.

shik
TO EAT
FOOD
9 S.
Rad. 184

 먹을 식

HIGH FREQUENCY COMPOUNDS

食口 식구 members of a family

食堂車 식당차 a dining car

食料品 식료품 a foodstuff

食事 식사 a meal; dinner

食卓 식탁 a dining table

主食 주식 staple food

MEANING AND SOUND

입 口 구 ku

집 堂 당 tang

헤아릴 料 료 ryo

일 事 사 sa

높을 卓 탁 t'ak

주인 主 주 chu

TYPICAL CONVERSATIONAL USAGE FOR READING AND TRANSLATION. EXERCISE:

1. 우리집은 食口가 적어서 生活費는 얼마 안 든다.
   Ours is a small family, so it does not cost us much for living.
2. 이 列車에는 食堂車가 연결되어 있읍니다.
   This train has a dining car attached to it.
3. 한국인의 主食은 쌀이다. The Korean's staple food is rice.
4. 금강산도 食後景 : 아무리 재미있는 일이라도 배가 부른 뒤에
   볼 일이라는 뜻. Even the Kŭmgang mountain must be seen
   on a full stomach.

When the grains of the rice plants have ripened and they are harvested, the stalks are cut, bundled, tied or stacked. This character represents these bundled stalks. It is also, the head of the rice plant (⁂).

米 쌀 미. (*Genesis* 37 : 5∼7)

mi
RICE
GRAIN
6 S.
Rad. 119

HIGH FREQUENCY COMPOUNDS

MEANING AND SOUND

米價 미가 the price of rice 값 價 가 ka

米穀商 미곡상 a rice and grain dealer 곡식 穀 곡 kok

米色 미색 pale yellow; straw yellow 빛깔 色 색 saek

米粉 미분 rice flour 가루 粉 분 pun

玄米 현미 unpolished rice 검을 玄 현 hyŏn

TYPICAL CONVERSATIONAL USAGE FOR READING AND TRANSLATION. EXERCISE:

1. 쌀광에서 人心난다 : 살림이 넉넉해야 남도 도울 수 있다.
   Charity comes from the granary. (Only a man of surplus wealth can help others.)

2. 우리의 主食이 쌀이기 때문에 쌀에 대한 명칭들이 많이 있다. 예를 들면 어린 싹을 모라고 하고 방아 찧지 않은 곡식을 벼라고 하며 精米所에서 방아 찧은 것을 쌀이라고 하고 飮食으로 먹을 때 밥이라고 부른다. Rice is our staple food, so there are many descriptive names for it. For example *mo* (in budding stage), *pyŏ* (unhulled), *ssal* (uncooked), and *pap* (steamed rice).

This character represents a rice plant during growth. The ears of the plant spread outward and the drooping rice corns on top come to be symbolized by the downward slanting dash on top.

禾 벼 화

hwa
RICE-PLANT
5 S.
Rad. 115

ノ 一 千 矛 禾

HIGH FREQUENCY COMPOUNDS	MEANING AND SOUND
穀物 곡물 grain; cereals	곡식 穀 곡 kok
稅金 세금 tax	세금 稅 세 se
秀才 수재 a talented man	빼어날 秀 수 su
收穫 수확 harvesting; a crop	거둘 穫 확 hwak
移轉 이전 moving	옮길 移 이 i
種子 종자 a seed	씨 種 종 chong

TYPICAL CONVERSATIONAL USAGE FOR READING AND TRANSLATION. EXERCISE:

1. 올해는 집을 샀기 때문에 稅金이 많이 나올 것으로 斟酌하고 있다. I assume there will be a lot of taxes this year because I have purchased a house.

2. 금년 收穫이 작년 收穫에 비해서 훨씬 많다. This year's crop is by far larger compared to last year's crop.

3. 우리 科가 지금 짓고 있는 校舍로 移轉할 것 같다.
It seems that our department will be moving into the school building that is now under construction.

This ideograph, the combination of the grain (禾) and a sickle (刂, 刀) suggests reaping, the harvest, i.e., benefit, profit, or interest. When the oyster and the heron fight, the saying goes, "The fisherman benefits." (漁夫之利)

利 이로울 리 benefits.

li, i
BENEFIT
GAIN
7 S.

丿 二 千 千 禾 利 利

HIGH FREQUENCY COMPOUNDS

利得 이득 profit; benefit

利用 이용 utilizing; making use of

利益 이익 profit; gains

利害得失 이해득실 profit and loss

權利 권리 a right; a claim

不利 불리 disadvantage

勝利 승리 victory; triumph

MEANING AND SOUND

얻을 得 득 tŭk

쓸 用 용 yong

더할 益 익 ik

해칠 害 해 hae

권세 權 권 kwon

아닐 不 불 pul

이길 勝 승 sŭng

TYPICAL CONVERSATIONAL USAGE FOR READING AND TRANSLATION. EXERCISE:

1. 눈앞에 利益이 보일 때 義理를 생각하여야 한다.
   When you see profits, you have to think about the integrity and morality behind it.

2. 그는 利로운 것과 不利한 것을 判別하지 못한다. He can not judge whether it will be profitable or disadvantageous for him.

3. 自身의 利益만을 위하여 行動하면 怨望을 많이 사게 된다. If you act only in the interest of your gain, you will be resented.

The radical *hwa* (禾) stands for grain, the man's staple food, a highly valued possession. The phonetic (厶), representing a silkworm hidden in its cocoon, symbolizes privacy. Grain in ancient days was used 私 사사 사 to pay taxes and the residue was personal (厶, 私) property.

sa
PRIVATE
PERSONAL
SELFISH
7 S.

ノ 二 チ 矛 禾 私 私

HIGH FREQUENCY COMPOUNDS **MEANING AND SOUND**

私立 사립 private; nongovernmental 설 立 립 rip

私事 사사 private affairs 일 事 사 sa

私生活 사생활 private life 날 生 생 saeng

私有財産 사유재산 private property 재물 財 재 chae

私債 사채 a private debt 빚 債 채 ch'ae

私宅 사택 one's residence 집 宅 택 t'aek

TYPICAL CONVERSATIONAL USAGE FOR READING AND TRANSLATION. EXERCISE:

1. 子女들을 私立學校에 보내려면 많은 돈이 필요합니다.
   If you send your children to a private school, the overall school expenses would have to be great.
2. 私事로운 일에 參見하는 것은 실례가 된다.
   Meddling into other's personal affairs is rude.
3. 요즘 중국에서도 私有財産의 소유를 허용하고 있다. These days even in China one is allowed to possess personal property.
4. 지금 살고 계시는 집은 私宅입니까, 公館입니까?

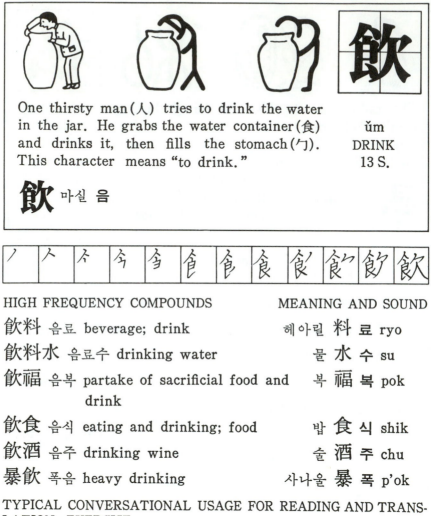

One thirsty man(人) tries to drink the water in the jar. He grabs the water container(食) and drinks it, then fills the stomach(勹). This character means "to drink."

ŭm
DRINK
13 S.

飲 마실 음

HIGH FREQUENCY COMPOUNDS

MEANING AND SOUND

飲料 음료 beverage; drink

飲料水 음료수 drinking water

飲福 음복 partake of sacrificial food and drink

飲食 음식 eating and drinking; food

飲酒 음주 drinking wine

暴飲 폭음 heavy drinking

헤아릴 料 료 ryo

물 水 수 su

복 福 복 pok

밥 食 식 shik

술 酒 주 chu

사나울 暴 폭 p'ok

TYPICAL CONVERSATIONAL USAGE FOR READING AND TRANS-LATION. EXERCISE:

1. 소금 먹은 놈이 물 켠다 : 죄 지은 놈이 罰을 당한다. Who had eaten salt drinks water. (Sinners suffer punishment.)

2. 배고픈 것은 飲食으로 채워지나 무식한 것은 研究로 채워진다. Hungry is cured by food, ignorance by study.

3. 飲食의 맛은 괜찮은데, 값이 너무 비싸요. The food is OK, but it's too expensive.

4. 暴飲은 健康에 害롭다. Heavy drinking is bad for the health.

The shape of an amphora or a wine pot used for distilling. The radical for liquid (氵) added to it indicates the jar is filled with liquor. But some says that (氵) is the drips alongside the bottle, added

酒 술 주 to give a "liquidity" feeling to it.

chu
WINE
LIQUOR
10 S.

HIGH FREQUENCY COMPOUNDS	MEANING AND SOUND

酒幕 주막 a tavern; an inn　　　　휘장 幕 막 mak

酒類 주류 beverages; alcoholic liquors　무리 類 류 ryu

酒色 주색 wine and women　　　　　빛 色 색 saek

酒神 주신 Bacchus; the god of wine　귀신 神 신 shin

酒宴 주연 a banquet　　　　　　　잔치 宴 연 yŏn

麥酒 맥주 beer　　　　　　　　　보리 麥 맥 maek

TYPICAL CONVERSATIONAL USAGE FOR READING AND TRANSLATION. EXERCISE:

1. 葡萄酒는 倨慢케 하는 것이요, 毒酒는 떠들게 하는 것이라.
   (잠언 20:1) Wine is a mocker, intoxicating drink arouses brawling. (*Proverbs* 20:1)

2. 뜨물 먹고 酒酊한다 : 취한 체하다. Drink rice-washing water and behave like a drunkard. (pretends to be drunk)

3. 契酒生面(계주생면) : 곗술에 낯내기 ; 여러 사람들의 共同物件을 가지고 自己의 생색을 낸다는 말. One uses public property in such a way that he gains favor from others.

This character depicts a mother feeding her baby on milk. The mother holds the baby with her arm. (⺈) represents the hand and (子) baby or child.

yu
MILK
8 S.

乳 젖 유

HIGH FREQUENCY COMPOUNDS

MEANING AND SOUND

乳房癌 유방암 cancer of the breast

乳業 유업 the dairy industry

乳業會社 유업회사 the dairy company

母乳 모유 mother's milk

牛乳 우유 cow's milk

방 房 방 pang

업 業 업 ŏp

모일 會 회 hoe

모일 社 사 sa

어머니 母 모 mo

소 牛 우 u

TYPICAL CONVERSATIONAL USAGE FOR READING AND TRANSLATION. EXERCISE:

1. 한국의 乳業會社들은 많은 製品들을 해외에 수출한다.
   The Korean dairy industry exports many products abroad.

2. 母乳를 먹고 자란 아이가 心理的으로 튼튼하다. The baby that is raised on mother's milk is the one who is mentally strong.

3. 미국인의 아침 食事는 보통 牛乳와 빵이다. Usually the American's breakfasts consist of milk and bread.

4. 口尙乳臭(구상유취) : 입에서 젖내가 난다 ; 말이나 행동이 幼稚하다는 뜻. Smelling of milk. (babyish; puerile)

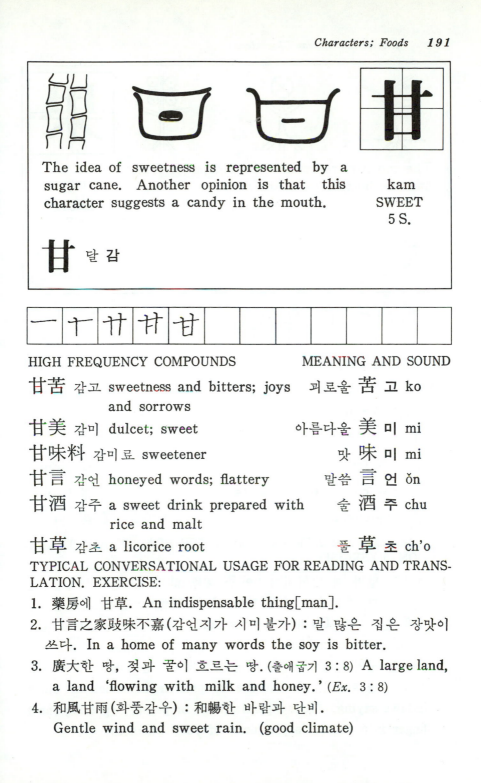

The idea of sweetness is represented by a sugar cane. Another opinion is that this character suggests a candy in the mouth.

kam
SWEET
5 S.

甘 달 감

一	十	廿	廿	甘					

HIGH FREQUENCY COMPOUNDS   MEANING AND SOUND

甘苦 감고 sweetness and bitters; joys and sorrows   괴로울 苦 고 ko

甘美 감미 dulcet; sweet   아름다울 美 미 mi

甘味料 감미료 sweetener   맛 味 미 mi

甘言 감언 honeyed words; flattery   말씀 言 언 ŏn

甘酒 감주 a sweet drink prepared with rice and malt   술 酒 주 chu

甘草 감초 a licorice root   풀 草 초 ch'o

TYPICAL CONVERSATIONAL USAGE FOR READING AND TRANSLATION. EXERCISE:

1. 藥房에 甘草. An indispensable thing[man].

2. 甘言之家豉味不嘉(감언지가 시미불가) : 말 많은 집은 장맛이 쓰다. In a home of many words the soy is bitter.

3. 廣大한 땅, 젖과 꿀이 흐르는 땅. (출애굽기 3 : 8) A large land, a land 'flowing with milk and honey.' (*Ex.* 3 : 8)

4. 和風甘雨(화풍감우) : 和暢한 바람과 단비. Gentle wind and sweet rain. (good climate)

The top part represents the cluster of fruits
and the bottom part, the roots.

kwa
FRUIT
8 S.

果 과실 과

丶	冂	曰	旦	甲	界	果					

HIGH FREQUENCY COMPOUNDS

果木 과목 a fruit tree

果樹園 과수원 an orchard

果實 과실 a fruit

果汁 과즙 fruit juice

結果 결과 consequence; results

效果 효과 effect

MEANING AND SOUND

나무 木 목 mok

동산 園 원 won

열매 實 실 shil

진액 汁 즙 chŭp

맺을 結 결 kyŏl

본받을 效 효 hyo

TYPICAL CONVERSATIONAL USAGE FOR READING AND TRANS-
LATION. EXERCISE:

1. 까마귀 날자 배 떨어진다 : 아무 關係 없이 한 일이 마침 어떤
   다른 일과 공교롭게 때가 같아 어떤 關係가 있는 것처럼 의
   심을 받게 됨. Up flew a crow and down fell a pear. (an
   unfortunate coincidence)

2. 사돈집 잔치에 감 놓아라 배 놓아라 한다. 남의 일에 부당한 干
   涉을 함을 이르는 말. At the banquet in the house of one's
   in-laws saying, "Bring persimmons or pears." (putting one's
   finger into another's pie; none of your business)

NAMES OF FRUITS

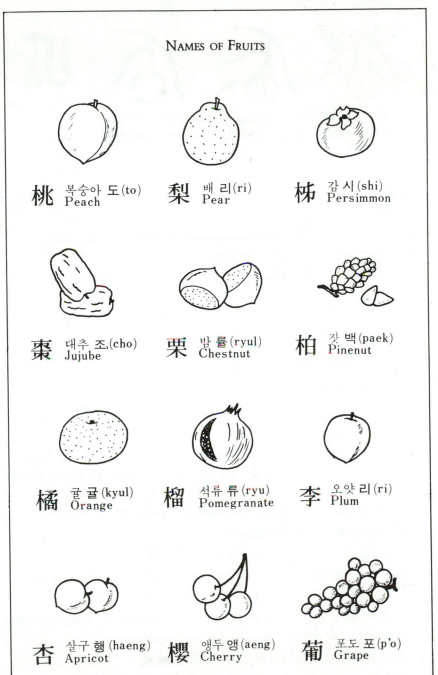

桃　복숭아 도(to)
Peach

梨　배 리(ri)
Pear

柿　감 시(shi)
Persimmon

棗　대추 조,(cho)
Jujube

栗　밤 률(ryul)
Chestnut

柏　잣 백(paek)
Pinenut

橘　귤 귤(kyul)
Orange

榴　석류 류(ryu)
Pomegranate

李　오얏 리(ri)
Plum

杏　살구 행(haeng)
Apricot

櫻　앵두 앵(aeng)
Cherry

葡　포도 포(p'o)
Grape

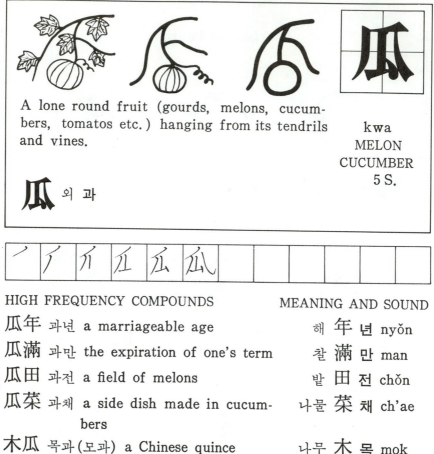

A lone round fruit (gourds, melons, cucumbers, tomatos etc.) hanging from its tendrils and vines.

kwa
MELON
CUCUMBER
5 S.

瓜 외 과

HIGH FREQUENCY COMPOUNDS

瓜年 과년 a marriageable age

瓜滿 과만 the expiration of one's term

瓜田 과전 a field of melons

瓜菜 과채 a side dish made in cucumbers

木瓜 목과 (모과) a Chinese quince

MEANING AND SOUND

해 年 년 nyŏn

찰 滿 만 man

밭 田 전 chŏn

나물 菜 채 ch'ae

나무 木 목 mok

TYPICAL CONVERSATIONAL USAGE FOR READING AND TRANSLATION. EXERCISE:

1. 수박 겉 핥기. Licking the outside skin of a watermelon. (superficiality; shallowness)

2. 허울 좋은 하눌타리 : 겉으로는 훌륭하나 속은 보잘것없는 것. A nice-looking snake gourd. (a thing not so good as it looks)

3. 瓜田不納履 (과전불납리) 참외밭 곁에서 신발을 고쳐 신지 말라 : 남에게 의심받을 행동을 하지 말라. Avoid a compromising position; Be careful not to invite suspicion.

4. 瓜熟蒂落 (과숙체락) : 참외가 익으면 저절로 떨어진다. When the melon is ripe, it will drop of itself.

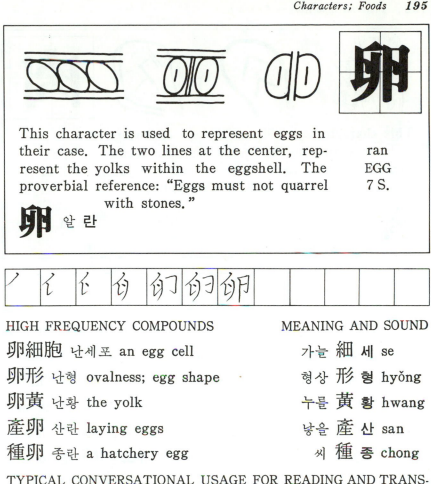

This character is used to represent eggs in their case. The two lines at the center, represent the yolks within the eggshell. The proverbial reference: "Eggs must not quarrel with stones."

ran
EGG
7 S.

卵 알 란

HIGH FREQUENCY COMPOUNDS

卵細胞 난세포 an egg cell

卵形 난형 ovalness; egg shape

卵黃 난황 the yolk

産卵 산란 laying eggs

種卵 종란 a hatchery egg

MEANING AND SOUND

가늘 細 세 se

형상 形 형 hyŏng

누를 黃 황 hwang

낳을 産 산 san

씨 種 종 chong

TYPICAL CONVERSATIONAL USAGE FOR READING AND TRANSLATION. EXERCISE:

1. 鷄卵有骨(계란유골) : 달걀에도 뼈가 있다는 뜻으로 일이 공교롭게 방해됨을 이르는 말. Disturbed unexpectedly.

2. 에디슨은 병아리를 孵化하려고 鷄卵을 품에 안고 있었다.
   Thomas A. Edison tried to hatch an egg on his bosom.

3. 닭이 먼저냐, 달걀이 먼저냐?
   Which was first, the chicken or the egg?

4. 以卵投石(이란투석) : 鷄卵으로 바위 치기 ; 抵抗하여도 到底히 이길 수 없음을 이르는 말. Using an egg to bash a stone.
   (overestimating one's strength)

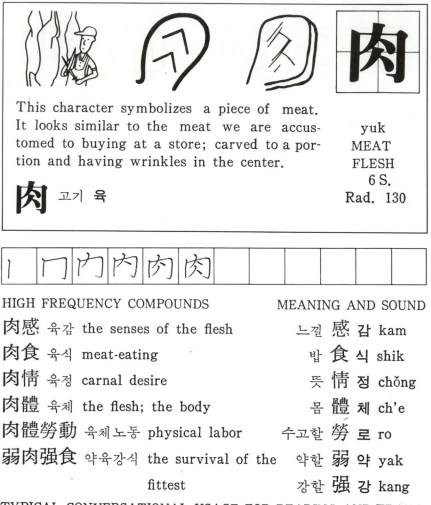

This character symbolizes a piece of meat. It looks similar to the meat we are accustomed to buying at a store; carved to a portion and having wrinkles in the center.

肉 고기 육

yuk
MEAT
FLESH
6 S.
Rad. 130

| 丨 | 冂 | 内 | 内 | 肉 | 肉 | | | | |

HIGH FREQUENCY COMPOUNDS

肉感 육감 the senses of the flesh

肉食 육식 meat-eating

肉情 육정 carnal desire

肉體 육체 the flesh; the body

肉體勞動 육체노동 physical labor

弱肉强食 약육강식 the survival of the fittest

MEANING AND SOUND

느낄 感 감 kam

밥 食 식 shik

뜻 情 정 chŏng

몸 體 체 ch'e

수고할 勞 로 ro

약할 弱 약 yak

강할 强 강 kang

TYPICAL CONVERSATIONAL USAGE FOR READING AND TRANSLATION. EXERCISE:

1. 건강한 肉體에 健康한 精神이 깃든다.
   A sound mind in a sound body.

2. 건강한 肉體는 靈魂의 寢室이지만 병든 육체는 영혼의 監獄이다. A healthy body is the guestchamber of the soul; a sick, its prison. (*Francis Bacon*)

3. 너희 온 영과 혼과 몸이 우리 주 예수 그리스도 降臨하실 때에 흠 없게 保全되기를 원하노라. (데살로니가 前書 5 : 23)

This character was from the figure of the shellfish with its two legs out of the shell. The shell was later used as the medium of financial exchange—thus, "treasure."

p'ae
SHELL
TREASURE
7 S.
Rad. 154

貝 조개 **패**

丨 冂 冂 目 目 貝 貝

HIGH FREQUENCY COMPOUNDS

貝殼 패각 a shell

貝物 패물 shell goods

貝石 패석 a fossil shell

貝塚 패총 a shell mound

眞珠貝 진주패 a pearl oyster

MEANING AND SOUND

껍질 殼 각 kak

만물 物 물 mul

돌 石 석 sŏk

무덤 塚 총 ch'ong

참 眞 진 chin

구슬 珠 주 chu

TYPICAL CONVERSATIONAL USAGE FOR READING AND TRANSLATION. EXERCISE:

1. 記念品店에는 많은 貝物들이 있다.
   There are many sea shell gifts in the souvenir store.
2. 텍사스에 있는 한 曠野에서 訓練을 받다가 貝石을 發見했다.
   While I was under training in a desert in Texas, I found a fossil shell.
3. 貝塚은 石器時代의 遺跡으로서 原始人들이 까 먹고 버린 조가비가 쌓여 이루어진 무더기이다. *P'aech'ong* is the relics of the Stone Age, composed of the shells which early men dumped.

12. 教育　교육　Education

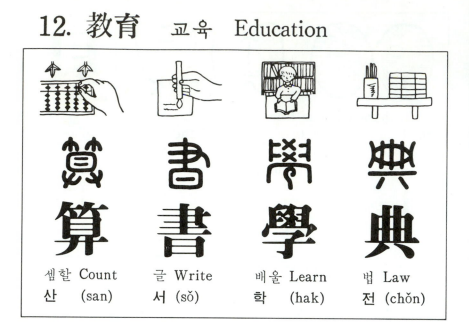

算	書	學	典
셈할 Count	글 Write	배울 Learn	법 Law
산 (san)	서 (sŏ)	학 (hak)	전 (chŏn)

누구든지 네 年少함을 업신여기지 못하게 하고 오직 말과 行實
과 사랑과 믿음과 貞節에 對하여 믿는 者에게 本이 되어 내가 이
를 때까지 읽는 것과 勸하는 것과 가르치는 것에 着念하라.
(디모데 前書 4 : 12～13)

　　Let no one despise your youth but be an example to the
believers in word, in conduct, in love, in spirit, in faith, in
purity. Till I come give attendance to reading, to exhortation,
to doctrine. (Ⅰ *Timothy* 4 : 12～13)

그러나 너는 배우고 確信한 일에 거하라. 네가 뉘에게서 배운 것
을 알며 또 네가 어려서부터 聖經을 알았나니 聖經은 能히 너로
하여금 그리스도 예수 안에 있는 믿음으로 말미암아 救援에 이르
는 智慧가 있게 하느니라. (디모데 後書 3 : 14～15)

　　You, however, must remain faithful in what you have
learned and are convinced of, aware from whom you learned
and how from childhood you have known the sacred scriptures
that are able to make you wise for salvation through faith
in Christ Jesus. (Ⅱ *Timothy* 3 : 14～15)

This character represents teaching, as when the father Abraham taught his son Isaac. The crosses at top and to the left, denote things marked incorrect, as in our own test grading. We also see the 敎 가르칠 교 father (父) watching over his son (子) as he receives his father's wisdom.

kyo
TO TEACH
11 S.

HIGH FREQUENCY COMPOUNDS

教授 교수 a professor

教育 교육 education

教師 교사 a teacher

教材 교재 teaching materials

教會 교회 church

MEANING AND SOUND

줄 授 수 su

기를 育 육 yuk

스승 師 사 sa

재목 材 재 chae

모일 會 회 hŏe

TYPICAL CONVERSATIONAL USAGE FOR READING AND TRANSLATION. EXERCISE:

1. 마땅히 행할 일을 아이에게 가르치라. 그리하면 늙어도 그것을 떠나지 아니하리라. (箴言 22 : 6) Train up a child in the way he should go; and when he is old, he will not depart from it. (*Proverbs* 22 : 6)

2. 가르침을 받는 자는 말씀을 가르치는 자와 모든 좋은 것을 함께 하라. (갈라디아서 6 : 6) The person who is being taught should share all good things with him who teaches the word. (*Galatians* 6 : 6)

3. 사람의 長點을 끌어내는 것이 敎育이다. Education draws out the best that is in one.

Here, we see a school boy sitting in front of the desk and looking at his books. Hence, the idea of diligent study and the learning that results, is conveyed.

hak
TO LEARN
TO STUDY
16 S.

學 배울 학   (學→学)

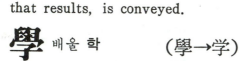

HIGH FREQUENCY COMPOUNDS

		MEANING AND SOUND
學校 학교 a school		학교 校 교 kyo
學歷 학력 an academic career		지낼 歷 력 ryŏk
學生 학생 a student		날 生 생 saeng
學說 학설 a theory; a doctrine		말씀 說 설 sŏl
博學 박학 extensive learning		넓을 博 박 pak
學位 학위 an academic degree		자리 位 위 wi

TYPICAL CONVERSATIONAL USAGE FOR READING AND TRANSLATION. EXERCISE:

1. 學校가 집에서 가까우므로 나는 자주 걸어다닌다.

   I often walk to school because it is close to our house.

2. 朴先生님은 무슨 學位를 가지고 있는지 아세요?

   Do you know what kind of degree Mr. Park has?

3. 地動說에 대한 學說은 누가 主唱했는지 알아?

   Do you know who put forth the heliocentric theory?

4. 博學多才(박학다재) : 學問이 넓고 재주가 많음.

   Extensive knowledge and great ability.

This character has the meaning of a letter or a document, which thought important in itself, takes on greater weight when seen with the many others designed to complement it. We can see this, as it developed from the idea of "one stitch which comprises part of a whole net."

文 글월 문

mun
LETTER
DOCUMENT
4 S.
Rad. 67

HIGH FREQUENCY COMPOUNDS

文官 문관 a civilian official

文教部 문교부 the Ministry of Education

文藝復興 문예부흥 the Renaissance

文獻 문헌 documentary records

文化 문화 culture

MEANING AND SOUND

벼슬 官 관 kwan

나눌 部 부 pu

재주 藝 예 ye

다시 復 부 pu

드릴 獻 헌 hŏn

화할 化 화 hwa

TYPICAL CONVERSATIONAL USAGE FOR READING AND TRANSLATION. EXERCISE:

1. 文學이란 文字를 통해 한 民族의 생각을 表現하는 것이다.
   Literature is "the expression of a nation's mind in writing."
   (*W. E. Channing*)

2. 貴重한 文獻들은 死藏되지 아니하고 硏究者들에 의하여 많이
   읽혀져야 한다. Important documents should not be hoarded but should be read by scholars.

3. 文化란 單純히 사람이 어떻게 살며, 習慣的으로 歷史에 어떻게
   連結되어 가는가 하는 것이다. (*L. R. Jones*)

Here, we see the character originally indicating a hand gripping a brush or a pencil. The feeling of a hand and stick still remains. Those markings at the very top relate that a brush or a pencil was made 筆 붓 필 from bamboo.

p'il
BRUSH
PENCIL

HIGH FREQUENCY COMPOUNDS

MEANING AND SOUND

筆記 필기 taking notes

기록할 記 기 ki

筆寫 필사 copying; transcription

베낄 寫 사 sa

筆硯 필연 brush and inkstone

벼루 硯 연 yŏn

筆者 필자 the writer; an author

놈 者 자 cha

筆筒 필통 a pencil case; a brush case

대통 筒 통 t'ong

大書特筆 대서특필 headline

특별할 特 특 t'ŭk

執筆 집필 writing

잡을 執 집 chip

TYPICAL CONVERSATIONAL USAGE FOR READING AND TRANSLATION. EXERCISE:

1. 붓은 칼보다 강하다. The pen is mightier than the sword.

2. 田博士의 講義를 듣지 못했으면 다른 學生의 筆記한 것이라도 빌려서 보아야 한다.
   If you could't follow Dr. Chŏn's lecture, then you must at least borrow and read notes taken by other students.

3. 다음 달부터 우리 新聞의 筆陣이 바뀌게 된다. Our newspaper's writing staff will be changed starting next month.

 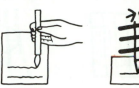

This character means a letter, a document, or "to write." The top radical represents a hand (⼺) holding a pen or a pencil. The radical below denotes "day" or "every day"(日).
So, the combination of the hand 書 글 서 radical and day radical is understood to be "correspondence."

sŏ
TO WRITE
LETTER
DOCUMENT
10 S.

HIGH FREQUENCY COMPOUNDS

書記 서기 a clerk; a secretary

書道 서도 calligraphy; penmanship

書目 서목 list of books

書店 서점 a bookstore; a bookseller's

書齋 서재 a study; a library

MEANING AND SOUND

기록할 記 기 ki

길 道 도 to

눈 目 목 mok

가게 店 점 chŏm

집 齋 재 chae

TYPICAL CONVERSATIONAL USAGE FOR READING AND TRANSLATION. EXERCISE:

1. 書堂 개 三年이면 풍월을 읊는다 : 아무리 무식한 사람이라도 유식한 사람과 오랫 동안 같이 있으면 다소 見聞이 트인다는 말.
   In three years a school dog is able to read compositions.

2. 이번에 書店에 들르면 우주 여행에 관한 책을 사겠다. If I stop by a bookstore this time, I will buy a book about space travel.

3. 書道는 國民學校에서도 주당 한 시간씩 練習을 하고 있다.
   Calligraphy is practiced one hour a week in elementary schools.

4. 제 書齋는 2층에 있어서 눈이 피로할 때 庭園을 바라보기 편리합니다.

In ancient times, the writer used thin, narrow slats of bamboo, starting at the top and writing downwards. Afterwards, connected slips were tied together, thus forming 册 책 a book, as is shown by the old character. "Document" may also be the interpretation.

ch'aek
BOOK
VOLUME
5 S.

册 책 책

|) | 刀 | 刀 | 刑 | 册 | | | | | |

HIGH FREQUENCY COMPOUNDS

MEANING AND SOUND

册匣 책갑 a bookcase   갑 匣 갑 kap

册櫃 책궤 a book box   궤 櫃 궤 kwe

册房 책방 a bookstore   방 房 방 pang

册床 책상 a desk; a table   평상 床 상 sang

册張 책장 a leaf of a book   베풀 張 장 chang

册欌 책장 a bookshelf   장 欌 장 chang

TYPICAL CONVERSATIONAL USAGE FOR READING AND TRANSLATION. EXERCISE:

1. 册房하고 書店은 같은 말입니다.
   Ch'aekpang and *sŏjŏm* mean the same thing.

2. 册床 위에 있는 册은 우리의 敎科書이다.
   The book on the desk is our textbook.

3. 册欌은 아름다우나 볼만한 册이 몇 권 없는 것 같다. The bookshelf is beautiful but there are only a few books worth reading.

4. 우리 學校 書店은 外國語 書籍만 取扱한다. Our school's bookstore only carries foreign language materials.

It represents an ancient canonical book (冊) that was placed on the table (冊). Ancient books were written on laths of bamboo, tied together (竹書). The scribes imagined the modern form (冊).

chŏn
CANONICAL
BOOK
8 S.

 典 법 전

HIGH FREQUENCY COMPOUNDS	MEANING AND SOUND
典當鋪 전당포 a pawnbroker's shop	가게 鋪 포 p'o
典雅 전아 elegance; refinement	아담할 雅 아 a
典章 전장 regulation; rules	문채 章 장 chang
典籍 전적 classical books	호적 籍 적 chŏk
典型的 전형적 typical	거푸집 型 형 hyŏng
古典 고전 a classic; old books	오랠 古 고 ko
辭典 사전 a dictionary; a lexicon	말 辭 사 sa

TYPICAL CONVERSATIONAL USAGE FOR READING AND TRANSLATION. EXERCISE:

1. 奎章閣에 장서된 典籍들을 하루속히 整理하고 飜譯하여 연구자들에게 널리 읽혔으면 좋겠다. I wish that all the classical books stored in Kyujanggak could quickly one day be arranged, translated, and widely read by researchers.

2. 저 분은 눈이 파랗고 선이 굵으며 키도 커서 典型的인 서구인처럼 보인다. That person's eyes are blue, his features are large, and he is tall, so he looks like a typical westerner.

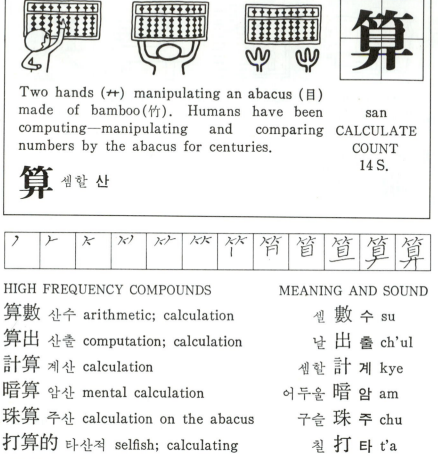

Two hands (艹) manipulating an abacus (目) made of bamboo(竹). Humans have been computing—manipulating and comparing numbers by the abacus for centuries.

san

CALCULATE
COUNT
14 S.

算 셈할 산

HIGH FREQUENCY COMPOUNDS

算數 산수 arithmetic; calculation

算出 산출 computation; calculation

計算 계산 calculation

暗算 암산 mental calculation

珠算 주산 calculation on the abacus

打算的 타산적 selfish; calculating

MEANING AND SOUND

셀 數 수 su

날 出 출 ch'ul

셈할 計 계 kye

어두울 暗 암 am

구슬 珠 주 chu

칠 打 타 t'a

TYPICAL CONVERSATIONAL USAGE FOR READING AND TRANSLATION. EXERCISE:

1. 國民學校 算數는 美國보다 韓國이 수준이 더 높다. The level of arithmetic in primary school is higher in Korea than in the U.S.

2. 珠算을 잘하는 사람은 거의 暗算도 빨리 한다. The man who uses an abacus well can do mental calculations almost as fast.

3. 現代人들은 珠算 대신 計算機를 利用하고 있다.
Modern people are using a calculator instead of an abacus.

4. 사람이 너무 打算的이면 친구 사귀기가 어렵다. If a person is too selfish, it is difficult for him to make friends.

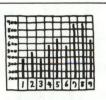 

This character originally meant a map, and later came to mean a matter written on paper, "to draw on paper" or "to project on paper." According to another opinion, it is the plans to be made to order one's granary (囗), when there are too many grains (啚) to be received therein.

圖 그림 도

to PICTURE CHART 14 S.

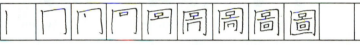

| | | | HIGH FREQUENCY COMPOUNDS | | | | | |

HIGH FREQUENCY COMPOUNDS

圖書 도서 books

圖書館 도서관 a library

圖案 도안 a design; a sketch

圖解 도해 an explanatory diagram

試圖 시도 implementation

地圖 지도 map

MEANING AND SOUND

글 書 서 sŏ

집 館 관 kwan

책상 案 안 an

풀 解 해 hae

시험할 試 시 shi

땅 地 지 chi

TYPICAL CONVERSATIONAL USAGE FOR READING AND TRANSLATION. EXERCISE:

1. 집은 圖書로, 庭園은 꽃으로 가득 채우라. A house full of books, and a garden of flowers. (*Andrew Lang*)

2. 冊 없는 房은 靈魂 없는 肉體와 같다. A room without books as a body without a soul. (*Cicero*)

3. 冊을 읽고 싶을 때 圖書館을 利用하세요.
When you want to read books, use the library.

4. 敎室마다 世界地圖가 하나씩 있고 여러 가지 圖解도 있다. Each classroom has a world map and various types of other charts.

13. 建物 전물 Architectural Structure

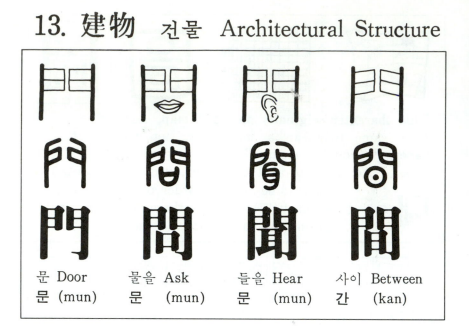

문 Door	물을 Ask	들을 Hear	사이 Between
문 (mun)	문 (mun)	문 (mun)	간 (kan)

솔로몬이 여호와의 이름을 위하여 殿을 建築하고 自己 權榮을
위하여 宮闕 建築하기를 決心하니라. (歷代下 2：1)

Solomon determined to build a temple in honor of the
name of the Lord, and a palace for himself. (Ⅱ *Chronicles*
2：1)

서로 말하되, 자 벽돌을 만들어 견고히 굽자 하고 이에 벽돌로
돌을 대신하며 瀝青으로 진흙을 代身하고 또 말하되, 자 城과 臺
를 쌓아 臺 꼭대기를 하늘에 닿게 하여 우리 이름을 내고 온 地面
에 흩어짐을 免하자 하였더니 여호와께서 人生들의 쌓는 城과 臺
를 보시려고 降臨하셨더라. (創世記 11：3～4)

They said to one another, "Come on! Let us mold bricks
and thoroughly bake them;" so they had brick for stone
and asphalt for mortar. Then they said, "Come on! Let us
build a city for ourselves with a tower whose top reaches
unto the heavens." And the Lord came down to see the city
and the tower, which the children of men builded.
(*Genesis* 11：3～4)

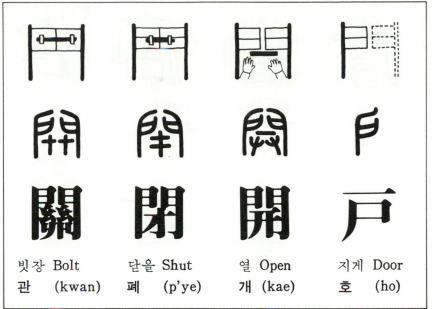

빗장 Bolt	닫을 Shut	열 Open	지게 Door
관 (kwan)	폐 (p'ye)	개 (kae)	호 (ho)

내가 門이니 누구든지 나로 말미암아 들어가면 救援을 얻고 또는 들어가며 나오며 꼴을 얻으리라. (요한福音 10 : 9)

I am the door. Whoever comes in through me will be saved; he will go in and out and find pasture. (*John* 10 : 9)

볼지어다 내가 門 밖에서 두드리노니 누구든지 내 音聲을 듣고 門을 열면 내가 그에게로 들어가 그로 더불어 먹고 그는 나로 더불어 먹으리라. (요한啓示錄 3 : 20)

Behold, I stand at the door and knock. If anyone listens to my voice and opens the door, I shall come in to him and dine with him and he with me. (*Revelation* 3 : 20)

그의 안에서 建物마다 서로 連結하여 主 안에서 聖殿이 되어가고 너희도 聖靈 안에서 하나님의 居하실 處所가 되기 위하여 예수 안에서 함께 지어져 가느니라. (에베소書 2 ; 21~22)

The whole building, framed together in him, raises into a temple that is holy in the Lord, in whom you also are built up together for a dwelling of God in the spirit. (*Ephesians* 2 : 21~22)

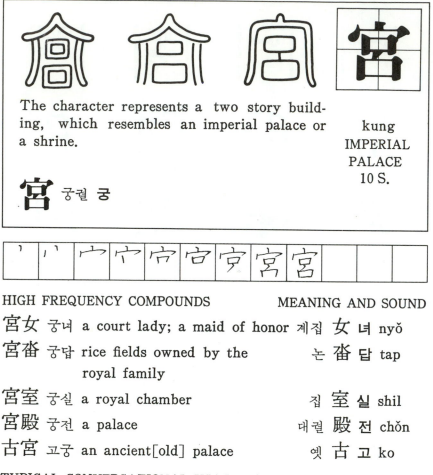

The character represents a two story building, which resembles an imperial palace or a shrine.

宮 궁궐 궁

kung
IMPERIAL
PALACE
10 S.

HIGH FREQUENCY COMPOUNDS

MEANING AND SOUND

宮女 궁녀 a court lady; a maid of honor   계집 女 녀 nyŏ

宮畓 궁답 rice fields owned by the royal family   논 畓 답 tap

宮室 궁실 a royal chamber   집 室 실 shil

宮殿 궁전 a palace   대궐 殿 전 chŏn

古宮 고궁 an ancient[old] palace   옛 古 고 ko

TYPICAL CONVERSATIONAL USAGE FOR READING AND TRANSLATION. EXERCISE:

1. 宮畓은 宮에 속한 논과 밭으로서 農事를 지어 宮에서 필요로 하는 것들을 供給하던 土地를 말한다. *Kungdap* is the rice paddys and fields attached to the palace, and by farming this piece of land they provided all goods needed in the palace.

2. 봄 가을에는 古宮마다 觀光客으로 붐빈다.
   In spring and fall, every old palace is packed with tourists.

3. 서울의 景福宮은 참으로 아름다운 古宮입니다.
   Kyŏngbokkung is one of the most beautiful palaces in Seoul.

高

This represents a very tall building or house with two stories. This is made use of as a radical.

ko
HIGH
10 S.
Rad. 189

高 높을 고

丶 亠 亠 亠 高 高 高 高

HIGH FREQUENCY COMPOUNDS

高見 고견 a valuable opinion

高官 고관 a high-ranking official

高級 고급 high-quality

高等考試 고등고시 the high civil
　　　　service examination

MEANING AND SOUND

볼 見 견 kyŏn

벼슬 官 관 kwan

등급 級 급 kŭp

등급 等 등 tŭng

상고할 考 고 ko

TYPICAL CONVERSATIONAL USAGE FOR READING AND TRANSLATION. EXERCISE:

1. 眼高手低(안고수저) : 能力은 없으면서 눈만 높다.
   High ideals, insufficient ability.
2. 내가 잘 아는 사람 하나는 高等考試를 세 번이나 보았으나 合格하지 못하고 말았다.
   A man who I know very well took the civil service examination three times but he could not pass it.
3. 天高馬肥(천고마비) : 하늘이 높고 말이 살찐다는 뜻으로, 가을이 썩 좋은 季節임을 일컫는 말.
   High sky and plump horses. (a splendid autumn)

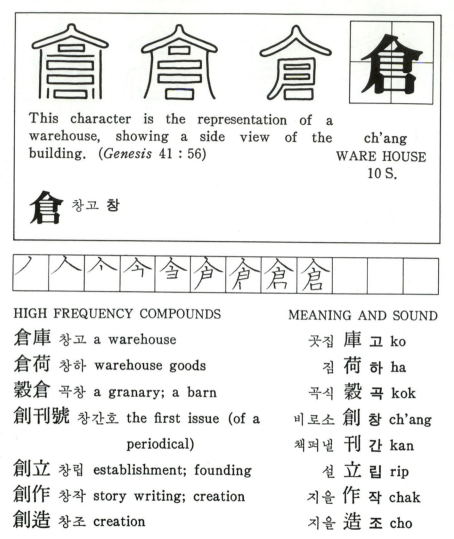

This character is the representation of a warehouse, showing a side view of the building. (*Genesis* 41 : 56)

ch'ang

WARE HOUSE
10 S.

倉　창고 **창**

HIGH FREQUENCY COMPOUNDS	MEANING AND SOUND

倉庫 창고 a warehouse

倉荷 창하 warehouse goods

穀倉 곡창 a granary; a barn

創刊號 창간호 the first issue (of a
　　　　　　 periodical)

創立 창립 establishment; founding

創作 창작 story writing; creation

創造 창조 creation

곳집 庫 고 ko

짐 荷 하 ha

곡식 穀 곡 kok

비로소 創 창 ch'ang

책펴낼 刊 간 kan

설 立 립 rip

지을 作 작 chak

지을 造 조 cho

TYPICAL CONVERSATIONAL USAGE FOR READING AND TRANS-LATION. EXERCISE:

1. 三南地方은 한국의 穀倉地帶이며 큰 절들도 많다.
   The three southern regions are Korea's "bread basket" and there are also many large temples in that region.

2. 太初에 하나님이 天地를 創造하시니라. (창세기 1 : 1)ˉIn the beginning God created the heaven and the earth. (*Genesis* 1 : 1)

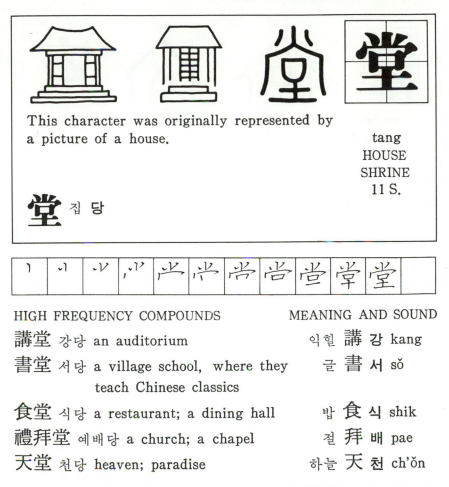

This character was originally represented by a picture of a house.

tang
HOUSE
SHRINE
11 S.

堂 집 당

HIGH FREQUENCY COMPOUNDS | MEANING AND SOUND

講堂 강당 an auditorium — 익힐 講 강 kang

書堂 서당 a village school, where they teach Chinese classics — 글 書 서 sŏ

食堂 식당 a restaurant; a dining hall — 밥 食 식 shik

禮拜堂 예배당 a church; a chapel — 절 拜 배 pae

天堂 천당 heaven; paradise — 하늘 天 천 ch'ŏn

TYPICAL CONVERSATIONAL USAGE FOR READING AND TRANSLATION. EXERCISE:

1. 금요일 오후부터는 講堂에서 學藝會를 할 예정이다.
   The art and science show is scheduled to be held in the auditorium starting Friday afternoon.

2. 20년 전의 韓國에는 아직도 書堂이 있었는데 千字文과 論語 등을 가르치고 있었다. Twenty years ago there were still village schools in Korea and they were teaching the *Thousand-Character Classic, Discourses of Confucius* etc.

3. 食堂이 어디에 있읍니까? Where is the restaurant?

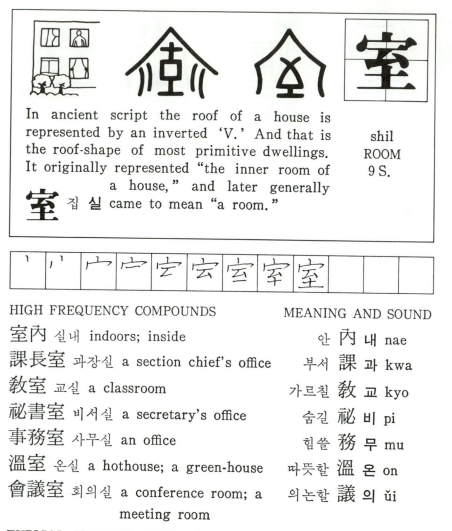

In ancient script the roof of a house is represented by an inverted 'V.' And that is the roof-shape of most primitive dwellings. It originally represented "the inner room of a house," and later generally 室 집 실 came to mean "a room."

shil
ROOM
9 S.

HIGH FREQUENCY COMPOUNDS

室內 실내 indoors; inside

課長室 과장실 a section chief's office

教室 교실 a classroom

祕書室 비서실 a secretary's office

事務室 사무실 an office

溫室 온실 a hothouse; a green-house

會議室 회의실 a conference room; a meeting room

MEANING AND SOUND

안 內 내 nae

부서 課 과 kwa

가르칠 教 교 kyo

숨길 祕 비 pi

힘쓸 務 무 mu

따뜻할 溫 온 on

의논할 議 의 ŭi

TYPICAL CONVERSATIONAL USAGE FOR READING AND TRANSLATION. EXERCISE:

1. 室內靜肅 (실내정숙) : Keep quiet indoors.

2. 우리 事務室은 大東 빌딩 5層에 자리잡고 있다. Our office is located on the 5th floor of the Taedong building.

3. 會議室에는 아직 司會者가 도착하지 못해서 우리는 조금 더 기다려 보기로 했다. The chairman had not arrived in the conference room yet, so we decided to wait a little longer.

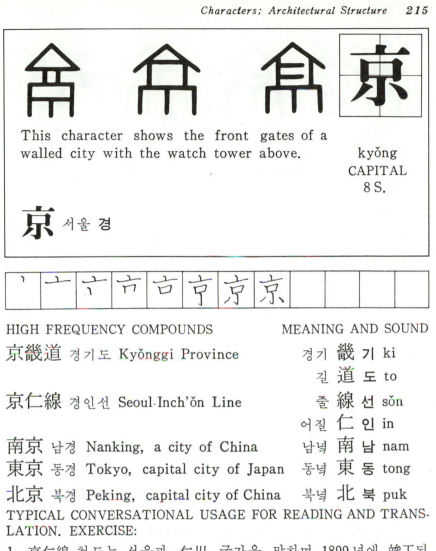

This character shows the front gates of a walled city with the watch tower above.

kyŏng
CAPITAL
8 S.

京 서울 경

```
丶  亠  宀  宀  古  亨  京  京
```

HIGH FREQUENCY COMPOUNDS

MEANING AND SOUND

京畿道 경기도 Kyŏnggi Province

경기 畿 기 ki

길 道 도 to

京仁線 경인선 Seoul·Inch'ŏn Line

줄 線 선 sŏn

어질 仁 인 in

南京 남경 Nanking, a city of China

남녘 南 남 nam

東京 동경 Tokyo, capital city of Japan

동녘 東 동 tong

北京 북경 Peking, capital city of China

북녘 北 북 puk

TYPICAL CONVERSATIONAL USAGE FOR READING AND TRANSLATION. EXERCISE:

1. 京仁線 철도는 서울과 仁川 구간을 말하며 1899년에 竣工되었다. The Seoul-Inch'ŏn line refers to the stretch of railway between Seoul and Inch'ŏn and was completed in 1899.

2. 美國에 오는 길에 東京을 들러서 3일 동안 觀光했다.
On the way to America, I stopped and did some sightseeing in Tokyo for 3 days.

3. 韓國에 있는 中國飲食店들은 거의 北京式이 많다.
The Chinese restaurants in Korea are almost all Peking style.

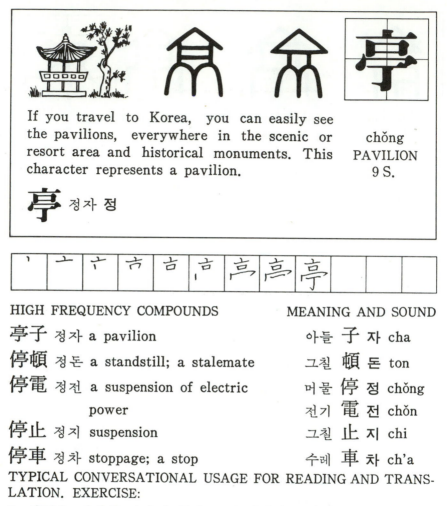

If you travel to Korea, you can easily see the pavilions, everywhere in the scenic or resort area and historical monuments. This character represents a pavilion.

chŏng
PAVILION
9 S.

亭 정자 정

HIGH FREQUENCY COMPOUNDS

亭子 정자 a pavilion

停頓 정돈 a standstill; a stalemate

停電 정전 a suspension of electric
power

停止 정지 suspension

停車 정차 stoppage; a stop

MEANING AND SOUND

아들 子 자 cha

그칠 頓 돈 ton

머물 停 정 chŏng

전기 電 전 chŏn

그칠 止 지 chi

수레 車 차 ch'a

TYPICAL CONVERSATIONAL USAGE FOR READING AND TRANSLATION. EXERCISE:

1. 亭子는 대부분 山水가 좋은 곳에 자리하고 있다. Pavilions are almost located in the places rich in natural beauty.

2. 停電이 되면 病院이나 큰 生産工場에서는 自家發電을 한다.
   If there is a power outage, hospitals and large production plants generate their own electricity.

3. 버스나 汽車를 타고 내릴 때에는 完全히 停車한 후에 내리고 또 乘車해야 한다.
   When you ride a bus or a train, you must wait until it is completely stopped before getting off and boarding it.

This character is a juxtaposition of a door(戶) and an axe(斤), and refers to the place where fuel is prepared. In olden times, the chopping of firewood with the axe(斤) was done near the door of a house(戶).

所 바 소 Hence the axe beside a house(所), meaning place or location.

so
PLACE
8 S.

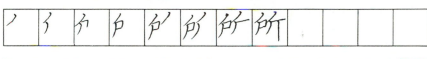

HIGH FREQUENCY COMPOUNDS

所感 소감 opinions; impression

所得稅 소득세 an income tax

所望 소망 desire; a wish

所産 소산 a product; outcome

所願 소원 one's prayer; a desire

所有 소유 possession; ownership

所持品 소지품 personal effects; one's baggage

MEANING AND SOUND

느낄 感 감 kam

얻을 得 득 tŭk

바랄 望 망 mang

낳을 産 산 san

원할 願 원 won

있을 有 유 yu

가질 持 지 chi

종류 品 품 p'um

TYPICAL CONVERSATIONAL USAGE FOR READING AND TRANSLATION. EXERCISE:

1. 믿음, 所望, 사랑 이 중에 第一은 사랑이라. (고린도전서 13 : 13)
   Faith, hope, and love; of these three the greatest is love.

2. 旅客機를 탈 때에는 檢閱臺 앞을 通過하면서 所持品을 다 내놓고 調査를 받아야 한다. When you travel by a passenger plane, you have to go through an inspection at the inspection point by showing them your possessions.

This character means winter. Winter is represented by icicles forming on the eaves of a Korean house.

tong
WINTER
5 S.

冬 겨울 동

ノ	ク	欠	冬	冬					

HIGH FREQUENCY COMPOUNDS

MEANING AND SOUND

冬季 동계 the winter season

冬眠 동면 hibernation

冬服 동복 winter clothes

冬至 동지 the winter solstice

越冬準備 월동준비 preparations for
the winter

철 季 계 kye

잠잘 眠 면 myŏn

옷 服 복 pok

이를 至 지 chi

넘을 越 월 wol

비길 準 준 chun

TYPICAL CONVERSATIONAL USAGE FOR READING AND TRANSLATION. EXERCISE:

1. 한국의 冬季節은 12월, 1월, 2월 기간인데 겨울 放學이 있다. December, January and February are the winter period in Korea and this is when they have their winter school vacation.

2. 전에는 대부분의 中高等學校에서 校服을 입었는데 季節에 따라 冬服과 夏服으로 구분되어 있었다.
Previously, almost all middle and high school students wore summer or winter school uniforms. The season decided which uniform was to be worn.

3. 한국에서의 越冬準備는 무엇보다도 김장과 땔감이 중요하다.

This ideograph is the combination of a house (··) and a woman (女). Since a woman makes homelife secure, this character means "peaceful or restful."

an
PEACEFUL
RESTFUL
6 S.

安 편안할 안

安 ＇ 宀 宄 安 安

HIGH FREQUENCY COMPOUNDS   MEANING AND SOUND

安寧 안녕 well-being; tranquility   편안할 寧 녕 nyŏng

安眠妨害 안면방해 disturbance of sleep   방해할 妨 방 pang

安息年 안식년 a sabbatical year   쉴 息 식 shik

安心 안심 peace of mind   마음 心 심 shim

安全裝置 안전장치 a safety device   둘 置 치 ch'i

安全第一 안전제일 safety first   차례 第 제 che

安定 안정 stability   정할 定 정 chŏng

TYPICAL CONVERSATIONAL USAGE FOR READING AND TRANSLATION. EXERCISE:

1. 安寧하십니까? 퍽 오래간만입니다!
   How are you? It's been a long time since I saw you last.

2. 일이 잘 되어 가니 安心하세요, 때가 되면 다 이루어지겠지요.
   The work is going well, so don't worry. In time it will turn out just fine.

3. 來年이 安息年인데 이스라엘로 聖地巡禮를 할까 합니다.
   Next year is my sabbatical year and I am thinking of going to the Holy Land of Israel.

A pig in a hut symbolizing a home. The pig is probably the earliest domesticated animal. The invention of this character probably took place in a fairly advanced stage of an agricultural society.

ka
HOUSE
HOME
10 S.

家 집 가 Year of the pig by the twelve animal signs: 1959, 1971, 1983, 1995···

HIGH FREQUENCY COMPOUNDS

家長 가장 the head of a family

家庭 가정 home; a family

家族 가족 a family

家畜 가축 a domestic animal

家訓 가훈 family precepts

國家 국가 a country; a nation

農家 농가 a farmhouse

MEANING AND SOUND

긴 長 장 chang

뜰 庭 정 chŏng

겨레 族 족 chok

기를 畜 축 ch'uk

가르칠 訓 훈 hun

나라 國 국 kuk

농사 農 농 nong

TYPICAL CONVERSATIONAL USAGE FOR READING AND TRANSLATION. EXERCISE:

1. 家和萬事成(가화만사성) : 집 안이 和睦하면 모든 일이 잘 되어 나간다. If you are living in your home in peace and harmony, everything will go well.

2. 東家食西家宿(동가식서가숙) : 떠돌아다니며 얻어 먹고 다니는 것. Begging for handouts from door to door.

3. 누구든지 自己親族, 특히 自己家族을 돌아보지 아니하면 믿음을 背反한 자요, 不信者보다 더 악한 자니라. (I *Tim.* 5 : 8)

This character represents a door with two leaves. Doors provide exits and entrances. It is also used as a counting unit for cannons. This is made use of as the radical number 169.

mun
DOOR
GATE
8 S.
Rad. 169

門 문 문

｜　「　Ｆ　Ｐ　Ｐ｜　門　門　門

HIGH FREQUENCY COMPOUNDS

守門將 a gatekeeper; a door-
　　　keeper

門外漢 문외한 an outsider

門牌 문패 a name plate; a doorplate

門下生 문하생 one's disciple; one's pupil

專門 전문 specialty; major in

MEANING AND SOUND

지킬 守 수 su

놈 漢 한 han

밖 外 외 oe

간판 牌 패 p'ae

날 生 생 saeng

오로지 專 전 chŏn

TYPICAL CONVERSATIONAL USAGE FOR READING AND TRANSLATION. EXERCISE:

1. 옛날에 大漢門에는 守門將으로 九尺長身의 巨人이 있었다.
   In old days, the guard at the Taehan gate was nine foot tall giant.

2. 그는 文學에는 造詣가 깊지만 電氣工學에는 門外漢이다.
   He is at home in literature but he knows nothing about electrical engineering.

3. 韓國에는 집집마다 門牌가 있다.
   Each house in Korea has a name plate on the door.

This character is a pictograph of one leaf of a door (戶). It is also symbolic of the house and the family. The radical part of the numerous characters relating to doors and the house.

戶 집 호

ho

DOOR
HOME
4 S.
Rad. 63

| ` | ⌐ | 亠 | 戶 | | | | | | | |

HIGH FREQUENCY COMPOUNDS

戶口 호구 houses and inhabitants

戶斂 호렴 house-tax

戶別 호별 house by house

戶籍 호적 a census register

戶主 호주 the head of a family

門戶 문호 the door or a family

MEANING AND SOUND

입 口 구 ku

거둘 斂 렴 ryŏm

다를 別 별 pyŏl

서적 籍 적 chŏk

주인 主 주 chu

문 門 문 mun

TYPICAL CONVERSATIONAL USAGE FOR READING AND TRANS-LATION. EXERCISE:

1. 選擧運動을 위하여 戶別訪問을 해야 된다.
   You have to campaign door to door for an election campaign.

2. 아기를 낳았으니까 戶籍에 올리러 區廳에 가야 한다.
   I have to go to the district office in order to make a family registration because I have had a baby.

3. 男便이 死亡하면 아내가 戶主로 될 수 있다.
   If the husband dies, then the wife can become the head of the family.

14. 道具　도구　Tools

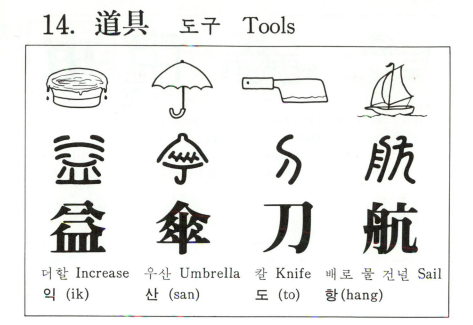

더할 Increase	우산 Umbrella	칼 Knife	배로 물 건널 Sail
익 (ik)	산 (san)	도 (to)	항(hang)

이 殿은 建築할 때에 돌을 뜨는 곳에서 治石하고 가져다가 建築하였으므로 建築하는 동안에 殿 속에서는 방망이나 도끼나 모든 鐵 연장 소리가 들리지 아니하였으며… (列王記上 6 : 7)

And the temple, when it was being built, was built with stone finished at the quarry, so that no hammer or chisel or any iron tool was heard in the temple while it was being built. (I *Kings* 6 : 7)

또 거기서 네 하나님 여호와를 爲하여 壇 곧 돌 壇을 쌓되 그것에 鐵器를 대지 말지니라. (申命記 27 : 5)

And there you shall build an altar of the Lord your God, an altar of stones; you shall not use any iron tool on them. (*Deuteronomy* 27 : 5)

이에 예수께서 이르시되 네 劍을 도로 집에 꽂으라 劍을 가지는 者는 다 劍으로 亡하느니라.(마태福音 26 : 52)

Then said to him, "put your sword in its place, for all who take the sword will perish by the sword." (*Matthew* 26 : 52)

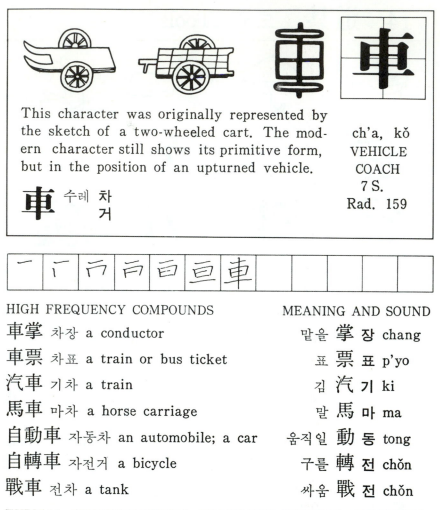

This character was originally represented by the sketch of a two-wheeled cart. The modern character still shows its primitive form, but in the position of an upturned vehicle.

車 수레 차
거

ch'a, kŏ
VEHICLE
COACH
7 S.
Rad. 159

HIGH FREQUENCY COMPOUNDS

	MEANING AND SOUND
車掌 차장 a conductor	맡을 掌 장 chang
車票 차표 a train or bus ticket	표 票 표 p'yo
汽車 기차 a train	김 汽 기 ki
馬車 마차 a horse carriage	말 馬 마 ma
自動車 자동차 an automobile; a car	움직일 動 동 tong
自轉車 자전거 a bicycle	구를 轉 전 chŏn
戰車 전차 a tank	싸움 戰 전 chŏn

TYPICAL CONVERSATIONAL USAGE FOR READING AND TRANSLATION. EXERCISE:

1. 車掌은 용산역을 지나서부터 汽車票 검사를 시작했다.
   After passing by Yongsan station the conductor started checking the passenger's train tickets.

2. 나는 텍사스에 있는 戰車部隊에서 二年間 근무했다.
   I worked for two years in an armored cavalry unit in Texas.

3. 서울의 電車는 오래 전부터 運行이 中止되었고 그 一部는 南山의 어린이 公園에서 전시되고 있다.

庫 庫 庫 庫

This character indicates a garage or warehouse, with a cart or other wheeled vehicle
inside.

ko
GARAGE
WAREHOUSE
10 S.

庫 창고 고

丶 亠 广 庐 庐 庐 庐 庐 庫

HIGH FREQUENCY COMPOUNDS

MEANING AND SOUND

金庫 금고 a safe

冷藏庫 냉장고 a refrigerator

文庫 문고 book collection; a library

書庫 서고 a library; a stack room

車庫 차고 a garage

倉庫 창고 a warehouse

쇠 金 금 kŭm

찰 冷 랭 raeng

감출 藏 장 chang

글 書 서 sŏ

수레 車 차 ch'a

곳집 倉 창 ch'ang

TYPICAL CONVERSATIONAL USAGE FOR READING AND TRANS-
LATION. EXERCISE:

1. 金庫의 번호를 모르면 아무도 利用할 수 없다. If the safe
   combination is unknown, no one can get into the safe.
2. 옛날 사람들은 冷藏庫 없이 얼마나 不便하게 살았을까!
   I wonder how people went without refrigerators in old days!
3. 우리 車庫에는 自動車 2 대와 4 대의 自轉車가 있다.
   There are two cars and four bicycles in our garage.
4. 倉庫는 生活에 必要한 物件들을 두는 곳이다. A storage house
   is a place where some of necessities of life are kept.

This ideograph combines the radical of the ship (舟), eight (八), and mouth (口). It represents the ark of Noah that means a ship or a boat. Noah built a ship and he took his eight people into his ark during the Deluge. (*Genesis* 7 : 6～9)

船 배 선

sŏn

SHIP, BOAT

11 S.

HIGH FREQUENCY COMPOUNDS

MEANING AND SOUND

船客 선객 a passenger

손 客 객 kaek

船室 선실 the passenger's quarters

집 室 실 shil

船員保險 선원보험 seamen's insurance

관원 員 원 won

船籍 선적 the nationality of a ship

서적 籍 적 chŏk

船便 선편 shipping service

편할 便 편 p'yŏn

漁船 어선 a fishing boat

고기잡을 漁 어 ŏ

TYPICAL CONVERSATIONAL USAGE FOR READING AND TRANSLATION. EXERCISE:

1. 노아는 잣나무로 배를 지었다.
   Noah made a boat from resinous wood.
2. 船便은 航空郵便보다 오래 걸리지만 값이 싸다. Surface mail takes more time for delivery but it is cheaper than air mail.
3. 저 배가 殊常한데 빨리 船籍을 알아보시오.
   That boat looks suspicious, quickly find out its nationality.
4. 日氣不順으로 인하여 두 隻의 漁船이 失踪됐다. Two fishing boats disappeared because of the inclement weather.

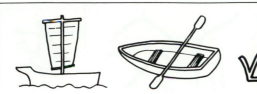

This character represents a sailing ship. The boat and the sail are returned to a more customary relationship from their juxtaposition in the Sino-Korean character for sailing on the water.

hang
SAIL
10 S.

航 배로
　物건널 **항**

HIGH FREQUENCY COMPOUNDS　　MEANING AND SOUND

航空 항공 aviation; flying　　빌 空 공 kong

航空母艦 항공모함 an aircraft carrier　싸움배 艦 함 ham

航空郵便 항공우편 airmail　　우편 郵 우 u

航空學 항공학 aeronautics　　배울 學 학 hak

航路 항로 a route; a course　　길 路 로 ro

航海 항해 a voyage; a sea trip　　바다 海 해 hae

TYPICAL CONVERSATIONAL USAGE FOR READING AND TRANSLATION. EXERCISE:

1. 사공이 많으면 배가 山으로 올라간다 : 지시하고 간섭하는 이 가 많으면 일이 뜻밖의 方向으로 進行하는 수가 있다. If you have too many steersmen, the boat will go up the hill.

2. 美國에서 韓國까지의 航空郵便은 약 一週日 걸린다. It takes about one week for a letter to get to Korea from the U.S. by airmail.

3. 제 큰 兄님은 大韓航空에서 二十年 동안 勤務했읍니다. My elder brother has been working at the Korean Airline for twenty years.

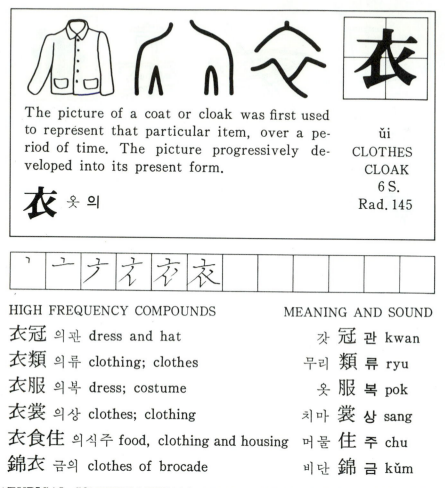

The picture of a coat or cloak was first used to represent that particular item, over a period of time. The picture progressively developed into its present form.

衣 옷 의

ŭi
CLOTHES
CLOAK
6 S.
Rad. 145

HIGH FREQUENCY COMPOUNDS

衣冠 의관 dress and hat

衣類 의류 clothing; clothes

衣服 의복 dress; costume

衣裳 의상 clothes; clothing

衣食住 의식주 food, clothing and housing

錦衣 금의 clothes of brocade

MEANING AND SOUND

갓 冠 관 kwan

무리 類 류 ryu

옷 服 복 pok

치마 裳 상 sang

머물 住 주 chu

비단 錦 금 kŭm

TYPICAL CONVERSATIONAL USAGE FOR READING AND TRANSLATION. EXERCISE:

1. 먹는 것은 自己自身을 즐겁게 하기 위함이요, 입는 것은 남을 즐겁게 하기 위함이다. Eat to please thyself, but dress to please others. (*Benjamin Franklin*)

2. 옷이 날개다 : 못난 사람도 옷을 잘 입으면 잘나 보인다는 뜻. Clothes are feathers. (If an ugly person dresses well, even he can look nice.)

3. 옷은 새 옷이 좋고 사람은 옛 사람이 좋다. New clothes are the best clothes, but an old friend is the best kind of friend.

The first one, represents two cocoons. The second, intertwining threads;collectively they are called silk.

sa
SILK
THREAD
12 S.
Rad. 120

絲 실 사

∠	幺	幺	糸	糸	絲	絲	絲	絲	絲

HIGH FREQUENCY COMPOUNDS	MEANING AND SOUND
絲管 사관 string and wind musical instruments	대롱 管 관 kwan
絲柳 사류 a weeping willow	버들 柳 류 ryu
絹絲 견사 silk thread	비단 絹 견 kyŏn
毛絲 모사 wool yarn	털 毛 모 mo
鐵絲 철사 wire; wiring	쇠 鐵 철 ch'ŏl

TYPICAL CONVERSATIONAL USAGE FOR READING AND TRANSLATION. EXERCISE:

1. 바늘 가는 데 실 간다. The thread must follow the needle. (Human beings with mutual love)

2. 明紬옷은 四寸까지 덥다. Silk clothing warms even a cousin. (the benefits of one's near relative's wealth)

3. 一絲一毫(일사일호) : 한 오리의 실과 한 오리의 털 ; 지극히 하 잘것없고 작은 일. An iota; a tiny bit.

4. 鐵絲줄을 엮어서 鐵網을 만든다. Steel wires are joined together to make a net called wire netting.

Shapes of an umbrella clearly defined. This character has evolved only little because of its simplicity and readily accessible meaning.

san
UMBRELLA
12 S.

 傘 우산 산

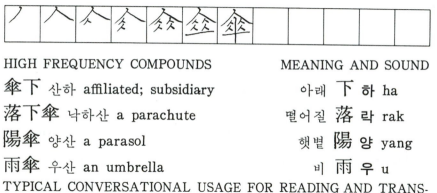

HIGH FREQUENCY COMPOUNDS

傘下 산하 affiliated; subsidiary

落下傘 낙하산 a parachute

陽傘 양산 a parasol

雨傘 우산 an umbrella

MEANING AND SOUND

아래 下 하 ha

떨어질 落 락 rak

햇볕 陽 양 yang

비 雨 우 u

TYPICAL CONVERSATIONAL USAGE FOR READING AND TRANSLATION. EXERCISE:

1. 유엔 難民 고등 辦務官은 국제적인 難民 문제를 解決하기 위한 유엔 傘下의 特別機構이다. UNHCR is a special organization under the umbrella of the U.N. which was set up to solve the problems of international refugees.

2. 落下傘은 第一次 世界大戰때 西洋에서 使用되었다. Parachutes were first used by the westerners in World War I.

3. 東洋女人들은 여름에 살결이 타는 것을 防止하기 위하여 陽傘 을 使用한다. Oriental women, in order to avoid getting sunburnt in the summer time, use parasols.

4. 바람에 그녀의 雨傘이 뒤집혔다. The wind blew her umbrella inside out.

This radical is a pictograph of a knife or sword. The proverb cautions: A knife that's too sharp easily cuts the fingers.

to
KNIFE
2 S.
Rad. 18

刀 칼 도

ㄱ	刀										

HIGH FREQUENCY COMPOUNDS

刀工 도공 a sword maker; swordsmith

果刀 과도 a dessert knife

粧刀 장도 an ornamental knife

長刀 장도 a long sword

菜刀 채도 a vegetable knife

MEANING AND SOUND

장인 工 공 kong

과실 果 과 kwa

꾸밀 粧 장 chang

긴 長 장 chang

나물 菜 채 ch'ae

TYPICAL CONVERSATIONAL USAGE FOR READING AND TRANSLATION. EXERCISE:

1. 單刀直入(단도직입) : 혼자서 칼을 휘두르고 거침없이 敵陣으로 쳐들어감. 文章이나 말의 너절한 虛頭를 빼고 바로 그 要點으로 풀이하여 들어감. Being straight forward.

2. 식칼이 제 자루를 못 깎는다 : 제가 제 자신의 일을 하기는 어려운 경우를 이르는 말. A kitchen knife cannot sharpen its own handle. (unable to do it all by himeself)

3. 대장장이 집에 식칼이 없다 : 마땅히 있어야 할 곳에 그 物件이 없을 때를 일컬음. No kitchen knife in a blacksmith's house; The cobbler's children go barefoot.

The shape of a horn, as it was originally drawn with realism, came also to mean "angle" through its usage.

kak
HORN
ANGLE
7 S.
Rad. 148

角 뿔 각

ノ   ク   ク   古   肖   角   角

HIGH FREQUENCY COMPOUNDS | MEANING AND SOUND

角度 각도 an angle

角氷 각빙 an ice cube

角柱 각주 a square pillar

角逐 각축 rivalry; competition

三角形 삼각형 a triangle

直角 직각 a right angle

법 度 도 to

얼음 氷 빙 ping

기둥 柱 주 chu

쫓을 逐 축 ch'uk

형상 形 형 hyŏng

곧을 直 직 chik

TYPICAL CONVERSATIONAL USAGE FOR READING AND TRANSLATION. EXERCISE:

1. 美國 國防省 建物은 五角形으로 지어졌다. The U. S. Department of Defense building was built in a pentagonal shape.

2. 이집트의 第三王朝는 신비스런 三角形의 피라밋을 지었다. In the third dynasty of Egypt, they built the mysterious triangular pyramids.

3. 90 度의 角을 直角이라고 한다.
   A ninety degree angle is called a right angle.

4. 커피에 넣는 설탕 중에는 角雪糖이 便利하다.
   Among the sugar put in coffee, sugar cubes are convenient.

This character combines the radical for horn (角) with knife(刀) and ox(牛).
To cleave the horn of an ox requires the use of a knife; hence (解).

hae
DIVIDE
UNTIE
EXPLAIN
13 S.

解 풀 해

ノ　ク　ク　ク　角　角　角　角　解　解　解

HIGH FREQUENCY COMPOUNDS

解決 해결 solution; disposing of

解雇 해고 layoff; discharge

解答 해답 an answer; a solution

解放 해방 liberation

解剖 해부 dissection

難解 난해 being difficult to understand

MEANING AND SOUND

정할 決 결 kyŏl

품살 雇 고 ko

대답할 答 답 tap

놓을 放 방 pang

나눌 剖 부 pu

어려울 難 난 nan

TYPICAL CONVERSATIONAL USAGE FOR READING AND TRANSLATION. EXERCISE:

1. 나의 問題解決의 열쇠는 祈禱밖에 없다.
   Prayer is the only key to solving my problems.

2. 景氣의 沈滯로 解雇 바람이 불고 있다. Due to the economic depression, there are many places laying off employees.

3. 이 퍼즐의 解答은 다음 호에 발표됩니다.
   The key to this puzzle will appear in the next issue.

4. 한국의 解放記念日은 8월 15일이다.
   Korea's liberation day is August fifteenth.

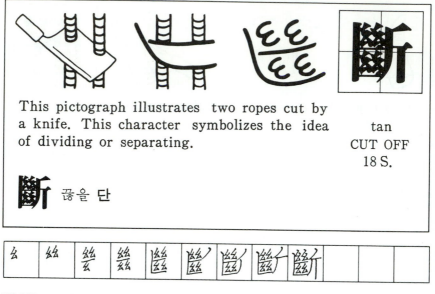

This pictograph illustrates two ropes cut by a knife. This character symbolizes the idea of dividing or separating.

tan
CUT OFF
18 S.

斷 끊을 단

HIGH FREQUENCY COMPOUNDS

斷交 단교 a break of friendship

斷念 단념 abandonment; giving up

斷面圖 단면도 a cross section

斷食療法 단식요법 a fasting cure

斷片的 단편적 fragmentary; scrappy

優柔不斷 우유부단 lack of decision

MEANING AND SOUND

사귈 交 교 kyo

생각 念 념 nyŏm

낯 面 면 myŏn

고칠 療 료 ryo

조각 片 편 p'yŏn

부드러울 柔 유 yu

TYPICAL CONVERSATIONAL USAGE FOR READING AND TRANSLATION. EXERCISE:

1. 박과장의 자제는 독일 留學 가려고 무척 노력하더니 結婚하더니만 斷念하고 말았더군! Section Chief Park's son worked very hard in order to go to Germany to study, but after he got married he gave up the idea.

2. 나는 너무 直線的이어서 優柔不斷한 사람은 相對하고 싶지 않아. I don't want to associate with a person who lacks decision as I am too straightforward.

3. 美國에서도 요즘 斷食療法으로 治療를 많이 하는 것 같아.

A boy cuts a watermelon which is mainly produced in July into seven pieces. This character is the combination of seven(七) and a knife(刀). Thus, (切) carries the meaning "to cut an object into pieces with a sword."

chŏl
CUT
4 S.

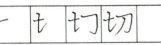
切 끊을 절
온·통 체

一	七	切	切								

HIGH FREQUENCY COMPOUNDS

切斷 절단 cutting

切望 절망 an earnest desire

切實 절실 acute; immediate

切品 절품 out of stock

一切 일절 absolutely

一切 일체 the whole

親切 친절 kindness; goodness

MEANING AND SOUND

끊을 斷 단 tan

바랄 望 망 mang

열매 實 실 shil

품수 品 품 p'um

한 一 일 il

친할 親 친 ch'in

TYPICAL CONVERSATIONAL USAGE FOR READING AND TRANSLATION. EXERCISE:

1. 切斷機를 使用하실 때 操心하세요.
   Be careful when you use the cutting machine.

2. 그 商品은 市中에 나오자마자 切品되었다. Those sales items ran out of stock, as soon as the sale started.

3. 오늘의 旅行案內者는 아주 親切합니다.
   Today's travel guide is very kind.

4. 切齒腐心(절치부심) : 憤을 못이겨 이를 갈고 속을 썩임.

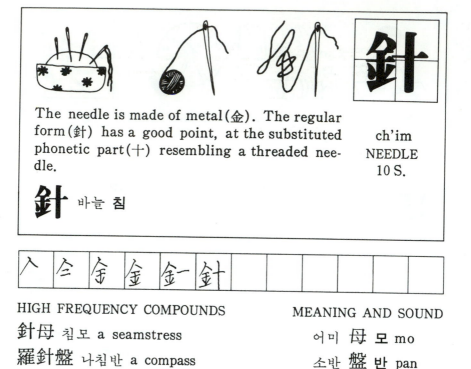

The needle is made of metal (金). The regular form (針) has a good point, at the substituted phonetic part (十) resembling a threaded needle.

ch'im
NEEDLE
10 S.

針 바늘 침

入 스 亼 金 金 金 針

HIGH FREQUENCY COMPOUNDS

針母 침모 a seamstress

羅針盤 나침반 a compass

針才 침재 talent in needlework (sewing)

短針 단침 the hour; hand (watch)

方針 방침 a policy; a line; a course

指針 지침 a pointer; an indicator

MEANING AND SOUND

어미 母 모 mo

소반 盤 반 pan

재주 才 재 chae

짧을 短 단 tan

모 方 방 pang

손가락 指 지 chi

TYPICAL CONVERSATIONAL USAGE FOR READING AND TRANSLATION. EXERCISE:

1. 一針見血 (일침견혈) : 단 한 번에 일을 처리함.
   To needle only once to reveal blood. (To come to the point)

2. 아무리 바빠도 바늘 허리 매어 쓰지 못한다 : 아무리 급한 일이라도 格式을 어기고는 행할 수 없다는 말. However pressed you may be for time, you must thread the needle, not tie it round the middle.

3. 針小棒大 (침소봉대) : 작은 일을 크게 허풍 떨어 말함.
   Exaggeration; hyperbole.

This character was originally a pictograph of a nail(丁). Clarified with the metal radical(金), it is now written (釘).

chŏng
NAIL
SPIKE
10 S.

釘 못 정

| ノ | ㇏ | ㇒ | 仐 | 牟 | 金 | 金 | 釘 | | |

HIGH FREQUENCY COMPOUNDS   MEANING AND SOUND

釘頭 정두 the head of a nail   머리 頭 두 tu

釘彫 정조 the decoration on the porcelain   새길 彫 조 cho

釘錘 정추 a hammer   저울 錘 추 ch'u

釘鞋 정혜 spiked shoes   신 鞋 혜 hye

押釘 압정 a thumbtack   누를 押 압 ap

TYPICAL CONVERSATIONAL USAGE FOR READING AND TRANSLATION. EXERCISE:

1. 튀어 나온 못은 두들겨 맞게 마련이다. A nail that sticks out is struck in. (Envy follows good fortune).

2. 선반을 만들려고 작은 못 몇 개를 鐵物店에서 사왔다.
I bought a few small nails from the hardware store in order to make a shelf.

3. 망치는 못을 치고 못은 나무를 뚫는다. The hammer hit the nail and the nail made a hole in the wood. (chain relation)

4. 揭示板에 時間表를 붙이는 데 押釘이 必要하다. Thumbtacks are wanted for putting the schedule on the bulletin board.

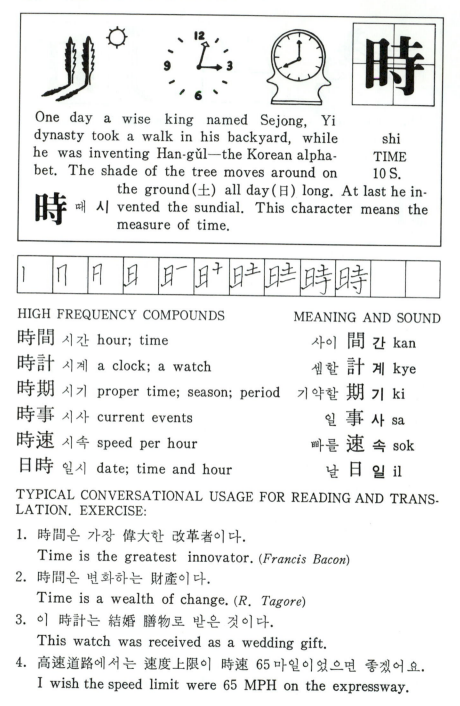

One day a wise king named Sejong, Yi
dynasty took a walk in his backyard, while   shi
he was inventing Han-gǔl—the Korean alpha-   TIME
bet. The shade of the tree moves around on   10 S.
the ground(土) all day(日) long. At last he in-
時 때 시 vented the sundial. This character means the
measure of time.

HIGH FREQUENCY COMPOUNDS

時間 시간 hour; time

時計 시계 a clock; a watch

時期 시기 proper time; season; period

時事 시사 current events

時速 시속 speed per hour

日時 일시 date; time and hour

MEANING AND SOUND

사이 間 간 kan

셈할 計 계 kye

기약할 期 기 ki

일 事 사 sa

빠를 速 속 sok

날 日 일 il

TYPICAL CONVERSATIONAL USAGE FOR READING AND TRANS-
LATION. EXERCISE:

1. 時間은 가장 偉大한 改革者이다.
   Time is the greatest innovator. (*Francis Bacon*)
2. 時間은 변화하는 財産이다.
   Time is a wealth of change. (*R. Tagore*)
3. 이 時計는 結婚 膳物로 받은 것이다.
   This watch was received as a wedding gift.
4. 高速道路에서는 速度上限이 時速 65마일이었으면 좋겠어요.
   I wish the speed limit were 65 MPH on the expressway.

A brush is seen here cleaning the vessel—conveying the idea that it is now empty of content. Hence, "exhaust," "finished," and "the end."

chin
EXHAUST
14 S.

盡 다할 진

HIGH FREQUENCY COMPOUNDS	MEANING AND SOUND

盡力 진력 endeavor; effort; exertion 　　　힘 力 력 ryǒk

盡誠 진성 giving one's whole heart 　　　정성 誠 성 sŏng

盡數 진수 the entire number; the whole 　　셀 數 수 su

盡心 진심 one's whole heart 　　　마음 心 심 shim

盡終日 진종일 all day long 　　　마칠 終 종 chong

賣盡 매진 a sellout 　　　　팔 賣 매 mae

消盡 소진 vanishing completely 　　없앨 消 소 so

TYPICAL CONVERSATIONAL USAGE FOR READING AND TRANSLATION. EXERCISE:

1. 一網打盡(일망타진) : 한꺼번에 모조리 잡음. To capture everything in only one casting of the net. (everything captured)

2. 無窮無盡(무궁무진) : There is no end nor exhaustion.

3. 그 商品은 市場에 나오자마자 賣盡되었다.
   That item was sold out as soon as it came out on the market.

4. 그는 너를 위해 百方으로 盡力하겠다고 約束했다.
   He has promised to use all his influence in your favor.

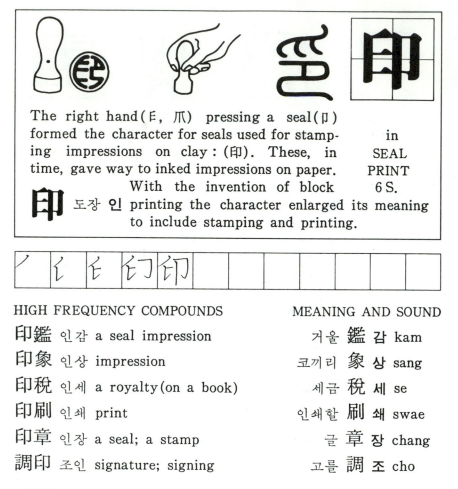

The right hand(ㅌ, 爪) pressing a seal(卩) formed the character for seals used for stamping impressions on clay : (印). These, in time, gave way to inked impressions on paper. With the invention of block 印 도장 **인** printing the character enlarged its meaning to include stamping and printing.

in
SEAL
PRINT
6 S.

HIGH FREQUENCY COMPOUNDS

印鑑 인감 a seal impression

印象 인상 impression

印税 인세 a royalty(on a book)

印刷 인쇄 print

印章 인장 a seal; a stamp

調印 조인 signature; signing

MEANING AND SOUND

거울 鑑 감 kam

코끼리 象 상 sang

세금 税 세 se

인쇄할 刷 쇄 swae

글 章 장 chang

고를 調 조 cho

TYPICAL CONVERSATIONAL USAGE FOR READING AND TRANSLATION. EXERCISE:

1. 첫 印象이 대단히 重要하다.
   There is a great deal in the first impressions.

2. 이 圖書의 印税는 어떻게 支拂하기로 했읍니까? How did you decide to pay the royalty about this book?

3. 韓國의 금속활자 印刷術은 西洋보다 二百年 앞섰다.
   Korea's printing history in movable type advanced 200 years than the western world.

4. 여기에 印章을 찍으세요. Put your seal here, please.

15. 測量　측량　Measurement

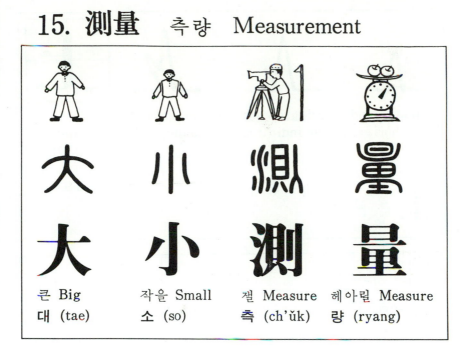

큰 Big	작을 Small	잴 Measure	헤아릴 Measure
대 (tae)	소 (so)	측 (ch'ŭk)	량 (ryang)

또 내게 지팡이 같은 갈대를 주며 말하기를 일어나서 하나님의
聖殿과 祭壇과 그 안에서 敬拜하는 者들을 尺量하되 聖殿 밖 마당
은 尺量하지 말고 그냥 두라 이것을 異邦人에게 주었은즉 저희가
거룩한 城을 마흔 두 달 동안 짓밟으리라. (요한啓示錄 11 : 1~2)

Rise and measure the temple of God, the altar, and those
who worship there. But leave out the court which is
outside the temple, and do not measure it, for it has been
given to the Gentiles. (*Revelation* 11 : 1~2)

네가 하나님의 奧妙를 어찌 能히 測量하며 全能者를 어찌 能히
穩全히 알겠느냐. (욥記 11 : 7)

Do you know the mind and purposes of God? Will long
searching make them known to you? Are you qualified to judge
the Almighty? (*Job* 11 : 7)

그 度量은 땅보다 크고 바다보다 넓으니라. (욥記 11 : 9)

Their measure is longer than the earth and broader than
the sea. (*Job* 11 : 9)

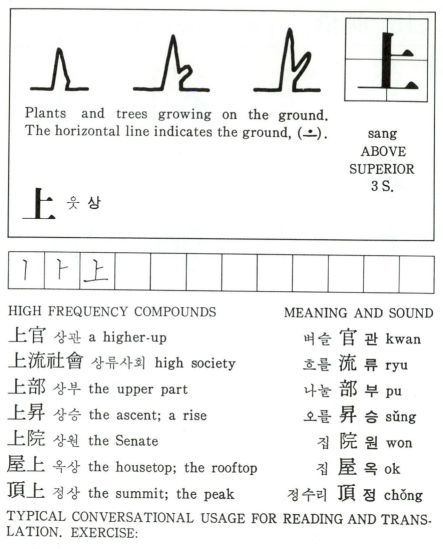

Plants and trees growing on the ground. The horizontal line indicates the ground, (一).

sang
ABOVE
SUPERIOR
3 S.

上 웃 상

丨 卜 上

HIGH FREQUENCY COMPOUNDS

上官 상관 a higher-up

上流社會 상류사회 high society

上部 상부 the upper part

上昇 상승 the ascent; a rise

上院 상원 the Senate

屋上 옥상 the housetop; the rooftop

頂上 정상 the summit; the peak

MEANING AND SOUND

벼슬 官 관 kwan

흐를 流 류 ryu

나눌 部 부 pu

오를 昇 승 sŭng

집 院 원 won

집 屋 옥 ok

정수리 頂 정 chŏng

TYPICAL CONVERSATIONAL USAGE FOR READING AND TRANSLATION. EXERCISE:

1. 안 되면 祖上의 탓 : 자기의 責任을 回避하고 다른 구실을 붙인다는 뜻. If a man fails, he blames his ancestors. (A fool blames others.)

2. 그 일은 내 임의로 할 수 없고 上部의 지시에 따라서 처리해야 하겠으니까 이번 週末까지 기다려 봅시다. I can not do that voluntarily because I have to do it in accordance with my superior's instructions, so let's wait until the end of this week.

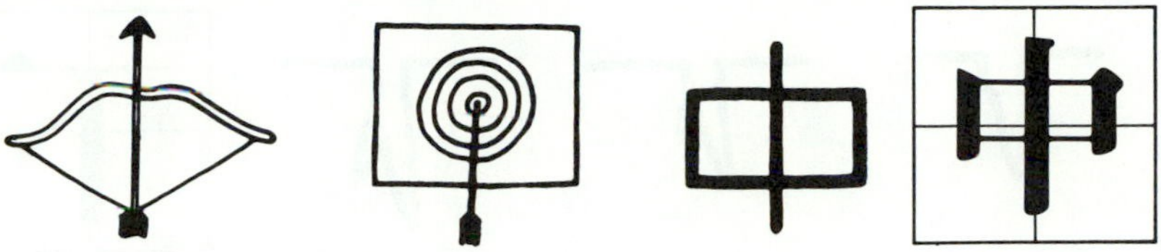

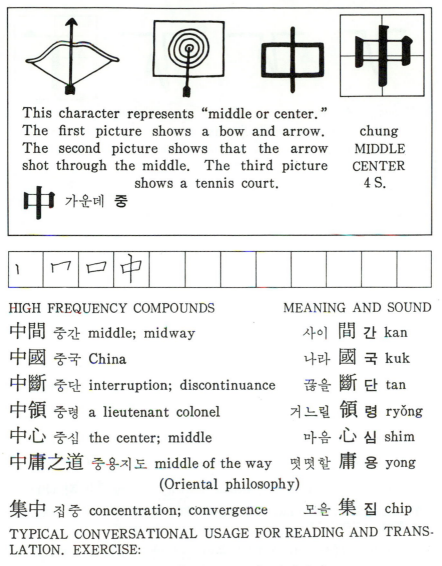

This character represents "middle or center." The first picture shows a bow and arrow. The second picture shows that the arrow shot through the middle. The third picture shows a tennis court.

chung
MIDDLE
CENTER
4 S.

中 가운데 중

丨	冂	口	中								

HIGH FREQUENCY COMPOUNDS — MEANING AND SOUND

中間	중간	middle; midway	사이 間 간	kan
中國	중국	China	나라 國 국	kuk
中斷	중단	interruption; discontinuance	끊을 斷 단	tan
中領	중령	a lieutenant colonel	거느릴 領 령	ryǒng
中心	중심	the center; middle	마음 心 심	shim
中庸之道	중용지도	middle of the way (Oriental philosophy)	떳떳할 庸 용	yong
集中	집중	concentration; convergence	모을 集 집	chip

TYPICAL CONVERSATIONAL USAGE FOR READING AND TRANSLATION. EXERCISE:

1. 몬트레이는 나성하고 桑港의 中間에 위치한다.
   Monterey is located between Los Angeles and San Francisco.
2. 朴中領이 우리 聯隊 부관으로 지난달에 赴任했다. Lt. Col. Park was assigned as our regimental adjutant last month.
3. 中國은 이제 다시 自由世界에 門戶를 開放하고 있다.
   China is now opening its doors to the free world again.

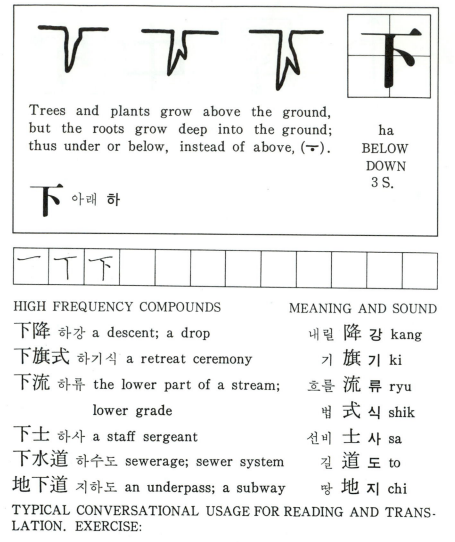

Trees and plants grow above the ground,
but the roots grow deep into the ground;
thus under or below, instead of above, (➖).

ha
BELOW
DOWN
3 S.

下 아래 **하**

HIGH FREQUENCY COMPOUNDS

下降 하강 a descent; a drop

下旗式 하기식 a retreat ceremony

下流 하류 the lower part of a stream;
lower grade

下士 하사 a staff sergeant

下水道 하수도 sewerage; sewer system

地下道 지하도 an underpass; a subway

MEANING AND SOUND

내릴 降 강 kang

기 旗 기 ki

흐를 流 류 ryu

법 式 식 shik

선비 士 사 sa

길 道 도 to

땅 地 지 chi

TYPICAL CONVERSATIONAL USAGE FOR READING AND TRANS-
LATION. EXERCISE:

1. 上濁下不淨(상탁하부정) : 윗물이 맑아야 아랫물이 맑다. 즉 위
   에 있는 사람이 잘못하면 아래에 있는 사람도 따라서 잘못하
   게 된다는 뜻. The upper waters of a river must be clear for
   the lower waters to be clear.

2. 下旗式 하는 동안 車나 사람은 모두 不動姿勢를 取해야 한다.
   During the retreat ceremony all vehicles and personnel must
   remain motionless.

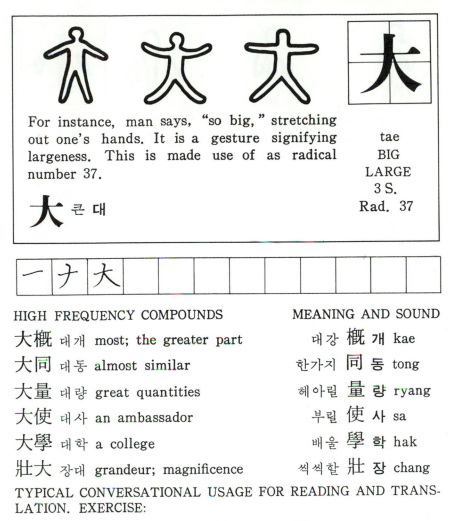

For instance, man says, "so big," stretching out one's hands. It is a gesture signifying largeness. This is made use of as radical number 37.

tae
BIG
LARGE
3 S.
Rad. 37

大 큰 대

一 ナ 大

HIGH FREQUENCY COMPOUNDS

大概 대개 most; the greater part

大同 대동 almost similar

大量 대량 great quantities

大使 대사 an ambassador

大學 대학 a college

壯大 장대 grandeur; magnificence

MEANING AND SOUND

대강 概 개 kae

한가지 同 동 tong

헤아릴 量 량 ryang

부릴 使 사 sa

배울 學 학 hak

씩씩할 壯 장 chang

TYPICAL CONVERSATIONAL USAGE FOR READING AND TRANSLATION. EXERCISE:

1. 現代社會는 모든 면에서 機械化되었기 때문에 大量生產을 쉽게 한다. In modern society everything has become mechanized, so it is easy to mass-produce things.

2. 美國 大使舘에 가려면 光化門에서 南쪽으로 十分쯤 걸어가면 된다. If you want to go to the American embassy, you have to walk ten minutes south from Kwanghwa Gate.

3. 大器晚成(대기만성) : 큰 그릇은 늦게 이루어짐 ; 크게 될 사람은 늦게 이루어짐. Great vessels are late in completion.

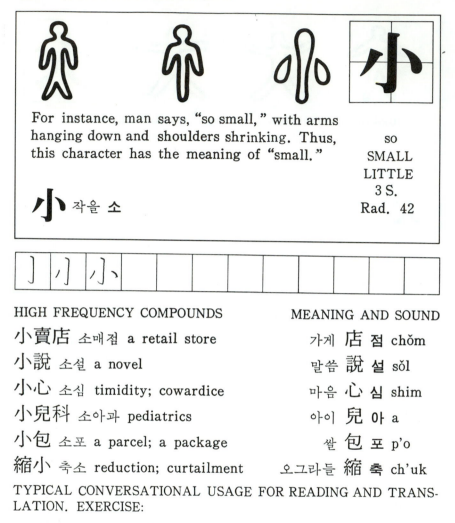

For instance, man says, "so small," with arms hanging down and shoulders shrinking. Thus, this character has the meaning of "small."

SO
SMALL
LITTLE
3 S.
Rad. 42

小 작을 소

HIGH FREQUENCY COMPOUNDS

小賣店 소매점 a retail store

小說 소설 a novel

小心 소심 timidity; cowardice

小兒科 소아과 pediatrics

小包 소포 a parcel; a package

縮小 축소 reduction; curtailment

MEANING AND SOUND

가게 店 점 chŏm

말씀 說 설 sŏl

마음 心 심 shim

아이 兒 아 a

쌀 包 포 p'o

오그라들 縮 축 ch'uk

TYPICAL CONVERSATIONAL USAGE FOR READING AND TRANSLATION. EXERCISE:

1. 小賣店은 都賣店에서 가져온 物件들을 파는 작은 가게이다.
   A retail store is a small store that sells goods brought from a wholesale store.

2. 小說의 유일한 存在 意義는 그것이 人生을 表現하려고 한다는 데에 있다. The only reason for the existence of a novel is that it does attempt to represent life.

3. 小兒科 醫師는 아이들의 病을 치료하지만 어른과 相談한다.
   A pediatrician treats children's sicknesses but counsels adults.

Originally, this character was a pictograph of a chisel or drill. A sharp point proceeds from a large(大) end to a small(小) end.

ch'ŏm
SHARP
POINT
6 S.

尖 뾰족할 **첨**

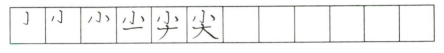

)	小	小	小	小	尖					

HIGH FREQUENCY COMPOUNDS

MEANING AND SOUND

尖端 첨단 a pointed end; a tip

끝 端 단 tan

尖刀 첨도 a sharp-pointed knife

칼 刀 도 to

尖兵 첨병 a vanguard

군사 兵 병 pyŏng

尖塔 첨탑 a pinnacle; a spire

탑 塔 탑 t'ap

TYPICAL CONVERSATIONAL USAGE FOR READING AND TRANSLATION. EXERCISE:

1. 宇宙旅行에 대한 研究는 尖端科學의 주요한 한 部門이다.
   Research concerning space travel is one important part of the advanced sciences.

2. 저쪽 진열장 안에 있는 尖刀는 보기만 해도 베어지는 것 같구나! Even when I am only looking at the knife in that showcase, it seems as if it is cutting me.

3. 尖兵은 敵 가까이 行軍할 때 行軍部隊의 前方에서 敵의 事情을 살피고 警戒하는 小部隊의 軍士이다. The vanguard is a small unit which marches in front of the main body of troops, observes the enemy situation, and protects the main body.

4. 尖塔의 避雷針은 벼락을 피하기 위해서 만들어졌다.

This character represents the center or the middle. The man(人) is standing in the center of the blackboard(口).

ang
CENTER
MIDDLE
5 S.

央 가운데 앙

| 丨 | 冂 | 冂 | 屮 | 央 | | | | | | |

HIGH FREQUENCY COMPOUNDS

中央 중앙 the center; the middle

中央情報部 중앙정보부 the Central
    Intelligence Agency(C. I. A.)

中央廳 중앙청 the Central Government
    Building

上映 상영 screening

快宿 앙숙 a cat-and-dog life

MEANING AND SOUND

가운데 中 중 chung

실상 情 정 chŏng

알릴 報 보 po

관청 廳 청 ch'ŏng

비칠 映 영 yŏng

앙심품을 快 앙 ang

잘 宿 숙 suk

TYPICAL CONVERSATIONAL USAGE FOR READING AND TRANSLATION. EXERCISE:

1. 나는 진열대 中央에 있는 것을 사고 싶다.
   I like to buy the one in the center of the display case.

2. 現在의 國立博物館 建物은 前에 中央廳이었다.
   The national museum was the Capitol Building previously.

3. 이번에 東邦劇場에서는 무슨 映畵를 上映합니까? What kind of movie plays at the Tongbang theater at this time.

4. 개와 고양이는 서로 快宿이라 늘 싸운다.

This character has a twofold meaning. The first is that of squareness or the quality of having four sides and four right angles. The second, however, suggests the concept of direction, as a boat which is able to steer its course by harnessing the wind.

pang
SQUARE
DIRECTION
4 S.
Rad. 70

方 모 방
　 방위 방

`丶 一 亍 方`

HIGH FREQUENCY COMPOUNDS

方法 방법 a method; a way

方言 방언 a dialect

方位 방위 a point of the compass

方程式 방정식 an equation

方向 방향 a direction; a way

方向探知機 방향탐지기 a direction finder

MEANING AND SOUND

법 法 법 pŏp

말씀 言 언 ŏn

자리 位 위 wi

과정 程 정 chŏng

향할 向 향 hyang

찾을 探 탐 t'am

틀 機 기 ki

TYPICAL CONVERSATIONAL USAGE FOR READING AND TRANSLATION. EXERCISE:

1. 여러 가지 方法을 다 써 봤으나 解決할 道理가 없다. I have tried all possible ways but there is no way to solve that problem.

2. 方言에 대한 敎訓으로는 고린도前書 14장에 使徒 바울의 記錄이 있다. A teaching concerning tongues is recorded by Apostle Paul in the 14th chapter of I *Corinthians*.

3. 天方地軸(천방지축) : 너무 바빠서 허둥지둥 내닫는 模樣. Being flustered from being too busy.

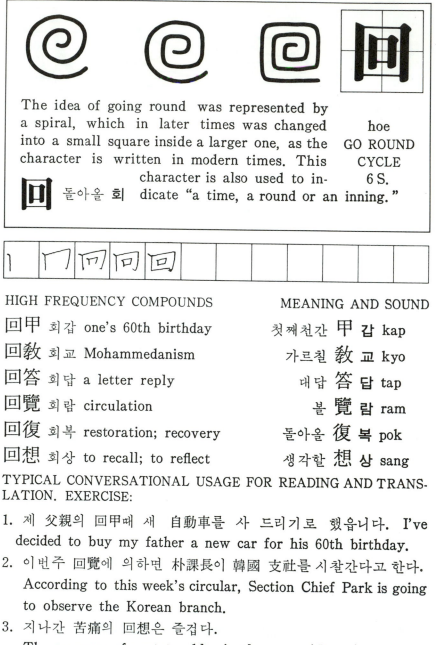

The idea of going round was represented by a spiral, which in later times was changed into a small square inside a larger one, as the character is written in modern times. This character is also used to indicate "a time, a round or an inning."

hoe
GO ROUND
CYCLE
6 S.

回 돌아올 회

HIGH FREQUENCY COMPOUNDS

回甲 회갑 one's 60th birthday

回教 회교 Mohammedanism

回答 회답 a letter reply

回覽 회람 circulation

回復 회복 restoration; recovery

回想 회상 to recall; to reflect

MEANING AND SOUND

첫째천간 甲 갑 kap

가르칠 教 교 kyo

대답 答 답 tap

볼 覽 람 ram

돌아올 復 복 pok

생각할 想 상 sang

TYPICAL CONVERSATIONAL USAGE FOR READING AND TRANSLATION. EXERCISE:

1. 제 父親의 回甲때 새 自動車를 사 드리기로 했읍니다. I've decided to buy my father a new car for his 60th birthday.

2. 이번주 回覽에 의하면 朴課長이 韓國 支社를 시찰간다고 한다. According to this week's circular, Section Chief Park is going to observe the Korean branch.

3. 지나간 苦痛의 回想은 즐겁다. The memory of past troubles is pleasant. (*Cicero*)

4. 回心轉意(회심전의) : 마음을 돌려먹고 뜻을 바꿈.

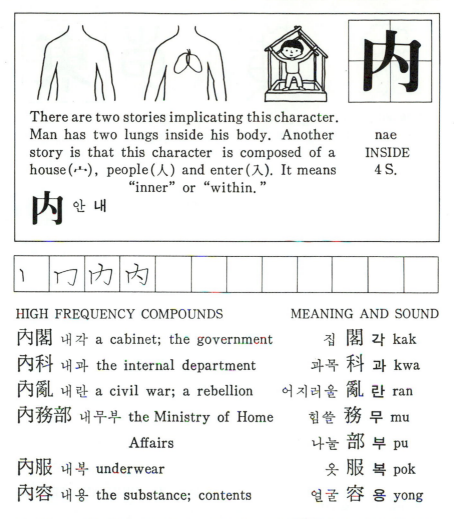

There are two stories implicating this character. Man has two lungs inside his body. Another story is that this character is composed of a house(宀), people(人) and enter(入). It means "inner" or "within."

nae

INSIDE

4 S.

内 안 내

丶 冂 内 内

HIGH FREQUENCY COMPOUNDS

内閣 내각 a cabinet; the government

内科 내과 the internal department

内亂 내란 a civil war; a rebellion

内務部 내무부 the Ministry of Home

Affairs

内服 내복 underwear

内容 내용 the substance; contents

MEANING AND SOUND

집 閣 각 kak

과목 科 과 kwa

어지러울 亂 란 ran

힘쓸 務 무 mu

나눌 部 부 pu

옷 服 복 pok

얼굴 容 용 yong

TYPICAL CONVERSATIONAL USAGE FOR READING AND TRANSLATION. EXERCISE:

1. 제 큰 兄님은 内務部에서 勤務하십니다.

My elder brother works at the Ministry of Home Affairs.

2. 南加州에서는 겨울에도 内服을 입을 必要가 없다.

We don't need to wear underwear in Southern California.

3. 무엇을 하든지 内容과 形式의 按排가 맞아야 한다. Whatever you do, you have to balance the contents and the forms.

The sun (日) peering through a tree (木) may also suggest direction—in this case, the east (東).

tong
EAST
8 S.

東 동녘 동

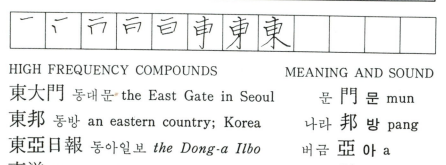

HIGH FREQUENCY COMPOUNDS

東大門 동대문 the East Gate in Seoul

東邦 동방 an eastern country; Korea

東亞日報 동아일보 *the Dong-a Ilbo*

東洋 동양 the Orient; the East

極東 극동 the Far East

近東 근동 the Near East

MEANING AND SOUND

문 門 문 mun

나라 邦 방 pang

버금 亞 아 a

큰 바다 洋 양 yang

다할 極 극 kŭk

가까울 近 근 kŭn

TYPICAL CONVERSATIONAL USAGE FOR READING AND TRANSLATION. EXERCISE:

1. 서울의 東大門 近處에는 커다란 규모의 市場이 있다.
   Near the East Gate in Seoul is a large scale market place.

2. 東亞日報는 많이 읽혀지는 日刊新聞의 하나이다. *The Dong-a Ilbo* is one of the most widely-read newspapers.

3. 東奔西走(동분서주) : 이리저리로 몹시 바쁘게 다니는 것을 말함. Busily going here and there.

4. 東征西伐(동정서벌) : 戰爭을 하여 여러 나라를 이리저리로 征伐하는 것. The subjugation of many countries.

This character came to express the direction "west." When the sun goes down in the west, the bird returns to its nest.

sŏ
WEST
6 S.

西 서녘 서

HIGH FREQUENCY COMPOUNDS	MEANING AND SOUND
西歐化 서구화 westernization; Europeanization	성 歐 구 ku
	화할 化 화 hwa
西紀 서기 the Christian era; Anno Domini(A.D.)	벼리 紀 기 ki
西獨 서독 West Germany	홀로 獨 독 tok
西洋式 서양식 an European style; western style	바다 洋 양 yang
西洋畫 서양화 western painting	그림 畫 화 hwa

TYPICAL CONVERSATIONAL USAGE FOR READING AND TRANSLATION. EXERCISE:

1. 西獨도 韓國과 같이 한 民族이면서 自由陣營과 共産世界로 兩斷된 슬픔을 안고 있다.

   West Germany is like South Korea in that it lives with the sadness of being a free nation that has a communist counterpart that is made up of people of the same race.

2. 鄭先生은 美術大學에서 西洋畫를 專攻했다고 한다.

   They say Mr. Chŏng majored in western art at an art school.

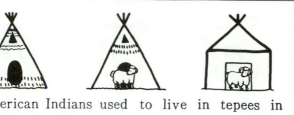

American Indians used to live in tepees in the South a lot. The door of a tepee is toward the south (南). One sheep (羊) stands in front of the door. This character represents the south.

nam
SOUTH
9 S.

南 남녘 남

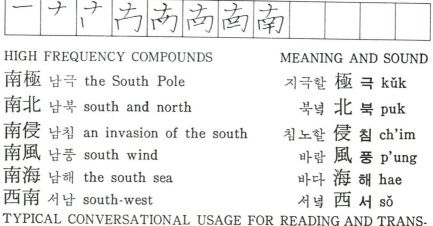

HIGH FREQUENCY COMPOUNDS

南極 남극 the South Pole

南北 남북 south and north

南侵 남침 an invasion of the south

南風 남풍 south wind

南海 남해 the south sea

西南 서남 south-west

MEANING AND SOUND

지극할 極 극 kŭk

북녘 北 북 puk

침노할 侵 침 ch'im

바람 風 풍 p'ung

바다 海 해 hae

서녘 西 서 sŏ

TYPICAL CONVERSATIONAL USAGE FOR READING AND TRANSLATION. EXERCISE:

1. 펭귄새는 南極의 神士이다.
   The penguin is the gentleman of the South Pole.

2. 南風이 불면 비가 온다는 말이 있다.
   They say when the south wind blows it is going to rain.

3. 韓國의 南海에는 약 三千個의 섬들이 있다.
   There are about 3,000 islands in the South Sea of Korea.

4. 南北對話는 韓半島의 緊張緩和에 도움이 될 것이다.
   The South-North talks will go far toward the easing of tensions on the Korean peninsula.

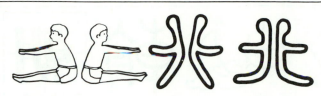

This character represents the north. The picture of two men seated back-to-back. In Korea, north has always been regarded as the back and south as the front. Thus, the house gate and the emperor's throne both face the south.

北 북녘 북
도망할 배

puk; pae
NORTH
DEFEATED
5 S.

HIGH FREQUENCY COMPOUNDS

北極星 북극성 the polar star

北方 북방 the northern regions

北魚 북어 a dried walleye pollack

北緯 북위 the north latitude

敗北 패배 defeated; beaten

MEANING AND SOUND

지극할 極 극 kŭk

방위 方 방 pang

고기 魚 어 ŏ

씨 緯 위 wi

패할 敗 패 p'ae

TYPICAL CONVERSATIONAL USAGE FOR READING AND TRANSLATION. EXERCISE:

1. 北쪽으로 가면 鴨綠江과 白頭山이 있다. When you head north, you will see the Yalu River and Mt. Paektu.

2. 韓國의 佳宅들은 北을 등지고 南을 向해 있는 것이 특징이다. A common feature of Korean houses is to have the back of the house facing the north and the front facing the south.

3. 저의 할머니는 北魚찜을 아주 좋아하십니다. My grandmother likes seasoned and steamed pollacks very much.

4. 서울은 北緯 37 도 3분 東經 127 도 4분에 위치하고 있다. Seoul is situated in lat. 37°3′N and long. 127°4′E.

Christian life should be Christ centric by day
(日) and by night(月). 朝鮮 was an old   cho
name for Korea. This character 鮮(선) is the   MORNING
combination of a fish(魚) and a sheep(羊).   12 S.
They are both symbols of Christianity. Thus,
朝 아침 조 朝 represents "the sinking moon and the
rising sun" and means "morning."

HIGH FREQUENCY COMPOUNDS   MEANING AND SOUND

朝刊 조간 a morning paper   책펴낼 刊 간 kan

朝飯 조반 breakfast   밥 飯 반 pan

朝夕 조석 morning and evening;   저녁 夕 석 sŏk
          breakfast and supper

朝鮮 조선 Korea's old name   고을 鮮 선 sŏn

朝會 조회 a morning gathering   모일 會 회 hoe

王朝 왕조 a dynasty   임금 王 왕 wang

TYPICAL CONVERSATIONAL USAGE FOR READING AND TRANS-
LATION. EXERCISE:

1. 金先生님 오늘 朝刊新聞 보셨어요?
   Mr. Kim, did you see this morning's newspaper?

2. "고요한 아침의 나라"라는 말은 朝鮮에서 왔다. The word
   "the land of the morning calm" comes from Chosŏn.

3. 우리는 月曜日 아침마다 九時에 朝會를 선다.
   We have a morning gathering each Monday at 9 o'clock.

4. 朝令暮改(조령모개): 아침에 命令을 내리고 저녁에 다시 고침.

春

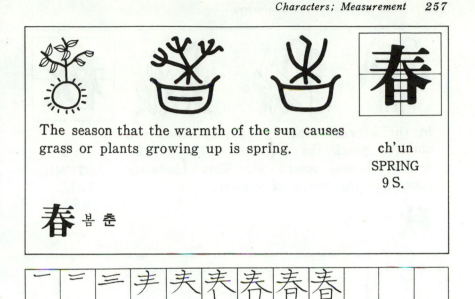

The season that the warmth of the sun causes grass or plants growing up is spring.

ch'un
SPRING
9 S.

春 봄 춘

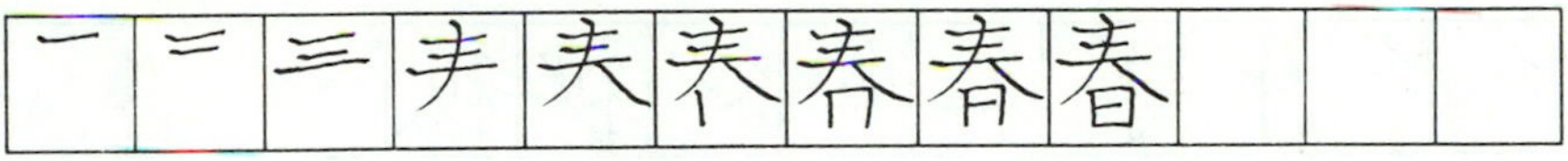

HIGH FREQUENCY COMPOUNDS	MEANING AND SOUND
春耕 춘경 spring plowing	밭갈 耕 경 kyŏng
春窮期 춘궁기 a hard time in spring	곤궁할 窮 궁 kung
春夢 춘몽 spring dreams; fantasies	꿈 夢 몽 mong
春分 춘분 the vernal equinox	나눌 分 분 pun
立春 입춘 the first day of spring	설 立 립 rip
青春 청춘 the spring time of life	푸를 青 청 ch'ŏng

TYPICAL CONVERSATIONAL USAGE FOR READING AND TRANSLATION. EXERCISE:

1. 봄 날씨의 變化는 계모(繼母)의 얼굴 같다.
   Spring is as changeable as a stepmother's face.
2. 一年의 計劃은 봄에 세우고, 하루 日課는 아침에 定한다.
   Make your whole year's plans in the spring, and your day's plans early in the morning.
3. 우리 옆집의 大門에는 立春大吉 네 글자가 씌어 있다.
   Written on the front door of our neighbor's is the four character expression meaning spring time prosperity.

In the harvest time, grains(禾) ripen and children pluck the grain out. They make a fire(火) and scorch it. This character represents the season of autumn.

ch'u
AUTUMN
FALL
9 S.

秋 가을 추

HIGH FREQUENCY COMPOUNDS · MEANING AND SOUND

秋分 추분 the autumnal equinox 　나눌 分 분 pun

秋收 추수 the harvest 　거둘 收 수 su

秋波 추파 autumn waves; an amorous glance 　물결 波 파 p'a

秋風 추풍 autumn breeze 　바람 風 풍 p'ung

秋毫 추호 a jot; a whit 　터럭 毫 호 ho

晚秋 만추 late autumn 　늦을 晚 만 man

春秋 춘추 spring and autumn; years; age 　봄 春 춘 ch'un

TYPICAL CONVERSATIONAL USAGE FOR READING AND TRANS-LATION. EXERCISE:

1. 어른의 나이는 春秋, 年歲 등으로 부른다.

   When we refer to an elder's age, we use the honorific expressions *ch'unch'u, yŏnse,* etc.

2. 秋收 때는 되었는데 곡식을 거두어 들일 일꾼이 不足하다.

   When harvest time has arrived, harvesting the crops is difficult due to a shortage of hands.

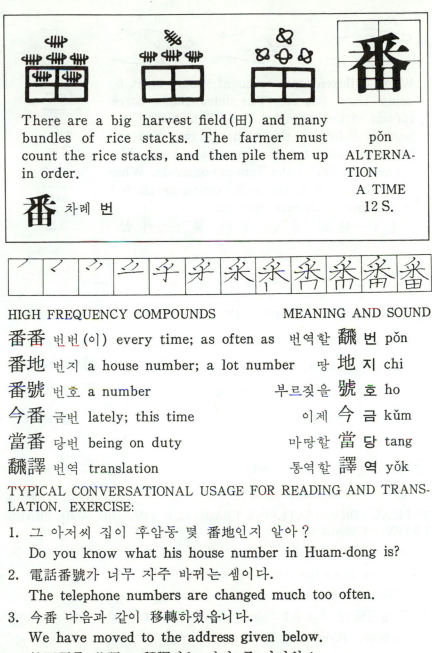

There are a big harvest field (田) and many bundles of rice stacks. The farmer must count the rice stacks, and then pile them up in order.

pŏn
ALTERNA-
TION
A TIME
12 S.

番 차례 번

HIGH FREQUENCY COMPOUNDS   MEANING AND SOUND

番番 번번(이) every time; as often as   번역할 飜 번 pŏn

番地 번지 a house number; a lot number   땅 地 지 chi

番號 번호 a number   부르짖을 號 호 ho

今番 금번 lately; this time   이제 今 금 kŭm

當番 당번 being on duty   마땅할 當 당 tang

飜譯 번역 translation   통역할 譯 역 yŏk

TYPICAL CONVERSATIONAL USAGE FOR READING AND TRANS-
LATION. EXERCISE:

1. 그 아저씨 집이 후암동 몇 番地인지 알아?
   Do you know what his house number in Huam-dong is?

2. 電話番號가 너무 자주 바뀌는 셈이다.
   The telephone numbers are changed much too often.

3. 今番 다음과 같이 移轉하였읍니다.
   We have moved to the address given below.

4. 韓國語를 英語로 飜譯하는 것이 좀 어려워요.
   Translating Korean into English is somewhat difficult.

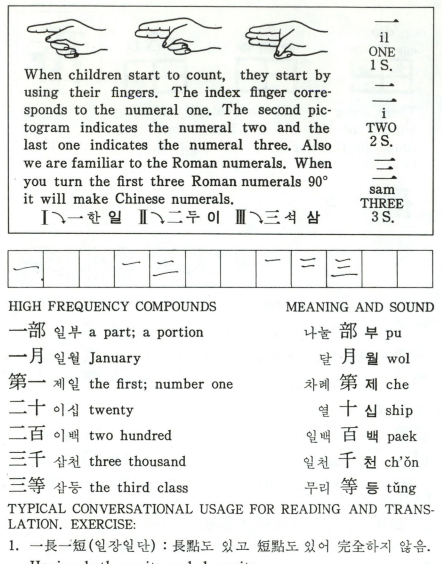

When children start to count, they start by using their fingers. The index finger corresponds to the numeral one. The second pictogram indicates the numeral two and the last one indicates the numeral three. Also we are familiar to the Roman numerals. When you turn the first three Roman numerals 90° it will make Chinese numerals.

Ⅰ〵一 한 일 Ⅱ〵二 두 이 Ⅲ〵三 석 삼

一
il
ONE
1 S.

二
i
TWO
2 S.

三
sam
THREE
3 S.

HIGH FREQUENCY COMPOUNDS

一部 일부 a part; a portion

一月 일월 January

第一 제일 the first; number one

二十 이십 twenty

二百 이백 two hundred

三千 삼천 three thousand

三等 삼등 the third class

MEANING AND SOUND

나눌 部 부 pu

달 月 월 wol

차례 第 제 che

열 十 십 ship

일백 百 백 paek

일천 千 천 ch'ŏn

무리 等 등 tŭng

TYPICAL CONVERSATIONAL USAGE FOR READING AND TRANSLATION. EXERCISE:

1. 一長一短 (일장일단) : 長點도 있고 短點도 있어 完全하지 않음. Having both merits and demerits.

2. 二重人格 (이중인격) : a man of dual personality.

3. 三綱五倫 (삼강오륜) : the three bonds and the five constant virtues. (Confucian moral principles)

4. 三位一體 (삼위일체) : the Trinity.

16. 軍事 군사 The Military

창 Spear	군사 Soldier	활 Bow	맡을 Preside
과 (kwa)	병 (pyŏng)	궁 (kung)	사 (sa)

그러므로 하나님의 全身甲冑를 取하라. 이는 惡한 날에 너희가 能히 對敵하고 모든 일을 行한 後에 서기 爲함이라. 그런즉 서서 眞理로 너희 허리띠를 띠고 義의 胸背를 붙이고 平安의 福音의 豫備한 것으로 신을 신고 모든 것 위에 믿음의 防牌를 가지고 이로써 能히 惡한 者의 모든 火箭을 消滅하고 救援의 투구와 聖靈의 劍 곧 하나님의 말씀을 가지라. (에베소書 6:13~17)

Take up, therefore, the whole armour of God so that you may be able to stand when you have done all the fighting. So stand your ground, with the belt of truth tightened around your waist, wearing the breastplate of righteousness on your body, with the readiness of the good news of peace bound on your feet; above all taking up the shield of faith, with which you will be able to extinguish all the flaming arrows of the evil one. And take the helmet of salvation and the sword of the spirit, which is the word of God.

(Ephesians 6:13~17)

This character combines the radical for vehicle (車) with the radical for cover (冖). The resulting idea of camouflaged vehicle has come to mean "military."

kun
MILITARY
9 S.

軍 군사 군

HIGH FREQUENCY COMPOUNDS

MEANING AND SOUND

軍紀 군기 military discipline

기강 紀 기 ki

軍納 군납 the purveyance of supplies or services for an army

들일 納 납 nap

모일 會 회 hoe

軍法會議 군법회의 a court martial

의논할 議 의 ŭi

軍需 군수 munitions

구할 需 수 su

國軍 국군 the national army

나라 國 국 kuk

美軍 미군 the U.S. Army

아름다울 美 미 mi

TYPICAL CONVERSATIONAL USAGE FOR READING AND TRANSLATION. EXERCISE:

1. 千軍萬馬 (천군만마) : 다수의 軍士와 軍馬. A massive army.

2. 형님의 會社는 작년부터 美軍에 納品하게 되어 흑자를 내고 있다. Since last year, my brother's company has been bringing a profit by supplying the U.S. Army.

3. 美軍은 每年 봄에 國軍과 함께 韓美聯合作戰을 한 달씩 하고 있다. Every spring the U.S. armed forces join the R.O.K. forces for one month to participate in Team Spirit.

This character is represented by two hands (艸, 六) brandishing a battle axe(斤)—symbol of the soldier.

pyŏng
SOLDIER
ARMY
7 S.

兵 군사 병

丿 亻 仁 斤 斤 丘 乒 兵

HIGH FREQUENCY COMPOUNDS

MEANING AND SOUND

兵科 병과 a branch of the service

兵器 병기 weapon; arms

兵力 병력 force of arms; military force

富國强兵 부국강병 to enrich the country and increase its military power

憲兵 헌병 military police(M. P.)

과목 科 과 kwa
그릇 器 기 ki
힘 力 력 ryŏk
부자 富 부 pu
강할 强 강 kang
법 憲 헌 hŏn

TYPICAL CONVERSATIONAL USAGE FOR READING AND TRANSLATION. EXERCISE:

1. 兵科마다 義務가 다르지만 平素에 專攻과 特技를 참조하여 訓練 받은 分野대로 任務를 遂行하게 된다. Each military occupational specialty is different and generally speaking, any prior study or specialized training is used as a reference for deciding what kind of training and duty a person will do in the military.

2. 憲兵 白車 한 대가 通路를 막고 民間人들을 調査하고 있다. A white M. P. car is blocking the road and the civilians are being inspected.

3. 草木皆兵(초목개병) : The grass and the trees as troops.

This character means troops. (阝) means flag and the radical (豕) a pig. The amusing analysis suggests that the nature of soldiers is somewhat unsavory and the flag denotes uniformity of thought and action. "The herd … two thousand." (*Mark* 5 : 13)

tae
TROOPS
BAND
12 S.

隊 떼 대

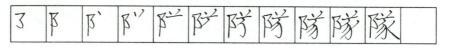

HIGH FREQUENCY COMPOUNDS

MEANING AND SOUND

隊列 대열 a rank; a file ・・・・・・・・・・・ 벌일 列 렬 ryŏl

軍隊 군대 an army; the troops ・・・・・・ 군사 軍 군 kun

入隊 입대 joining the army; enrollment ・・・ 들 入 입 ip

除隊 제대 discharge from the military service ・・・ 제할 除 제 che

中隊 중대 a company; a troop ・・・・・・ 가운데 中 중 chung

TYPICAL CONVERSATIONAL USAGE FOR READING AND TRANSLATION. EXERCISE:

1. 査閲式 때에 모든 隊列은 칼로 자른 듯이 반듯하다.

   During a military parade every file is lined up perfectly straight as if it were cut by knife.

2. 나는 高等學校를 卒業하자마자 機甲兵으로 入隊했다.

   As soon as I graduated from the high school, I enlisted into an armored unit.

3. 除隊한 後에는 自動車 정비사로 열심히 일할 예정이다.

   After being discharged from the service, I am planning on working really hard in auto maintenance.

By combining the derived form for cupped hand (ㅋ) with the radical for mouth (ㅁ), the character for "command" was formed.

sa

PRESIDE
COMMAND
5 S.

司 맡을 사

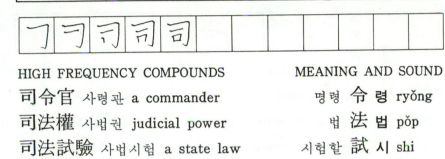

HIGH FREQUENCY COMPOUNDS	MEANING AND SOUND

司令官 사령관 a commander
명령 令 령 ryŏng

司法權 사법권 judicial power
법 法 법 pŏp

司法試驗 사법시험 a state law examination
시험할 試 시 shi

경험할 驗 험 hŏm

司書 사서 a librarian
글 書 서 sŏ

司會者 사회자 the chairman; m. c.
모일 會 회 hoe

TYPICAL CONVERSATIONAL USAGE FOR READING AND TRANSLATION. EXERCISE:

1. 저분이 새로 부임한 제 2 사단 司令官입니다.
   That person is the newly assigned 2nd Division Commander.

2. 내 大學同窓 하나가 이번 司法試驗에 合格하였다. One of my classmates at college passed the state law examination lately.

3. 우리 圖書館 司書들은 일도 잘하고 퍽 친절합니다.
   Our librarians work hard and also are very kind.

4. 그녀는 인기있는 TV 쇼 프로그램에서 司會를 맡고 있다.
   She acts as m. c. for a popular television show.

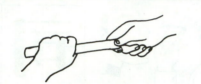

This character means fighting or struggle. One man holding a stick, and another person trying to take it away.

chaeng
FIGHTING
CONTEST
8 S.

爭 다툴 쟁

HIGH FREQUENCY COMPOUNDS

MAENING AND SOUND

爭論 쟁론 an argument

의논할 論 론 ron

爭點 쟁점 a point of contention

점 點 점 chŏm

爭取 쟁취 gain in a contest; obtaining

취할 取 취 ch'wi

爭奪戰 쟁탈전 a struggle; a contest

빼앗을 奪 탈 t'al

戰爭 전쟁 a war; a battle

싸울 戰 전 chŏn

TYPICAL CONVERSATIONAL USAGE FOR READING AND TRANSLATION. EXERCISE:

1. 戰爭은, 설사 大勝利를 거둔다 해도 國家的 不幸이 아닐 수 없다. A war, even the most victorious, is a national misfortune.

2. 러시아의 大文豪 톨스토이는 歷史小說인 《戰爭과 平和》를 써서 世界的인 名聲을 얻었다.
The renowned Russian writer Leo Tolstoy wrote the historical novel *War and Peace* and received worldwide fame.

3. 軍隊란 사람을 잡는 凶器요, 戰爭은 德을 거스르는 것이며, 將帥는 죽음을 내리는 官吏이다. The military means lethal weapons, war means that which is not virtuous, and a general officer is an official who creates death.

This character is the combination of (人) and a spear or weapon (戈). The character represents the idea that a soldier holds a weapon and attacks, or destroys.

pŏl
ATTACK
6 S.

伐 칠벌

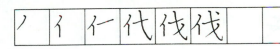

HIGH FREQUENCY COMPOUNDS

伐木 벌목 felling; hewing; logging

伐採 벌채 timber cutting

伐草 벌초 weeding a grave

殺伐 살벌 bloodiness; savage

征伐 정벌 conquest; subjugation

討伐 토벌 suppression

MEANING AND SOUND

나무 木 목 mok

캘 採 채 ch'ae

풀 草 초 ch'o

죽일 殺 살 sal

칠 征 정 chŏng

칠 討 토 t'o

TYPICAL CONVERSATIONAL USAGE FOR READING AND TRANSLATION. EXERCISE:

1. 세 사람이 하루 종일 伐木했는데 아직 끝내지 못했다. **Three people logged trees all day long, but they did not finish it.**

2. 밭을 만들기 위해 伐木作業이 必要하다.
   We need to clean the land to make it into farmlands.

3. 韓國戰爭때 洛東江 地域에서 殺伐한 戰鬪가 행해졌다.
   During the Korean War, a bloody battle was fought at the Naktong River area.

3. 豫備軍은 共匪 討伐作戰을 成功的으로 遂行했다. **The Reserve Army had a successful operation fighting with Red guerrillas.**

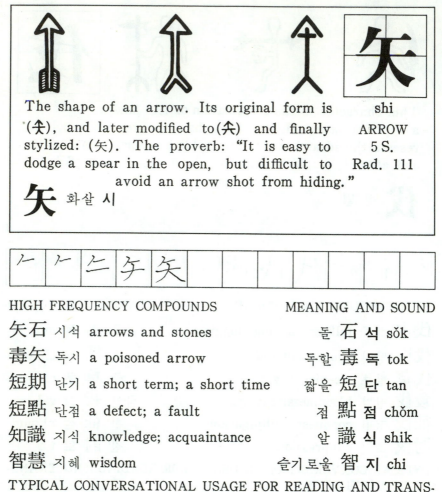

The shape of an arrow. Its original form is (大), and later modified to (大) and finally stylized: (矢). The proverb: "It is easy to dodge a spear in the open, but difficult to avoid an arrow shot from hiding."

shi
ARROW
5 S.
Rad. 111

矢 화살 시

HIGH FREQUENCY COMPOUNDS

矢石 시석 arrows and stones

毒矢 독시 a poisoned arrow

短期 단기 a short term; a short time

短點 단점 a defect; a fault

知識 지식 knowledge; acquaintance

智慧 지혜 wisdom

MEANING AND SOUND

돌 石 석 sŏk

독할 毒 독 tok

짧을 短 단 tan

점 點 점 chŏm

알 識 식 shik

슬기로울 智 지 chi

TYPICAL CONVERSATIONAL USAGE FOR READING AND TRANSLATION. EXERCISE:

1. 그 親舊는 나도 모르는 사이에 쏜살같이 쫓아왔다. I did not know that my friend had come back as quickly as an arrow.

2. 明哲한 者의 마음은 知識을 얻고, 智慧로운 者의 귀는 知識을 求하느니라. (箴言 18 : 15) An intelligent mind acquires knowledge, and the ear of the wise seeks knowledge. (*Proverbs* 18 : 15)

3. 여호와를 敬畏하는 것이 智慧의 根本이요, 거룩하신 者를 아는 것이 明哲이라. The fear of the Lord is the beginning of wisdom, and the knowledge of the Holy one is insight.

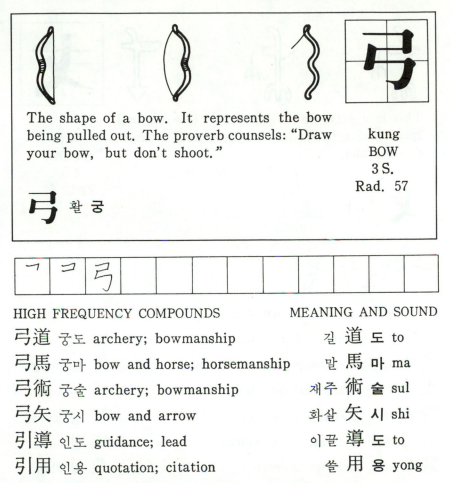

The shape of a bow. It represents the bow being pulled out. The proverb counsels: "Draw your bow, but don't shoot."

kung
BOW
3 S.
Rad. 57

弓 활 궁

HIGH FREQUENCY COMPOUNDS

弓道	궁도	archery; bowmanship
弓馬	궁마	bow and horse; horsemanship
弓術	궁술	archery; bowmanship
弓矢	궁시	bow and arrow
引導	인도	guidance; lead
引用	인용	quotation; citation

MEANING AND SOUND

길	道	도	to
말	馬	마	ma
재주	術	술	sul
화살	矢	시	shi
이끌	導	도	to
쏠	用	용	yong

TYPICAL CONVERSATIONAL USAGE FOR READING AND TRANSLATION. EXERCISE:

1. 韓國 女子 弓道 팀은 1984년에 열린 나성 五輪大會에서 優勝 했다. The Korean women's archery team won first place in the 1984 Olympic Games held in Los Angeles.

2. 新羅時代 花郎들은 學問뿐만 아니라 弓馬에도 능해야 했다. The Hwarang (Knights) of the Shilla dynasty had to be proficient in not only general knowledge but also in archery horsemanship.

3. 徐執事님은 지난 主日에 한 姉妹를 우리 敎會에 引導했다. Deacon Sŏ led one sister to our church last Sunday.

This is a pictograph of a spear. The original spear had a horizontal bayonet and a three-prong stand.

kwa
SPEAR
4 S.
Rad. 62

戈 창 과

HIGH FREQUENCY COMPOUNDS	MEANING AND SOUND
戈甲 과갑 spear and armour	갑옷 甲 갑 kap
戈鋒 과봉 the sharp point of a spear	칼날 鋒 봉 pong
戈盾 과순 spear and buckler	방패 盾 순 sun
警戒 경계 precaution; warning	경계할 警 경 kyŏng
成功 성공 success; achievement	이룰 成 성 sŏng
截斷 절단 cutting; severance	끊을 截 절 chŏl

TYPICAL CONVERSATIONAL USAGE FOR READING AND TRANSLATION. EXERCISE:

1. 失敗는 成功의 어머니다. Failure teaches success.

2. 日本은 第二次大戰에서 敗亡하였지만 지금은 經濟大國이 되었다. Japan was totally destroyed in World War Ⅱ, but now it has become an economic superpower.

3. 창과 방패 그리고 활은 인디안의 武器이다.
   Spears, shields and arrows are Indian's weapons.

4. 强風으로 電信線이 截斷되었다.
   The gale tore up telegraph wires.

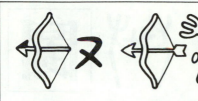

To shoot an arrow(矢): (身) is the representation of a bow with an arrow. (矢) was
transformed into (寸) used to mean the hand
(⺕). Some says that the character is the
combination of a body(身) and
an arrow(寸) aimed at it.

sa

SHOOT

10 S.

射 쏠 사

丿 亻 竹 自 自 身 身 射 射

HIGH FREQUENCY COMPOUNDS

MEANING AND SOUND

射擊 사격 firing; shooting

칠 擊 격 kyŏk

射殺 사살 killing by shooting

죽일 殺 살 sal

射手 사수 a gunner

손 手 수 su

反射 반사 reflection; reverberation

돌이킬 反 반 pan

放射 방사 radiation

놓을 放 방 pang

注射 주사 to inject

물멜 注 주 chu

感謝 감사 gratitude; thanks

사례할 謝 사 sa

TYPICAL CONVERSATIONAL USAGE FOR READING AND TRANS-
LATION. EXERCISE:

1. 射擊訓練을 받는 동안 제일 어려웠던 것은 夜間射擊이었다.
   During the firing exercise the most difficult thing was the
   night fire.

2. 基本訓練 받을 때에 一等射手의 메달을 取得했다.
   I got an expert marksmanship medal during the basic training.

3. 流行性感氣가 돌면 豫防注射를 맞아야 한다.
   You must get inoculated if the flu is going around.

This character represents the fighting between two people. During their practice in Korean Taekwondo, they spar against each other. It means "to fight." The simplified character is (鬪).

t'u
FIGHT
20 S.

鬪　싸울 투

(鬪→鬪)

| 丨 | 厂 | 匚 | 匸 | 匡 | 匡丁 | 匡王 | 匡冂 | 鬥 | 鬧 | 鬪 | 鬪 |

HIGH FREQUENCY COMPOUNDS

鬪犬 투견 a dogfight

鬪技 투기 a contest; a match

鬪病 투병 a struggle against a disease

鬪爭 투쟁 fighting

鬪志 투지 a fighting spirit

激鬪 격투 a severe fight

拳鬪 권투 boxing; pugilism

MEANING AND SOUND

개 犬 견 kyŏn

재주 技 기 ki

병들 病 병 pyŏng

다툴 爭 쟁 chaeng

뜻 志 지 chi

심할 激 격 kyŏk

주먹 拳 권 kwon

TYPICAL CONVERSATIONAL USAGE FOR READING AND TRANSLATION. EXERCISE:

1. 惡戰苦鬪(악전고투) : 죽을 힘을 다하여 몹시 싸움.
   Hard fighting; a hard battle.

2. 그도 젊었을 때는 鬪志가 만만했다.
   He was much of a fighter in his younger day.

3. 부부 싸움은 칼로 물 베기 : 내외간의 싸움은 칼로 물을 베어도 痕迹이 없듯이 쉬 和合하는 것이라는 말. Husband and wife quarrels are like cutting the water with a knife.

A shepherd named David carried a slingshot to take care of flock. When David fought with Goliath, the stone hit Goliath and killed him. The origin of the character is the wrapping (包) of a stone (石) by the belt. It now represents the idea of a cannon.

砲 대포 포

p'o
CANNON
10 S.

一 丁 ア 石 石 矴 矴 砲 砲

HIGH FREQUENCY COMPOUNDS

砲擊 포격 bombardment; an artillery attack

砲兵 포병 an artilleryman

砲聲 포성 the boom of a gun

砲手 포수 a hunter

砲丸 포환 a cannonball; a slug

大砲 대포 a cannon; a gun

MEANING AND SOUND

칠 擊 격 kyŏk

군사 兵 병 pyŏng

소리 聲 성 sŏng

손 手 수 su

알 丸 환 hwan

큰 大 대 tae

TYPICAL CONVERSATIONAL USAGE FOR READING AND TRANSLATION. EXERCISE:

1. 韓國戰爭때 砲擊 소리에 귀가 먹었다. I lost my hearing because of the bombardment during the Korean War.

2. 나는 砲兵으로 三年間 勤務한 일이 있다. I have had the experience in serving as an artilleryman for three years.

3. 砲煙彈雨 (포연탄우) : 大砲의 煙氣와 빗발 같은 탄알 ; 激烈한 戰鬪를 뜻하는 말. Cannon smoke and a shower of shells. (a furious battle)

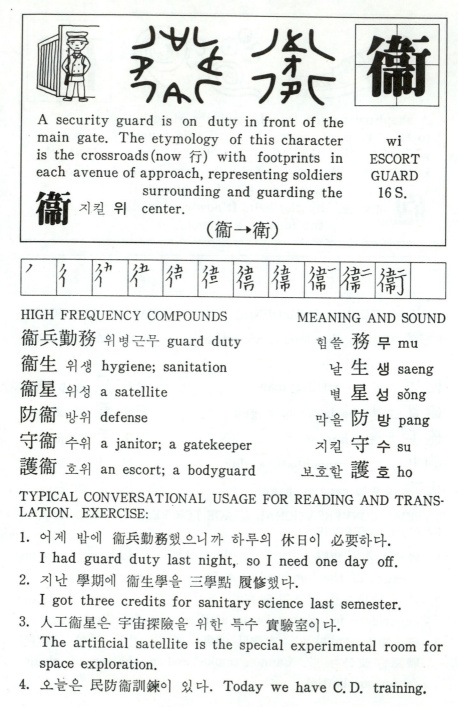

A security guard is on duty in front of the main gate. The etymology of this character is the crossroads (now 行) with footprints in each avenue of approach, representing soldiers surrounding and guarding the center.

衛 지킬 위

wi
ESCORT
GUARD
16 S.

(衞→衛)

HIGH FREQUENCY COMPOUNDS

衞兵勤務 위병근무 guard duty

衞生 위생 hygiene; sanitation

衞星 위성 a satellite

防衞 방위 defense

守衞 수위 a janitor; a gatekeeper

護衞 호위 an escort; a bodyguard

MEANING AND SOUND

힘쓸 務 무 mu

날 生 생 saeng

별 星 성 sŏng

막을 防 방 pang

지킬 守 수 su

보호할 護 호 ho

TYPICAL CONVERSATIONAL USAGE FOR READING AND TRANSLATION. EXERCISE:

1. 어제 밤에 衞兵勤務했으니까 하루의 休日이 必要하다.
   I had guard duty last night, so I need one day off.

2. 지난 學期에 衞生學을 三學點 履修했다.
   I got three credits for sanitary science last semester.

3. 人工衞星은 宇宙探險을 위한 특수 實驗室이다.
   The artificial satellite is the special experimental room for space exploration.

4. 오늘은 民防衞訓鍊이 있다. Today we have C. D. training.

17. 藝術 예술 Arts

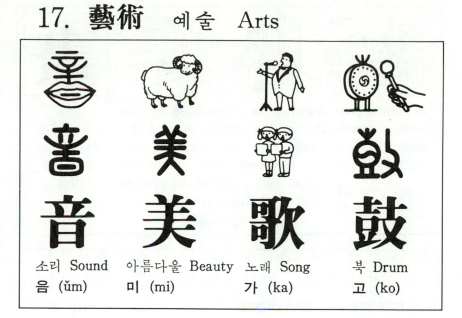

소리 Sound　아름다울 Beauty　노래 Song　북 Drum
음 (ŭm)　미 (mi)　가 (ka)　고 (ko)

너희 義人들아 여호와를 즐거워하라. 讚頌은 正直한 자의 마땅
히 할 바로다. 竪琴으로 여호와께 感謝하고 열 줄 琵琶로 讚頌할
지어다. 새 노래로 그를 노래하며 즐거운 소리로 工巧히 演奏할
지어다. (詩篇 33 : 1〜3)

Sing for joy in the Lord, O you righteous ones; Praise is
becoming to the upright. Give thanks to the Lord with the
lyre; Sing praises to Him with a harp of ten strings. Sing to
Him a new song; Play skillfully with a shout of joy.
(*Psalms* 33 : 1〜3)

나팔 소리로 讚揚하며 琵琶와 竪琴으로 讚揚할지어다. 小鼓 치
며 춤추어 讚揚하며 絃樂과 洞簫로 讚揚할지어다. 큰 소리 나는
提琴으로 讚揚하며 높은 소리 나는 提琴으로 讚揚할지어다.
(詩篇 150 : 3〜5)

Praise Him with trumpet sound; Praise Him with harp and
lyre. Praise Him with timbrel and dancing; Praise Him with
stringed instuments and pipe. Praise Him with loud cymbals;
Praise with resounding cymbals. (*Psalms* 150 : 3〜5)

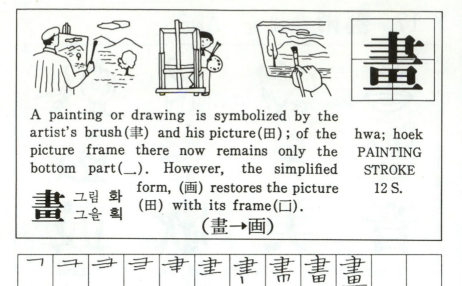

A painting or drawing is symbolized by the artist's brush(聿) and his picture(田); of the picture frame there now remains only the bottom part(_). However, the simplified form, (画) restores the picture (田) with its frame(囗).

hwa; hoek
PAINTING
STROKE
12 S.

畫   그림 화
      그을 획

(畫→画)

ㄱ ㄱ ㄱ ㄱ 肀 聿 聿 書 畵 畫

HIGH FREQUENCY COMPOUNDS

畫家 화가 an artist; a painter

畫面 화면 TV or movie screen

漫畫 만화 a cartoon; a comic picture

名畫 명화 a famous picture

壁畫 벽화 a fresco; a wall painting

MEANING AND SOUND

통한이 家 가 ka

낯 面 면 myŏn

부질없을 漫 만 man

이름 名 명 myŏng

벽 壁 벽 pyŏk

TYPICAL CONVERSATIONAL USAGE FOR READING AND TRANSLATION. EXERCISE:

1. 모든 畫家는 自己의 영혼에 붓을 적셔서 自己의 참모습을 그림에 옮긴다.

   Every artist dips his brush in his own soul, and paints his own nature into his pictures. (*Henry W. Beechers*)

2. 畫中之餠(화중지병) : 그림에 떡 ; 실지로 利用할 수 없고 欲求를 채울 수 없음을 가리키는 말.

   A rice cake in the painting. (something unavailable)

3. 新聞마다 재미있는 漫畫가 실려 있다.

   Each newspaper has an interesting cartoon on it.

The movie projector is one of the best tools for the audio-visual education. When you operate the projector, you need a screen which reflects a man in action. This character means "to reflect." (映) is the combination of light (日) and a man (人) in the center (中).

yǒng
REFLECT
9 S.

映 비칠 영

| ㅣ | ㄇ | 日 | 映 | 映 | 映 | 映 | 映 | | | | |

HIGH FREQUENCY COMPOUNDS

映寫 영사 projection

映像 영상 image; reflection

映畵 영화 a movie

映畵俳優 영화배우 a cinema [movie] actor[actress]

反映 반영 reflection

上映 상영 showing; screening

MEANING AND SOUND

베낄 寫 사 sa

형상 像 상 sang

그릴 畵 화 hwa

광대 俳 배 pae

광대 優 우 u

돌이킬 反 반 pan

위 上 상 sang

TYPICAL CONVERSATIONAL USAGE FOR READING AND TRANSLATION EXERCISE:

1. 나는 視聽覺敎育 시간에 映寫機 使用法에 대해서 배웠다.
   I learned how to operate the projector during the audio-visual education class.

2. 그 映畵는 亞細亞 映畵祭에서 金賞을 받았다. That movie received the gold award from the Asian Movie Contest.

3. 그 映畵는 지금 단성사에서 上映中이다.
   The film is now on show at Tansŏngsa.

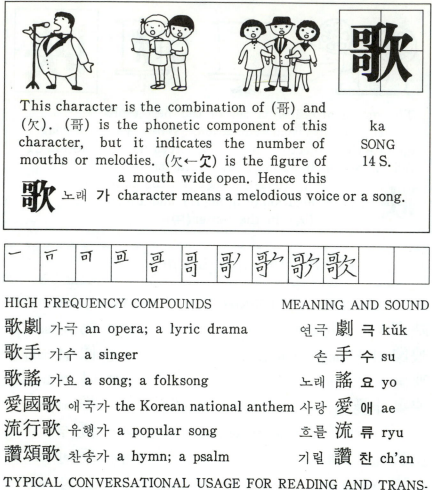

This character is the combination of (哥) and
(欠). (哥) is the phonetic component of this
character, but it indicates the number of
mouths or melodies. (欠←欠) is the figure of
a mouth wide open. Hence this
歌 노래 **가** character means a melodious voice or a song.

ka
SONG
14 S.

一 口 可 叿 哥 哥 哥 歌 歌 歌

HIGH FREQUENCY COMPOUNDS

歌劇 가극 an opera; a lyric drama

歌手 가수 a singer

歌謠 가요 a song; a folksong

愛國歌 애국가 the Korean national anthem

流行歌 유행가 a popular song

讚頌歌 찬송가 a hymn; a psalm

MEANING AND SOUND

연극 劇 극 kŭk

손 手 수 su

노래 謠 요 yo

사랑 愛 애 ae

흐를 流 류 ryu

기릴 讚 찬 ch'an

TYPICAL CONVERSATIONAL USAGE FOR READING AND TRANS-
LATION. EXERCISE:

1. 有名한 歌手들 中에는 福音傳道者로 轉向한 사람이 몇 있다.
   Among the famous singers, there are a few who have switched
   to Gospel singing.

2. 四面楚歌 (사면초가) : Songs are heard on four sides. (surrounded on all sides by enemies)

3. 敎會마다 聖歌隊가 있다. Each church has a choir.

4. 韓國의 愛國歌는 안 익태씨가 作曲했다.
   The Korean national anthem was composed by An Ik-t'ae.

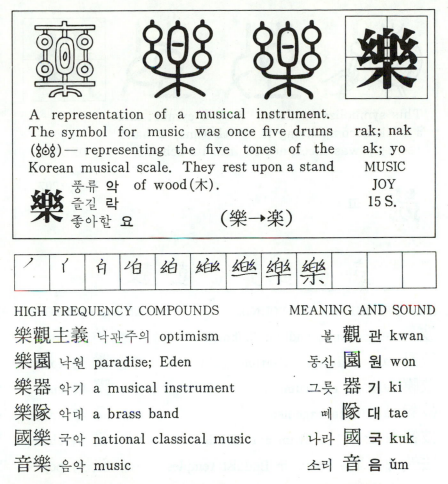

A representation of a musical instrument. The symbol for music was once five drums (𢀖) — representing the five tones of the Korean musical scale. They rest upon a stand 풍류 **악** of wood(木).

즐길 **락**

좋아할 **요**

(樂→楽)

rak; nak

ak; yo

MUSIC

JOY

15 S.

HIGH FREQUENCY COMPOUNDS

樂觀主義 낙관주의 optimism

樂園 낙원 paradise; Eden

樂器 악기 a musical instrument

樂隊 악대 a brass band

國樂 국악 national classical music

音樂 음악 music

MEANING AND SOUND

볼 觀 관 kwan

동산 園 원 won

그릇 器 기 ki

떼 隊 대 tae

나라 國 국 kuk

소리 音 음 ŭm

TYPICAL CONVERSATIONAL USAGE FOR READING AND TRANSLATION. EXERCISE:

1. 좋은 노래도 늘 들으면 싫다. Even a sweet song, sung over much, becomes disagreeable. (limitation)

2. 나의 아저씨는 陸軍 軍樂隊에서 지휘를 十年間 하셨다.
My uncle conducted a military band for ten years.

3. 喜怒哀樂(희로애락) : 기쁨과 노염과 슬픔과 즐거움.
Pleasure, anger, sorrow and joy—the passions.

4. 仁子樂山(인자요산) : 어진 사람은 山을 좋아한다.
The benevolent like mountains.

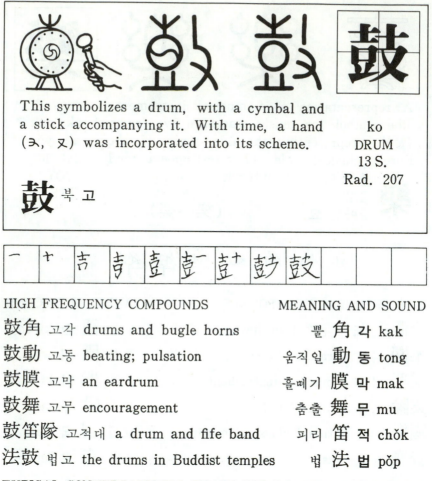

This symbolizes a drum, with a cymbal and a stick accompanying it. With time, a hand (ㅈ, ㅈ) was incorporated into its scheme.

ko
DRUM
13 S.
Rad. 207

鼓 북 고

HIGH FREQUENCY COMPOUNDS

鼓角 고각 drums and bugle horns

鼓動 고동 beating; pulsation

鼓膜 고막 an eardrum

鼓舞 고무 encouragement

鼓笛隊 고적대 a drum and fife band

法鼓 법고 the drums in Buddist temples

MEANING AND SOUND

뿔 角 각 kak

움직일 動 동 tong

홀떼기 膜 막 mak

춤출 舞 무 mu

피리 笛 적 chŏk

법 法 법 pŏp

TYPICAL CONVERSATIONAL USAGE FOR READING AND TRANSLATION. EXERCISE:

1. 좋은 북은 세게 칠 필요가 없다.
   You don't need to beat a good drum vigorously.
2. 동네 북 치듯 한다 : 여러 사람이 달려들어 함부로 때리는 모양. To make a combined attack on a person.
3. 왼쪽 가슴에 손을 얹어 보면 심장의 鼓動이 느껴진다. Placing your hand on the left chest, you can feel the beating of heart.
4. 韓國戰爭때 中共軍의 鼓笛隊를 본 일이 있다.
   I saw a Chinese drum and fife band during the Korean War.

This character is the hieroglyphic figure of a dancer flapping her sleeves with a fan and decorations. Korean shaman dancer is significantly related to folklore.

mu
DANCE
14 S.

 춤출 무

HIGH FREQUENCY COMPOUNDS

舞曲 무곡 a dance tune; dance music

舞臺 무대 the stage; the arena

舞蹈會 무도회 a dance party

舞扇 무선 a dancer's fan

舞踊 무용 a dance; dancing

歌舞 가무 singing and dancing

MEANING AND SOUND

굽을 曲 곡 kok

돈대 臺 대 tae

밟을 蹈 도 to

부채 扇 선 sŏn

뛸 踊 용 yong

노래 歌 가 ka

TYPICAL CONVERSATIONAL USAGE FOR READING AND TRANSLATION. EXERCISE:

1. 춤은 音樂과 사랑의 子女이다.
   Dancing, the child of music and of love. (*Sir John Davies*)

2. 舞踊은 가장 高尙하고 가장 感動的이며 가장 아름다운 藝術이다. Dancing is the loftiest, the most moving, the most beautiful of the arts. (*Havelok Ellis*)

3. 龍飛鳳舞(용비봉무) : 龍이 날고 鳳凰이 춤춤 ; 山川이 수려하고 신령한 氣勢. Dragon's flying and phoenix's dancing. (a mysterious features of mountains and streams)

"Punjae," the art of raising miniature trees in shallow pots (皿) is an offshoot of the art of gardening, which is so much like the Japanese culture. It has roots in China through Korea. This character means a flower-pot, or basin.

盆 동이 분 pot, or basin.

pun
BASIN
POT
9 S.

HIGH FREQUENCY COMPOUNDS

MEANING AND SOUND

盆景 분경 a tray landscape; a miniature garden — 볕 景 경 kyŏng

盆臺 분대 a flowerpot saucer — 돈대 臺 대 tae

盆栽 분재 growing in a pot — 심을 栽 재 chae

盆種 분종 potting; planting — 심을 種 종 chong

盆地 분지 a basin; a valley; a hollow — 땅 地 지 chi

花盆 화분 a flowerpot — 꽃 花 화 hwa

TYPICAL CONVERSATIONAL USAGE FOR READING AND TRANSLATION. EXERCISE:

1. 오늘은 비가 오니까 盆種하기에 좋은 時間이다. Today is raining, so it is good time to plant a flower in the pot.

2. 大邱는 盆地이니까, 겨울에는 춥고 여름에는 덥다.
The city of Taegu is cold in the winter and warm in the summer comparing to other cities

3. 나의 房을 淸掃하다가 花盆을 깨뜨렸다.
When I cleaned my room, I broke a flowerpot.

18. 職業　직업　Occupations

創世記에 記錄된 九名의 創業者들
Nine of the earliest recorded inventors

아벨은 羊치는 者의 始祖(創世記 4 : 2)
  Abel invented shepherding.

가인은 農事하는 者의 始祖(創世記 4 : 2)
  Cain invented farming.

가인은 都市 開發의 始祖(創世記 4 : 17)
  Cain invented the city.

야발은 帳幕에 居하는 者의 始祖(創世記 4 : 20)
  Jabal invented tents.

유발은 하프와 오르간의 始祖(創世記 4 : 21)
  Jubal invented the harp and organ.

두발가인은 金屬工의 始祖(創世記 4 : 22)
  Tubal Cain invented metal working with brass and iron.

노아는 方舟와 動物學의 始祖(創世記 6 : 14)
  Noah invented the Ark and zoology.

노아는 葡萄酒 生産의 始祖(創世記 9 : 20, 21)
  Noah invented wine.

니므롯은 사냥꾼의 始祖(創世記 10 : 8, 9)
  Nimrod invented hunting.

This character is the combination of (牛) and (攵). (牛) is the hieroglyph of the head of an ox with horns and means a cow or an ox. (攵) is a transformation of (父) which is the right hand holding a rod. It means a shepherd or "to feed."

牧 기를 목

mok
PASTURE
SHEPHERD
8 S.

丿 亠 牛 牛 牛 牛 牧 牧

HIGH FREQUENCY COMPOUNDS

牧童 목동 a herd boy; a shepherd boy

牧師 목사 a pastor; reverend; a minister

牧場 목장 a pasture; a ranch

牧畜業 목축업 stock farming

牧會 목회 pastoral duties

放牧 방목 pasturage

MEANING AND SOUND

아이 童 동 tong

스승 師 사 sa

마당 場 장 chang

기를 畜 축 ch'uk

모일 會 회 hoe

놓을 放 방 pang

TYPICAL CONVERSATIONAL USAGE FOR READING AND TRANSLATION. EXERCISE:

1. 내가 또 마음에 合하는 牧者를 너희에게 주리니 그들이 知識과 明哲로 너희를 養育하리라. (예레미야 3 : 15) And I will give you pastors according to mine heart, which shall feed you with knowledge and understanding. (*Jeremiah* 3 : 15)

2. 어제는 金牧師님과 한 時間 동안 結婚相談을 했다. Yesterday I consulted with Rev. Kim about the matrimony for one hour.

3. 욥의 牧場에는 羊이 七千이요, 약대가 三千이요, 소가 五百 겨리요, 암나귀가 五百이었다. (욥記, *Job* 1 : 3)

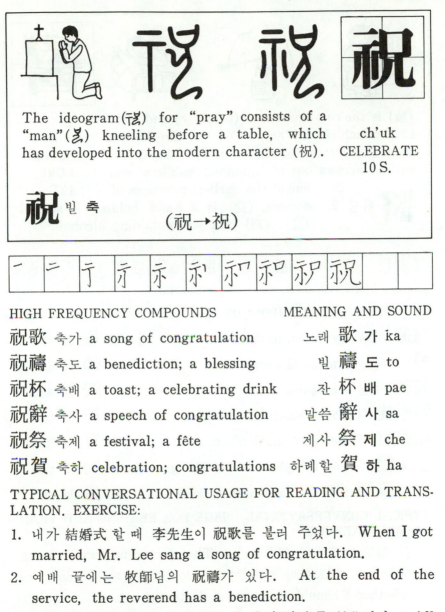

The ideogram (祝) for "pray" consists of a "man" (兄) kneeling before a table, which has developed into the modern character (祝).

ch'uk

CELEBRATE

10 S.

祝 빌 축

(祝→祝)

HIGH FREQUENCY COMPOUNDS

祝歌 축가 a song of congratulation

祝禱 축도 a benediction; a blessing

祝杯 축배 a toast; a celebrating drink

祝辭 축사 a speech of congratulation

祝祭 축제 a festival; a fête

祝賀 축하 celebration; congratulations

MEANING AND SOUND

노래 歌 가 ka

빌 禱 도 to

잔 杯 배 pae

말씀 辭 사 sa

제사 祭 제 che

하례할 賀 하 ha

TYPICAL CONVERSATIONAL USAGE FOR READING AND TRANSLATION. EXERCISE:

1. 내가 結婚式 할 때 李先生이 祝歌를 불러 주었다. When I got married, Mr. Lee sang a song of congratulation.

2. 예배 끝에는 牧師님의 祝禱가 있다. At the end of the service, the reverend has a benediction.

3. 모든 祝賀客들은 먼저 祝杯를 한 후에 食事를 始作했다. All guests had a toast first, and then started dinner together.

4. 우리 大學의 祝祭는 每年 九月에 열린다.
Our college festival is held in September every year.

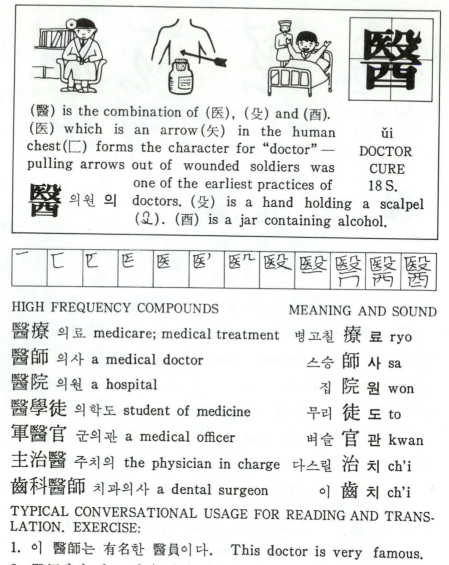

(醫) is the combination of (医), (殳) and (酉).
(医) which is an arrow(矢) in the human chest(匚) forms the character for "doctor" — pulling arrows out of wounded soldiers was one of the earliest practices of doctors. (殳) is a hand holding a scalpel (요). (酉) is a jar containing alcohol.

ǔi
DOCTOR
CURE
18 S.

醫　의원 의

| 一 | 匚 | 匸 | 医 | 医 | 医' | 医ㄴ | 医殳 | 医殳 | 医殳 | 医殳 | 医殳 |

HIGH FREQUENCY COMPOUNDS

MEANING AND SOUND

醫療 의료 medicare; medical treatment　병고칠 療 료 ryo

醫師 의사 a medical doctor　　　　스승 師 사 sa

醫院 의원 a hospital　　　　　　　집 院 원 won

醫學徒 의학도 student of medicine　무리 徒 도 to

軍醫官 군의관 a medical officer　벼슬 官 관 kwan

主治醫 주치의 the physician in charge　다스릴 治 치 ch'i

齒科醫師 치과의사 a dental surgeon　이 齒 치 ch'i

TYPICAL CONVERSATIONAL USAGE FOR READING AND TRANS-LATION. EXERCISE:

1. 이 醫師는 有名한 醫員이다.　This doctor is very famous.

2. 醫師에게 가 보아야 할지 어떨지 모르겠읍니다.　I don't know whether I should go to see a doctor or not.

3. 그가 몇 年 동안 軍醫官으로 勤務하고 있는지 아세요? Do you know how many years he's worked as an army surgeon.

4. 제 四寸同生은 齒科醫師로 第七師團에 있읍니다.
My cousin is a dentist in the 7th Division.

One man gets sick in bed. This character is
the combination of (疒) and (丙). (疒) is
formed from (爿, a bed) and (人, a man),
representing the person who is ill in bed.

pyŏng
DISEASE
10 S.

病 병들 병

` 一 广 疒 疒 疒 病 病 病

HIGH FREQUENCY COMPOUNDS

MEANING AND SOUND

病暇 병가 sick leave

병리학 pathology
病理學

病勢 병세 condition of a disease

病身 병신 a cripple; deformity

病院 병원 a hospital; an infirmary

傳染病 전염병 an infectious disease

겨를 暇 가 ka

다스릴 理 리 ri

기세 勢 세 se

몸 身 신 shin

집 院 원 won

물들 染 염 yŏm

TYPICAL CONVERSATIONAL USAGE FOR READING AND TRANS-
LATION. EXERCISE:

1. 醫師는 제 病 못 고친다.   A physician is careless of his own
   health. (the physician of others)

2. 金先生은 벌써 病院에 入院한 지 두 週日이 된다.
   Mr. Kim has been in the hospital since two weeks ago.

3. 健康한 者에게 醫師가 必要하지 않으나 病者에게는 必要하다.
   (마태福音 9 : 12) The healthy have no need of a physician,
   but the sick. (*Matt.* 9 : 12)

4. 同病相憐(동병상련) : Misery loves company.

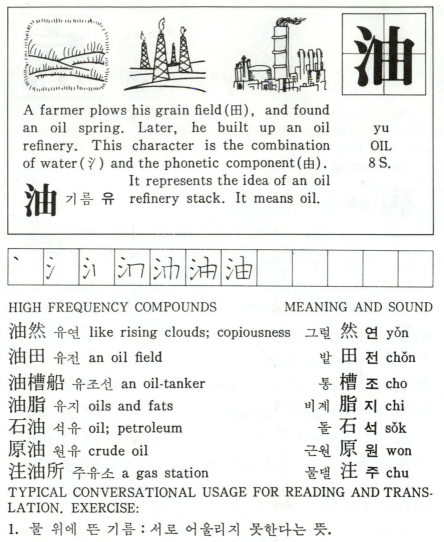

A farmer plows his grain field(田), and found an oil spring. Later, he built up an oil refinery. This character is the combination of water(氵) and the phonetic component(由).
It represents the idea of an oil

油 기름 유   refinery stack. It means oil.

yu
OIL
8 S.

丶 氵 氵 氵 沪 汩 油 油

HIGH FREQUENCY COMPOUNDS   MEANING AND SOUND

油然 유연 like rising clouds; copiousness   그럴 然 연 yŏn

油田 유전 an oil field   밭 田 전 chŏn

油槽船 유조선 an oil-tanker   통 槽 조 cho

油脂 유지 oils and fats   비계 脂 지 chi

石油 석유 oil; petroleum   돌 石 석 sŏk

原油 원유 crude oil   근원 原 원 won

注油所 주유소 a gas station   물댈 注 주 chu

TYPICAL CONVERSATIONAL USAGE FOR READING AND TRANSLATION. EXERCISE:

1. 물 위에 뜬 기름 : 서로 어울리지 못한다는 뜻.
   Oil on the water. (Someone does not mix.)

2. 國內에도 油田이 많으니까, 中東原油를 輸入할 必要는 없다.
   We don't need to import crude oil from the Mideast because we have a lot of domestic oil fields.

3. 우리 동네에도 注油所가 하나 있다.
   Our village has a gas station.

4. 揮發油를 넣어야겠어요. I'll have to fill it up with gas.

A plumber(人) maintains a sink. He uses a
wrench whose shape resembles(乍). It means   chak
"to make."   MAKE
                                               7 S.

作 지을 작

丿 亻 𠂉 𠂆 𠂉 作 作

HIGH FREQUENCY COMPOUNDS

作家 작가 an author; a writer

作別 작별 leave-taking; good-by

作戰 작전 a military operation

作品 작품 production; a work

名作 명작 a masterpiece

始作 시작 beginning; start

豐作 풍작 a good harvest

MEANING AND SOUND

통한이 家 가 ka

다를 別 별 pyŏl

싸울 戰 전 chŏn

품수 品 품 p'um

이름 名 명 myŏng

비로소 始 시 shi

풍년 豐 풍 p'ung

TYPICAL CONVERSATIONAL USAGE FOR READING AND TRANS-
LATION. EXERCISE:

1. 作家는 人間 영혼의 技師이다.   The writer is an engineer of
   the human soul. (*Joseph Stalin*)

2. 晝夜作業(주야작업) : To work day and night.

3. 始作이 半이다 : 무슨 일이든 始作하기가 어렵지 일단 손을 대
   면 반 이상 한 것이나 다름없다는 말. Well begun is half done.

4. 作心三日(작심삼일) : 決心이 사흘을 가지 못함.
   A resolution good for only three days.

The metals are born from the earth. The original seal form (釜) showed the presence of four gold nuggets (全), concealed under the earth (土). The regular form reveals only two nuggets (金). It is one of the radicals of high frequency, found in a group of characters for metals.

金 쇠 금 / 성 김

kŭm; kim
GOLD
METAL
8. S.
Rad. 167

HIGH FREQUENCY COMPOUNDS

金剛石 금강석 a diamond

金額 금액 an amount of money

金言 금언 a maxim; a golden saying

金銀 금은 gold and silver

金婚式 금혼식 the 50th year, golden wedding anniversary

稅金 세금 taxes

貯金 저금 savings

MEANING AND SOUND

굳셀 剛 강 kang

이마 額 액 aek

말씀 言 언 ŏn

은 銀 은 ŭn

혼인할 婚 혼 hon

세금 稅 세 se

쌓을 貯 저 chŏ

TYPICAL CONVERSATIONAL USAGE FOR READING AND TRANSLATION. EXERCISE:

1. 黃金時代 (황금시대) : The golden age.
2. 돈이 돈을 낳는다. Money begets money.
3. 돈을 빌려주면 친구를 잃는다.
   Lend your money and lose your friend.
4. 美國 販賣稅의 稅率은 現在 6%이다.
   In the U.S. the rate of sales tax is 6 per cent now.

Three components make up the character for skin: (又), the hand that flays; (丿), the animal skin; and (刀), the knife. It is the 107th radical of characters relating to the skin or leather.

皮 가죽 피

p'i
SKIN
LEATHER
5 S.
Rad. 107

| 一 | 厂 | 广 | 皮 | 皮 | | | | | | | |

HIGH FREQUENCY COMPOUNDS

皮帶 피대 a conveyor belt

皮膚 피부 the skin

皮膚科 피부과 dermatology

皮相的 피상적 superficial; shallow

皮革 피혁 leather; hides

脫皮 탈피 casting off; peeling off

MEANING AND SOUND

띠 帶 대 tae

살갗 膚 부 pu

과목 科 과 kwa

서로 相 상 sang

가죽 革 혁 hyŏk

벗을 脫 탈 t'al

TYPICAL CONVERSATIONAL USAGE FOR READING AND TRANSLATION. EXERCISE:

1. 그는 바나나 껍질에 미끄러져 넘어졌다.
   He stepped on a banana skin and slipped.

2. 겉에는 羊가죽 옷을 입었으나 속에는 이리 마음이 있다.
   Outside he is clothed in a sheep's skin; inside his heart is a wolf's.

3. 後進國에서 脫皮하려면 經濟 발전과 政治安定이 必要하다.
   If you want to advance out of an underdeveloped country, you need economic advances and political stability.

This character is represented by a student carrying three book boxes(耳) by the hand (又). According to another story, it is a person holding an ear, which has probably been cut off. It was not unusual for a victor to cut off an ear of the vanquished in order to claim merit.

ch'wi
TAKE
8 S.

取 가질 취

一 丆 F 耳 耳 取 取

HIGH FREQUENCY COMPOUNDS

MEANING AND SOUND

取扱 취급 handling; treatment; dealing · · · · 다룰 扱 급 kŭp

取得 취득 acquisition; purchase · · · · 얻을 得 득 tŭk

取捨選擇 취사선택 adoption or rejection · · · · 가릴 選 선 sŏn

取消 취소 cancellation; revocation · · · · 끌 消 소 so

取材 취재 collection of data; coverage · · · · 재목 材 재 chae

奪取 탈취 capture; seizure · · · · 빼앗을 奪 탈 t'al

TYPICAL CONVERSATIONAL USAGE FOR READING AND TRANSLATION. EXERCISE:

1. 다음 週末의 見學計劃을 取消해 주세요.
   Please cancel next weekend's field trip.

2. 朴教授는 昨年 봄에 博士學位를 取得했다.
   Professor Park got a Ph. D. last spring.

3. 李記者는 올림픽 경기 取材에 아주 바쁘다.
   Reporter Lee is too busy collecting the Olympic records.

4. 다윗이 아말렉 사람의 取하였던 모든 것을 도로 찾았다. David recovered all that Amalekites had taken. (I *Samuel* 30 : 18)

It is manlike in form, with a large and fearful head. Also it has a tail on it. It came to express the meaning of a demon.

kwi
DEMON
GHOST
10 S.

鬼 귀신 **귀**

HIGH FREQUENCY COMPOUNDS

鬼神 귀신 a ghost; a demon

鬼形 귀형 a ghostly figure

鬼火 귀화 fatuous fires; an elf fire

鬼話 귀화 a story of the ghost

魔鬼 마귀 Satan; an evil spirit

惡鬼 악귀 a demon; a devil

MEANING AND SOUND

귀신 神 신 shin

형상 形 형 hyŏng

불 火 화 hwa

말할 話 화 hwa

마귀 魔 마 ma

악할 惡 악 ak

TYPICAL CONVERSATIONAL USAGE FOR READING AND TRANSLATION. EXERCISE:

1. 神出鬼沒(신출귀몰) : 忽然히 나타났다 홀연히 사라짐. Sudden appearance and disappearance, of supernatural swiftness.

2. 낮에 난 도깨비 : 체면 없이 난잡한 짓을 하는 사람. Evil spirit of the daylight. (a shameless bastard)

3. 魔鬼로 틈을 타지 못하게 하라. (에베소書 4 : 27) Do not give the devil an opportunity. (*Ephesians* 4 : 27)

4. 有錢使鬼神(유전사귀신) : 돈만 있으면 鬼神도 부릴 수 있다. Money controls even the orders of the ghost.

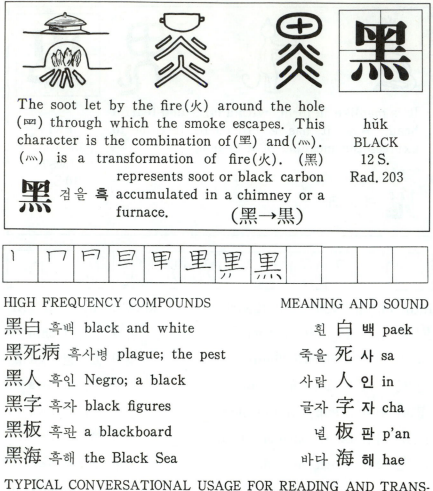

The soot let by the fire(火) around the hole (囪) through which the smoke escapes. This character is the combination of (里) and (灬). (灬) is a transformation of fire(火). (黑) represents soot or black carbon accumulated in a chimney or a furnace.

黑 검을 흑

黑 hŭk
BLACK
12 S.
Rad. 203

(黑→黒)

ㄱ 冂 冃 旦 甲 里 黒 黒

HIGH FREQUENCY COMPOUNDS

黑白 흑백 black and white

黑死病 흑사병 plague; the pest

黑人 흑인 Negro; a black

黑字 흑자 black figures

黑板 흑판 a blackboard

黑海 흑해 the Black Sea

MEANING AND SOUND

흰 白 백 paek

죽을 死 사 sa

사람 人 인 in

글자 字 자 cha

널 板 판 p'an

바다 海 해 hae

TYPICAL CONVERSATIONAL USAGE FOR READING AND TRANSLATION. EXERCISE:

1. 黑白分明(흑백 분명) : 善惡의 구별이 分明함.
   A clear distinction between black and white. (no confusion; separating the sheep from the goats)
2. 美國의 黑人들은 주로 都市와 南쪽에 많이 산다.
   American Negroes mainly live in the metropolitan and the southern areas.
3. 修業이 끝나면 黑板을 지워 주세요.
   Would you erase the blackboard when school is over?

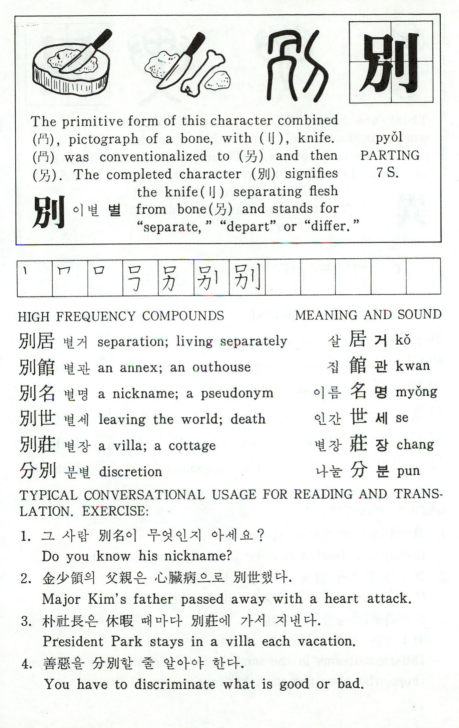

The primitive form of this character combined (凸), pictograph of a bone, with (刂), knife. (凸) was conventionalized to (另) and then (另). The completed character (別) signifies the knife(刂) separating flesh from bone(另) and stands for "separate," "depart" or "differ."

別 이별 별

py**ŏ**l

PARTING

7 S.

㇀	㇆	口	弓	另	別	別				

HIGH FREQUENCY COMPOUNDS

MEANING AND SOUND

別居 별거 separation; living separately   살 居 거 kŏ

別館 별관 an annex; an outhouse   집 館 관 kwan

別名 별명 a nickname; a pseudonym   이름 名 명 my**ŏ**ng

別世 별세 leaving the world; death   인간 世 세 se

別莊 별장 a villa; a cottage   별장 莊 장 chang

分別 분별 discretion   나눌 分 분 pun

TYPICAL CONVERSATIONAL USAGE FOR READING AND TRANSLATION. EXERCISE:

1. 그 사람 別名이 무엇인지 아세요?
   Do you know his nickname?
2. 金少領의 父親은 心臟病으로 別世했다.
   Major Kim's father passed away with a heart attack.
3. 朴社長은 休暇 때마다 別莊에 가서 지낸다.
   President Park stays in a villa each vacation.
4. 善惡을 分別할 줄 알아야 한다.
   You have to discriminate what is good or bad.

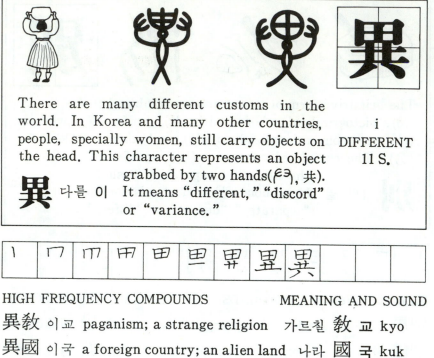

There are many different customs in the world. In Korea and many other countries, people, specially women, still carry objects on the head. This character represents an object grabbed by two hands(ʔʒ, 共).

異 다를 이 It means "different," "discord" or "variance."

i
DIFFERENT
11 S.

| 丶 | 冂 | 冂 | 甲 | 田 | 田 | 畀 | 畐 | 異 | | | |

HIGH FREQUENCY COMPOUNDS

MEANING AND SOUND

異教 이교 paganism; a strange religion　　가르칠 教 교 kyo

異國 이국 a foreign country; an alien land　　나라 國 국 kuk

異論 이론 a divergent view　　논의할 論 론 ron

異議 이의 an objection　　의논할 議 의 ŭi

異質的 이질적 heterogeneous; unusual　　바탕 質 질 chil

精神異狀 정신이상 mental derangement　　가릴 精 정 chŏng

TYPICAL CONVERSATIONAL USAGE FOR READING AND TRANSLATION. EXERCISE:

1. 異國生活은 외롭지만 재미가 있다.

   Living in a foreign country is lonely but interesting.

2. 異議가 있으면 會長님께 問議하세요.

   If you have an objection, talk to the chairman.

3. 同床異夢(동상이몽) : 起居를 함께 하면서 서로 다른 생각을 함 ; 같은 立場·일인데도 目標가 저마다 다름.

   Different dreams in the same bed. (different aims between those who have the same business)

The man takes a shower in the bathroom. This character is the combination of water (氵), (公) and (口). (氵) is the transformation of (水), (公) is the figure of water dripping down. The mouth(口) rep-resents a chap singing.

浴 목욕할 욕

yok
BATHE
10 S.

`丶 氵 氵 氵 沙 浐 浐 浴 浴`

HIGH FREQUENCY COMPOUNDS

浴室 욕실 a bathroom

浴衣 욕의 a bathrobe

浴化 욕화 the influence of virtue

沐浴湯 목욕탕 a bath; a bathhouse

日光浴 일광욕 a sun bath

海水浴 해수욕 a sea-bathing

MEANING AND SOUND

집 室 실 shil

옷 衣 의 ŭi

화할 化 화 hwa

머리감을 沐 목 mok

빛 光 광 kwang

바다 海 해 hae

TYPICAL CONVERSATIONAL USAGE FOR READING AND TRANSLATION. EXERCISE:

1. 나는 이번 週末에 浴衣를 하나 살까 한다.
   I am thinking of buying a bathrobe this weekend.

2. 美國人들은 잔디밭 위에서 日光浴을 많이 하는 편이다.
   Americans generally sun-bathe a lot on the lawn.

3. 물이 너무 차니까 여름일지라도 海水浴을 할 수가 없다.
   We can not swim in the ocean even though it is summer time because the water is too cold.

4. 沐浴齋戒(목욕재계) : ablutions; a purification ceremony.

A hand(彐) grasping two stalks(禾) of grain at once. By extension, it means combining several together, or a whole.

kyŏm
BOTH
COMBINE
10 S.

兼 겸할 겸

HIGH FREQUENCY COMPOUNDS

兼備 겸비 combining; having both

兼床 겸상 a table for two

兼用 겸용 combined use in both

兼全 겸전 being perfect in both

兼職 겸직 a concurrent office[position]

謙遜 겸손 humility; modesty

MEANING AND SOUND

갖출 備 비 pi

평상 床 상 sang

쓸 用 용 yong

온전 全 전 chŏn

직분 職 직 chik

겸손할 遜 손 son

TYPICAL CONVERSATIONAL USAGE FOR READING AND TRANSLATION. EXERCISE:

1. 趙博士는 知識과 德行을 兼備한 분이시다.
   Dr. Cho has knowledge and virtue of actions.

2. 시골에서는 손님 待接을 할 때 兼床을 많이 차린다.
   In the countryside, there are many treatments for guests making a table for two.

3. 이것은 아이들에게 有用한, 그네틀과 들것의 兼用物이다.
   This is a useful tool for children which combines a swing set and a baby carriage.

Two men sitting with a dish of food 皀(食) between them. The special meaning derives from the idea of a community festival and banquet. It means countryside, village, one's native place.

hyang
VILLAGE
COUNTRY-
SIDE
13 S.

鄕 시골 향

(鄕→鄕)

HIGH FREQUENCY COMPOUNDS

			MEANING AND SOUND
鄕校	향교	a Confucian temple[school]	학교 校 교 kyo
鄕愁	향수	homesickness; nostalgia	근심 愁 수 su
故鄕	고향	hometown	연고 故 고 ko
同鄕	동향	same village and town	한가지 同 동 tong
他鄕	타향	an alien land	다를 他 타 t'a
還鄕	환향	returning home	돌아올 還 환 hwan

TYPICAL CONVERSATIONAL USAGE FOR READING AND TRANSLATION. EXERCISE:

1. 鄕校는 儒敎의 敎育機關이었다. The Confucian school was the educational organization of Confucianism.

2. 오래간만에 故鄕에 돌아왔다.
   I have returned to my hometown after a long time.

3. 故鄕에 계신 어머님을 보고 싶어 죽겠어요! I want to see my mother who is in my hometown, very much!

4. 朴先生님과 나는 同鄕人이어서 더욱 親近하다. Because Mr. Park and I are from the same hometown we are closer friends.

商　商　商　**商**

A picture of a merchant opening a box to display his wares. Thus it means business.

sang
BUSINESS
TRADE
11 S.

商 장사 상

丶　亠　产　产　产　产　商　商　商

HIGH FREQUENCY COMPOUNDS

商工會議所 상공회의소 the Chamber
　　　　　　　　of Commerce

商船 상선 a merchant ship

商業銀行 상업은행 a commercial bank

商人 상인 a merchant

商店 상점 a store, a shop

商品 상품 commercial products; goods

MEANING AND SOUND

의논할 議 의 ŭi

곳 所 소 so

배 船 선 sŏn

은 銀 은 ŭn

사람 人 인 in

가게 店 점 chŏm

품수 品 품 p'ŭm

TYPICAL CONVERSATIONAL USAGE FOR READING AND TRANSLATION. EXERCISE:

1. 17 世紀 末葉에는 많은 外國商船들이 韓國 西海岸을 往來했다.
   At the end of the 17th century, a lot of foreign merchant ships visited the western coast of Korea.

2. 資本主義 經濟의 社會에서는 모든 財貨나 서비스가 商品으로 서 生産되고 交換된다.
   In capitalistic economic society, all goods and services are produced and exchanged as commodities.

The shape of a dancing girl. It means "to get acquainted with another."

kyo
ASSOCIATE
CROSS
6 S.

交 사귈 교

` 亠 亣 六 亣 交

| | | | |

HIGH FREQUENCY COMPOUNDS

MEANING AND SOUND

交代 교대 alternation; shift; relief

대신할 代 대 tae

交流 교류 circuit; an alternating current

흐를 流 류 ryu

交涉 교섭 negotiation; bargaining

건널 涉 섭 sŏp

交通信號 교통신호 a traffic light

통할 通 통 t'ong

交換教授 교환교수 an exchange
　　　　　　　professor

바꿀 換 환 hwan

줄 授 수 su

絕交 절교 a breach; a rupture

끊을 絕 절 chŏl

TYPICAL CONVERSATIONAL USAGE FOR READING AND TRANS-LATION. EXERCISE:

1. 貿易協定의 交涉은 지난週 韓國의 貿易使節團이 워싱턴을 訪問했을 때 열렸다. Negotiations for the trade agreement were opened in Washington during the visit of Korean trade mission there last week.

2. 네거리의 交通信號가 고장이 나서 警察官이 交通整理를 하고 있었다. The traffic light at the intersection broke, so the policeman was regulating traffic.

PART IV

RADICALS

Oracle bone. A specimen of many
thousands of pieces of inscribed
bones and tortoise shells from which
it is possible to reconstruct much of
the life of Shang dynasty (1520-
1030B.C.), China.

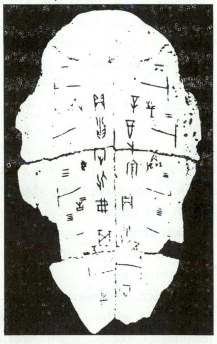

Radicals 部首(부수)

It is very useful, when the student has reached the dictionary stage, to know the number of strokes in each radical.

The earliest Chinese work, so far as is known which can properly be called a dictionary is the *Shuo-wen Chie-tzu*(說文解字 설문해자), published in 121 A.D. During the Han dynasty, this was modified by Hsu Sheng(許慎 허신, 30–124 A.D.) in his 15-volume paleographical work. In this the characters are distributed under five hundred and forty radicals.

Later lexicographers thought that it would be more convenient to have fewer groups. They therefore gradually reduced the number of the radicals, till at last there were only two hundred and fourteen.

About one hundred and forty of the total number of radicals are common everyday words, such as man(人), hand(手), ox(牛), horse(馬), etc., which must sooner or later form part of many characters.

What then, it may be asked, is the true function of the radicals, and where and why do they come into use? The answer is that, as they stand, they are nothing more than keys which will enable a reader to discover, approximately, the position of any given character in a Chinese dictionary; much in the same way, but not so unerringly, as that in which the letters of the alphabet guide the searcher in an English dictionary straight to the word required. For this purpose, and for this alone, they were originally selected and arranged in groups according to the number of strokes of which each is constructed; and thus they appear in Chinese dictionaries without any reference to their sounds, tones, or meanings, except when treated as substantive words. In conclusion it may be noted that the colloquial Chinese term for radical is *Soo Bu*(首部), head of a tribe.

List of the Radicals 部首一覽(부수일람)

(1) The radicals marked with an (*) have modified forms, which are used instead of the originals in the composition of other characters. These are shown at the right side of the originals.

(2) The radicals marked with a (†) are now obsolete, or rarely met with by beginners. Those left unmarked in this way have both a literary and a colloquial value, and should be carefully studied, however imperfectly, with the help of the following exercises, as has been suggested above, when some progress has already been made.

1 stroke			16†	几	안석궤	a bench		
1	一	한일	one	17†	凵	위튼 입구몸	a receptacle	
2†	丨	뚫을곤	a down stroke	18	刀*刂	칼도	a knife	
3†	丶	점	a point	19	力	힘력	strength	
4†	丿	삐침	a stroke to the left	20†	勹	쌀포몸	to wrap up	
5†	乙*乚	새을	a hook	21†	匕	비수비	a spoon	
6†	亅	갈고리궐	a barb	22†	匚	튼 입구몸	a box	
2 strokes				23†	匸	감출혜몸	to conceal	
7	二	두이	two	24	十	열십	ten	
8†	亠	돼지해 머리	above	25	卜	점복	to divine	
9	人*亻	사람인	a man	26†	卩*㔾	병부절	a joint	
10†	儿	어진 사람인발	a man	27†	厂	민엄호	a cliff	
11	入	들입	to enter	28†	厶	마늘모	selfish	
12	八	여덟팔	eight	29	又	또우	also; again	
13†	冂	멀경몸	a limit	**3 strokes**				
14†	冖	민갓머리	to cover	30	口	입구	a mouth	
15†	冫	이수변	icicle	31†	囗	큰입구몸	to enclose	

32	土	흙토	earth	57	弓	활궁	a bow
33	士	선비사	a scholar	58†	⼹*彑ㅋ튼가로왈		pig's head
34†	夂	뒤져올치	to follow	59†	彡	터럭삼방	feathers
35†	夊	천천히 걸을쇠발	to walk slowly	60†	彳	두인변	a step with the left foot
36†	夕	저녁석	evening				
37	大	큰대	great				
38	女	계집녀	a woman		**4 strokes**		
39	子	아들자	a son; an enclitic; a philosopher, etc.	61	心*忄忄	마음심	a heart
				62	戈	창과	a spear
				63	戶	지게호	a door
40†	宀	갓머리	a covering	64	手*扌	손수	a hand
41	寸	마디촌	an inch	65	支	지탱할지	a branch
42	小	작을소	small	66†	攴*攵	등글월문	to tap
43†	尢*尣兀	절름발이 왕	a lame	67	文	글월문	stripes; picture; characters; composition
44	尸	주검시엄	corpse				
45†	屮	왼손좌	left hand	68	斗	말두	a peck
46	山	메산	a mountain	69	斤	날근	a pound; an axe
47	巛*川巜	개미허리	a stream				
48	工	장인공	labour	70	方	모방	square; then
49	己	몸기	self				
50	巾	수건건	napkin	71	无*旡	이미기방	negative
51	干	방패간	a shield; to concern	72	日	날일	sun; a day
				73	曰	가로왈	to say
52†	幺	작을요	immature	74	月	달월	moon; a month
53†	广	엄호밑	a projecting roof	75	木	나무목	wood; a tree
54†	廴	민책받침	to move on	76	欠	하품흠방	to owe
55†	廾	스물입발	hands folded	77	止	그칠지	to stop
56†	弋	주살익	a dart	78	歹*歺	죽을사변	bad

79†	殳	갖은둥글월문	to kill	104†	疒	병질엄	disease

No.	Radical	Korean	English
79†	殳	갖은둥글월문	to kill
80†	毋	말무	do not
81	比	견줄비	to compare
82	毛	털모	hair
83	氏	각씨씨	family
84†	气	기운기엄	breath
85	水*氵水	물수	water
86	火*灬	불화	fire
87	爪*爫	손톱조머리	claws
88	父	아비부	father
89†	爻	점괘효	crosswise
90†	爿	장수장변	a contraction of 牀 sang, a bed
91	片	조각편	a slice or slip
92	牙	어금니아	back teeth
93	牛*牜	소우변	an ox
94	犬*犭	개견	a dog

5 strokes

No.	Radical	Korean	English
95†	玄	검을현	dark
96	玉*王	구슬옥	jade stone
97	瓜	외과	gourd
98	瓦	기와와	a tile
99	甘	달감	sweet
100	生	날생	to produce to live
101	用	쓸용	to use
102	田	밭전	field
103	疋	필필	a piece of cloth

No.	Radical	Korean	English
104†	疒	병질엄	disease
105†	癶	필발머리	back to back
106	白	흰백	white
107	皮	가죽피	skin
108†	皿	그릇명밑	a dish
109	目*罒	눈목	an eye
110†	矛	창모	a lance
111	矢	화살시	an arrow
112	石	돌석	stone
113	示*礻	보일시변	divine intimations; to proclaim
114†	内	짐승발자국유	footprint
115	禾	벼화	growing corn
116	穴	구멍혈	a cave
117	立	설립	to set up

6 strokes

No.	Radical	Korean	English
118	竹*⺮	대죽	bamboo
119	米	쌀미	rice
120†	糸	실사	silk
121†	缶	장군부	earthenware
122†	网*罒㓁	그물망	a net
123	羊*⺶	양양	sheep
124†	羽	깃우	feathers
125	老*耂	늙을로	old
126	而	말이을이	and; but
127†	耒	가래뢰	a plough

128	耳	귀이	an ear
129†	聿	붓율	a pen
130	肉*月月	고기육	flesh
131	臣	신하신	a minister
132	自	스스로자	from; self
133	至	이를지	to go to
134†	臼	절구구	a mortar
135	舌	혀설	tongue
136†	舛*牟	어그러질천	contradictory
137	舟	배주	boat
138†	艮	괘이름간	perverse
139	色	빛색	colour
140†	艸*艹	초두	grass
141†	虍	범호밑	tiger
142	虫	벌레훼	insect
143	血	피혈	blood
144	行	다닐행	to do; to go
145	衣*衤	옷의	clothes
146†	襾	덮을아	to cover; secondary

7 strokes

147	見	볼견	to see; to perceive
148	角	뿔각	a horn; an angle
149	言	말씀언	words; to speak
150	谷	골곡	a valley
151	豆	콩두	beans
152†	豕	돼지시	a pig

153†	豸	발없는 벌레치	reptile
154	貝	조개패	cowry; precious
155	赤	붉을적	flesh colour
156	走	달아날주	to go
157	足	발족	feet; enough
158	身	몸신	a body
159	車	수레거	a cart
160	辛	매울신	bitter
161	辰	별신	time; 7 to 9 a. m.
162†	辵*辶	책받침	to walk
163†	邑*阝	고을읍	a city
164	酉	닭유	5 to 7 p.m.
165†	釆	분별할채	to distinguish
166	里	마을리	a Korean mile

8 strokes

167	金	쇠금	gold; metal
168	長*镸	길장	long
169	門	문문	a gate; a door
170†	阜阝	언덕부	a mound
171†	隶	미칠이	to reach
172†	隹	새추	short-tailed birds
173	雨*⻗	비우	rain
174	靑	푸를청	the colour of nature; green; blue-black

175	非	아닐비	not; wrong		197†	鹵	잔땅로	salt
		9 strokes			198	鹿	사슴록	a deer
					199	麥	보리맥	wheat
176	面	낯면	face		200	麻	삼마	hemp
177†	革	가죽혁	rawhide					
178†	韋	다룬가죽위	leather			**12 strokes**		
179†	韭	부추구	leeks		201	黃	누를황	yellow
180	音	소리음	sound		202	黍	기장서	glutinous millet
181	頁	머리혈	a leaf of a book		203	黑	검을흑	black
182	風	바람풍	wind		204†	黹	바느질치	embroidery
183	飛	날비	to fly					
184	食*	(𩙿)밥식	to eat; food			**13 strokes**		
185	首	머리수	a head		205†	黽	맹꽁이맹	a frog
186	香	향기향	fragrant		206	鼎	솥정	a tripod
		10 strokes			207	鼓	북고	a drum
					208	鼠	쥐서	a rat
187	馬	말마	a horse			**14 strokes**		
188	骨	뼈골	bone		209	鼻	코비	a nose
189	高	높을고	high		210	齊	가지런할제	even; equal
190†	髟	터럭발밑	long hair					
191	鬥	싸움투	to fight			**15 strokes**		
192†	鬯	울창주창	fragrant herbs		211	齒	이치	front teeth
						16 strokes		
193†	鬲	오지병격	a caldron					
194	鬼	귀신귀	spirits of the dead		212	龍	용룡	a dragon
					213	龜	거북귀 (구)	a tortoise
		11 strokes				**17 strokes**		
195	魚	고기어	fish		214†	龠	피리약변	a flute
196	鳥	새조	a bird					

PART V
THEOLOGICAL & BIBLICAL TERMS

A page of the Bible in combination of Han-gŭl and Sino-Korean characters.

Theology 신학 神學

Apocalyptic Literature
계시 문학　啓示文學

Apologetics 변증학　辨證學

Biblical Archaeology
성경 고고학　聖經考古學

Biblical Criticism
성경 비평학　聖經批評學

Biblical Theology
성경 신학　聖經神學

Christian Art & Literature
기독교 문예　基督敎文藝

Christian Philosophy
기독교 철학　基督敎哲學

Comparative Religion
비교 종교학　比較宗敎學

The Death of God Theology
사신 신학　死神神學

Existential Theology 실존주
의적 신학　實存主義的 神學

Hermeneutics 성경 해석 방법
론　聖經解釋方法論

Historical Theology
역사 신학　歷史神學

Modernism Theology
현대주의 신학　現代主義神學

Natural Theology
자연 신학　自然神學

Neo-Orthodoxy
신정통 신학　新正統神學

Orthodoxy
정통 신학　正統神學

Pastoral Counseling
목회 상담　牧會相談

Pastoral Theology
목회학　牧會學

Pauline Theology
바울 신학　～神學

Practical Theology
실천 신학　實踐神學

Preaching, Homiletics
설교, 설교학　說敎, 說敎學

Reformed Theology
개혁주의 신학　改革主義神學

Religious Philosophy
종교 철학　宗敎哲學

Religious Psychology
종교 심리학　宗敎心理學

Systematic Theology
조직 신학　組織神學

Theology of Hope
희망의 신학　希望～神學

Asceticism
금욕주의　禁慾主義

Atheism 무신론　無神論

Christian Socialism 기독교 사
회주의　基督敎社會主義

Dispensationalism
시대주의　時代主義

Evangelicalism
복음주의　福音主義

Fundamentalism

근본주의 根本主義   무교회주의 無敎會主義
Gnosticism 영지주의 靈知主義   Pietism 경건주의 敬虔主義
Hellenism 헬레니즘   Polytheism 다신론 多神論
Judaism 유태주의 猶太主義   Puritanism
Legalism 율법주의 律法主義   청교도주의 淸敎徒主義
Liberalism   Rationalism
  자유주의 自由主義   합리주의 合理主義
Millennialism   Secularism 세속주의 世俗主義
  천년왕국설 千年王國說   Syncretism 혼합주의 混合主義
Mysticism 신비주의 神秘主義   Shamanism 샤머니즘
New Evangelicalism   Theism 유신론 有神論
  신복음주의 新福音主義   Unitarianism
Non-Church Movement   유니테리언주의 ～主義

Clergy 성직자 聖職者
Hospital Chaplain 원목 院牧   Missionary 선교사 宣敎師
Military Chaplain 군목 軍牧   Police Chaplain 경목 警牧
Minister, Reverend   Pastor 담임목사 擔任牧師
  목사 牧師

Doctrine 교리 敎理
Antichrist 적 (敵)그리스도   Catechism
Apostle 사도 使徒   요리 문답 要理問答
Atonement 속죄 贖罪   Catechumen
Authority 권위 權威   학습 교인 學習敎人
Baptism 세례 洗禮   Christological Controversy
Baptism in the Holy Spirit   기독론 논쟁 基督論論爭
  성령세례 聖靈洗禮   Communion of Saints
Baptismal Regeneration   성도의 교제 聖徒～交際
  중생의 세례 重生～洗禮   Confession of Faith
Calling, Vocation 소명 召命   신앙 고백서 信仰告白書
Canon 정경 正經   Covenant 언약 言約

Conversion 회심 回心

Creation 창조 創造

Creeds 신조 信條

Dead Sea Scrolls

　사해 문헌 死海文獻

Death 죽음 死亡(사망)

Decalogue 십계명 十誡命

Demythologization

　비신화화 非神話化

Eschatology 종말론 終末論

Eternity 영원 永遠

Faith 믿음 信仰(신앙)

Faith-Healing 신유 信癒

Fall 타락 墮落

Forgiveness 사죄 赦罪

Freedom and Free Will 자유,

　자유의지 自由, 自由意志

God 하나님

Good and Evil

　선과 악 善～惡

Good Works 선행 善行

Grace 은혜 恩惠

Hands, Laying on of

　안수 按手

Hell 지옥 地獄

Holy Spirit 성령 聖靈

Hope 소망 所望

Idolatry 우상 숭배 偶像崇拜

Image of God

　하나님의 형상 ～形象

Incarnation 성육 成肉

Indigenization 토착화 土着化

Infant Baptism

　유아 세례 幼兒洗禮

Infallibility 성경 무오의 교리

　聖經無誤～敎理

Inspiration of the Scriptures

　성경 영감설 聖經靈感說

Jesus Christ 예수 그리스도

Judgment 심판 審判

Justify 칭의 稱義

Kingdom of God

　하나님의 나라

Laity 평신도 平信徒

Labor 노동 勞動

Law 율법 律法

Life 생명 生命

Lord 주 主

Lord's Day 주일 主日

Love 사랑

Martyrdom, Martyr 순교,

　순교자 殉敎, 殉敎者

Miracle 이적 異蹟

Missions 선교 宣敎

Mystery 신비 神秘

Paganism 이교 異敎

Predestination 예정론 豫定論

Prophecy 예언 豫言

Providence 섭리 攝理

Regeneration 중생 重生

Relief 구제 救濟

Repentance 회개 悔改

Resurrection 부활 復活

Revelation 계시 啓示

Righteousness 의 義   Trinity 삼위일체 三位一體
Salvation 구원 救援   Truth 진리 眞理
Sanctification 성화 聖化   Vow, Oath, Promise 서원, 맹
Satan 사탄(사단)   세, 서약 誓願, 盟誓, 誓約
Sin 죄 罪   Will of God
Soul 영혼 靈魂   하나님의 의지 ～意志
Secularization 세속화 世俗化 Wisdom 지혜 智慧
Suffering 고난 苦難   Witness 증거 證據
Tongues 방언 方言

Denomination 교파 敎派

Anglican Church   Holiness Church
　성공회 聖公會   　성결 교회 聖潔敎會
Assembly of God   Methodist Church
　순복음 교회 順福音敎會   　감리 교회 監理敎會
Baptist Church   Lutheran Church
　침례 교회 浸禮敎會   　루터 교회 ～敎會
Church of the Brethren   Church of the Nazarene
　형제 교회 兄弟敎會   　나사렛 교회 ～敎會
Church of Christ   Presbyterian Church
　그리스도의 교회 ～敎會   　장로 교회 長老敎會

Roman Catholic Church 로마 카톨릭 교회 ～敎會

Archbishop 대주교 大主敎   Pope 교황 敎皇
Bishop 주교 主敎   Priest, Father 신부 神父
Brother 수사 修士   Sermon 강론 講論
Church 성당 聖堂   Sister 수녀 修女

Church Government 교회 정치 敎會政治

Church Councils   Ecumenism 에큐메니즘
　교회 협의회 敎會協議會   Campus Crusade for Christ
Discipline 권징 勸懲   　대학생 선교회 大學生宣敎會

The International Council of Christian-Church; ICCC
국제 기독교 연합회 國際基督教聯合會

Intervarsity Fellowship
복음주의 학생연맹 福音主義學生聯盟

National Association of Evan-gelicals; NAE 복음주의자 협의회 福音主義者協議會

Overseas Missionary Fellow-ship; OMF
해외 선교회 海外宣教會

World Council of Churches
세계 교회 협의회 世界教會協議會

The Officers of the Church 교회의 직분 教會職分

Deacon 집사 執事   deaconess 권사 勸師

Elder 장로 長老   Teacher 교사 教師

Church Organization 교회 기관 教會機關

Church Choir 성가대 聖歌隊   부인회 婦人會

Sunday School   Young Man Group
주일 학교 主日學校   청년회 靑年會

Women of the Church

Worship Service 예배 禮拜

Apostle Creed
사도신경 使徒信經

Benediction 축도 祝禱

Bible Reading
성경 봉독 聖經奉讀

Bible Study
성경 공부 聖經工夫

Hymn 찬송 讚頌

Lord's Prayer

주기도문 主祈禱文

Offering 헌금 獻金

Prayer 기도 祈禱

Responsive Reading
교독문 交讀文

Revival Service
부흥회 復興會

Sermon, Preaching
설교 說教

Christian Year 교회력 教會曆

Christmas 성탄절 聖誕節   Easter 부활절 復活節

Lent 사순절 四旬節   Thanksgiving
Pentecost 오순절 五旬節   추수감사절 秋收感謝節

Holy Bible 성경 聖經

Acts 사도행전 使徒行傳   New Testament
Chronicles 역대 상하 歷代上下   신약 성서 新約聖書
Deuteronomy 신명기 申命記   Numbers 민수기 民數記
Ecclesiastes 전도서 傳道書   Old Testament
Exodus 출애굽기 出～記   구약 성서 舊約聖書
Genesis 창세기 創世記   Proverbs 잠언 箴言
Gospel 복음서 福音書   Psalm 시편 詩篇
Kings 열왕기 상하 列王記上下

The Holy Bible Contents 성경 전서 목록 聖經全書目錄
1. Old Testament Contents

Genesis	창세기	(창)	50장
Exodus	출애굽기	(출)	40장
Leviticus	레위기	(레)	27장
Numbers	민수기	(민)	36장
Deuteronomy	신명기	(신)	34장
Joshua	여호수아	(수)	24장
Judges	사사기	(삿)	21장
Ruth	룻기	(룻)	4장
1 Samuel	사무엘상	(삼상)	31장
2 Samuel	사무엘하	(삼하)	24장
1 Kings	열왕기상	(왕상)	22장
2 Kings	열왕기하	(왕하)	25장
1 Chronicles	역대상	(대상)	29장
2 Chronicles	역대하	(대하)	36장
Ezra	에스라	(스)	10장
Nehemiah	느헤미야	(느)	13장
Esther	에스더	(에)	10장

Job	욥기	(욥)	42장
Psalms	시편	(시)	150장
Proverbs	잠언	(잠)	31장
Ecclesiastes	전도서	(전)	12장
Song of Songs	아가서	(아)	8장
Isaiah	이사야	(사)	66장
Jeremiah	예레미야	(렘)	52장
Lamentations	예레미야애가	(애)	5장
Ezekiel	에스겔	(겔)	48장
Daniel	다니엘	(단)	12장
Hosea	호세아	(호)	14장
Joel	요엘	(욜)	12장
Amos	아모스	(암)	9장
Obadiah	오바댜	(옵)	1장
Jonah	요나	(욘)	4장
Micah	미가	(미)	7장
Nahum	나훔	(나)	3장
Habakkuk	하박국	(합)	3장
Zephaniah	스바냐	(습)	3장
Haggai	학개	(학)	2장
Zechariah	스가랴	(슥)	14장
Malachi	말라기	(말)	4장

2. New Testament Contents

Matthew	마태복음	(마)	28장
Mark	마가복음	(막)	16장
Luke	누가복음	(눅)	24장
John	요한복음	(요)	21장
Acts	사도행전	(사)	28장
Romans	로마서	(롬)	16장
1 Corinthians	고린도전서	(고전)	16장
2 Corinthians	고린도후서	(고후)	13장
Galatians	갈라디아서	(갈)	6장

Ephesians	에베소서	(엡)	6장
Philippians	빌립보서	(빌)	4장
Colossians	골로새서	(골)	4장
1 Thessalonians	데살로니가전서	(살전)	5장
2 Thessalonians	데살로니가후서	(살후)	3장
1 Timothy	디모데전서	(딤전)	6장
2 Timothy	디모데후서	(딤전)	4장
Titus	디도서	(딛)	3장
Philemon	빌레몬서	(몬)	1장
Hebrews	히브리서	(히)	13장
James	야고보서	(약)	5장
1 Peter	베드로전서	(벧전)	5장
2 Peter	베드로후서	(벧후)	3장
1 John	요한일서	(요일)	5장
2 John	요한이서	(요이)	1장
3 John	요한삼서	(요삼)	1장
Jude	유다서	(유)	1장
Revelation	요한계시록	(계)	22장

올 래 (rae)
come

Jesus was crucified at Calvary. There were three crosses: Big man on the central cross and either side two thieves. One thief said to Jesus, "Remember me Jesus, when you **come** as King." Jesus said to him, "I promise you that today you will be in paradise with me. (*Luke* 23)

Adam and Eve in the garden of Eden. The Lord God called the man, and said to him, "where are you?" And he said I heard the sound of Thee in the garden, but I was afraid because I was naked, and I hid myself (*Gen.* 3:9, 10). At this point, they **came** forth from among the trees.

Hunmin chŏng-ŭm (Proper Sounds to Instruct the People), the origin of the Korean alphabet, Han-gŭl, devised by King Sejong in 1443.

THE KOREAN ALPHABET WITH ROMANIZATION
한글 기본 음절표

모음 V. 자음 C.	ㅏ a	ㅑ ya	ㅓ ŏ	ㅕ yŏ	ㅗ o	ㅛ yo	ㅜ u	ㅠ yu	ㅡ ŭ	ㅣ i
ㄱ k	가 ka	갸 kya	거 kŏ	겨 kyŏ	고 ko	교 kyo	구 ku	규 kyu	그 kŭ	기 ki
ㄴ n	나 na	냐 ya	너 nŏ	녀 nyŏ	노 no	뇨 nyo	누 nu	뉴 nyu	느 nŭ	니 ni
ㄷ t(d)	다 ta	댜 tya	더 tŏ	뎌 tyŏ	도 to	됴 tyo	두 tu	듀 tyu	드 tŭ	디 ti
ㄹ r(l)	라 ra	랴 rya	러 rŏ	려 ryŏ	로 ro	료 ryo	루 ru	류 ryu	르 rŭ	리 ri
ㅁ m	마 ma	먀 mya	머 mŏ	며 myŏ	모 mo	묘 myo	무 mu	뮤 myu	므 mŭ	미 mi
ㅂ p(b)	바 pa	뱌 pya	버 pŏ	벼 pyŏ	보 po	뵤 pyo	부 pu	뷰 pyu	브 pŭ	비 pi
ㅅ s	사 sa	샤 sya	서 sŏ	셔 syŏ	소 so	쇼 syo	수 su	슈 syu	스 sŭ	시 shi
ㅇ ng	아 a	야 ya	어 ŏ	여 yŏ	오 o	요 yo	우 u	유 yu	으 ŭ	이 i
ㅈ ch	자 cha	쟈 chya	저 chŏ	져 chyŏ	조 cho	죠 chyo	주 chu	쥬 chyu	즈 chŭ	지 chi
ㅊ ch'	차 ch'a	챠 ch'ya	처 ch'ŏ	쳐 ch'yŏ	초 ch'o	쵸 ch'yo	추 ch'u	츄 ch'yu	츠 ch'ŭ	치 ch'i
ㅋ k'	카 k'a	캬 k'ya	커 k'ŏ	켜 k'yŏ	코 k'o	쿄 k'yo	쿠 k'u	큐 k'yu	크 k'ŭ	키 k'i
ㅌ t'	타 t'a	탸 t'ya	터 t'ŏ	텨 t'yŏ	토 t'o	툐 t'yo	투 t'u	튜 t'yu	트 t'ŭ	티 t'i
ㅍ p'	파 p'a	퍄 p'ya	퍼 p'ŏ	펴 p'yŏ	포 p'o	표 p'yo	푸 p'u	퓨 p'yu	프 p'ŭ	피 p'i
ㅎ h	하 ha	햐 hya	허 hŏ	혀 hyŏ	호 ho	효 hyo	후 hu	휴 hyu	흐 hŭ	히 hi

1. The Korean Alphabet—Names and Sounds

Simple Vowels

Letters	Names	Romanization	English sounds
ㅏ	아	a	as *ah*
ㅓ	어	ŏ	as h*u*t
ㅗ	오	o	as *oh*
ㅜ	우	u	as d*o*
ㅡ	으	ŭ	as tak*e*n
ㅣ	이	i	as *i*nk
ㅐ	애	ae	as h*a*nd
ㅔ	에	e	as m*e*t
ㅚ	외	oe	as K*ö*ln

Compound Vowels

Letters	Names	Romanization	English sounds
ㅑ	야	ya	as *ya*rd
ㅕ	여	yŏ	as *yea*rn
ㅛ	요	yo	as *yo*ke
ㅠ	유	yu	as *you*
ㅒ	얘	yae	as *ya*m
ㅖ	예	ye	as *ye*s
ㅟ	위	wi	as *wi*eld
ㅢ	의	ŭi	as tak*e*n + *we*
ㅘ	와	wa	as *wa*n
ㅙ	왜	wae	as *wa*g
ㅝ	워	wo	as *wo*n
ㅞ	웨	we	as *we*t

Simple Consonants

Letters	Names	Romanization	English sounds
ㄱ	기역	k(g)	as *k*ing or *gr*ocer
ㄴ	니은	n	as *n*ame
ㄷ	디귿	t(d)	as *t*oy or *d*epend
ㄹ	리을	r(l)	as *r*ain or *l*ily
ㅁ	미음	m	as *m*other
ㅂ	비읍	p(b)	as *p*in or *b*ook
ㅅ	시옷	s(sh)	as *s*ome
ㅇ	이응	ng	as *ah* or ki*ng*
ㅈ	지읒	ch(j)	as *J*ohn
ㅊ	치읓	ch'	as *ch*ur*ch*
ㅋ	키읔	k'	as *k*ite
ㅌ	티읕	t'	as *t*ank
ㅍ	피읖	p'	as *p*um*p*
ㅎ	히읗	h	as *h*igh

Double Consonants

Letters	Names	Romanization	English sounds
ㄲ	쌍기역	kk	as s*k*y or Ja*ck*
ㄸ	쌍디귿	tt	as s*t*ay
ㅃ	쌍비읍	pp	as s*p*y
ㅆ	쌍시옷	ss	as e*ss*ence
ㅉ	쌍지읒	tch	as *j*oy

초성 (初聲)

가

초성 (初聲)   중성 (中聲)

각

종성 (終聲)

2. Korean National Anthem*

Translated from the Korean words of Yun Ch'i-ho

1. Till Paektu Mountain[1] wears away
   or the Eastern Sea has dried,

   May Korea prosper forever,
   God be at our side.

2. As armoured, stand the Namsan[2] pines,
   changeless thru winds and frost.

   Strong and dauntless, Korea's spirit
   Is unchanging too!

(refrain)
   Flow'ring *mugunghwa*,[3] this our symbol
   o'er three thousand *ri*[4]

   We'll preserve our beautiful homeland,
   Thru eternity.

1. Paektu Mountain(Whitehead), Korea's highest peak, is near the Yalu River in northern Korea.
2. Namsan is South Mountain on the center of Seoul City.
3. The *mugunghwa*, or rose of Sharon, is the national flower of Korea, and means, literally, "flower of eternity."
4. *Ri* is a measurement of distance equivalent of about 1/3 mile.

* The Korean national anthem was adopted after inauguration of the Republic of Korea in 1948.

애 국 가
Aegukka

안 익태 작곡
Music by Ik-t'ae An

1. 동 해 물 과 백 두 산 이 마 르 고닳 도 록
2. 남 산 위 에 저 소 나 무 철 갑 을 두 른 듯
1. Tong hae mulgwa Paektu sa ni ma rŭgo tal t'o rok
2. Namsan wi e chŏ so na mu ch'ŏl gabŭl tu rŭn dŭt

하 느 님 이 보 우 - 하 사 우 리 나 라 만 세
바 람 서 리 불 변 - 함 은 우 리 기 상 일 세
Ha nŭ nim i po- u -ha sa u ri na ra man se
Pa ram sŏ ri pul byŏn ham ŭn u ri ki sang il se

무 - 궁 화 삼 - 천 리 화 려 강 - 산
Mu - gung hwa sam - ch'ŏlli hwaryŏ kang - san

대 한 사 람 대 한 - 으 로 길 이 보 전 하 세
Tae han sa ram tae han - ŭ ro ki ri po jŏn ha se

3. 가을 하늘 공활한데 높고 구름 없이
　 밝은 달은 우리 가슴 일편단심일세
4. 이 기상과 이 맘으로 충성을 다하여
　 괴로우나 즐거우나 나라 사랑하세

3. Kaŭl hanŭl konghwalhande nopko kurŭm ŏpshi
　 Palgŭn tarŭn uri kasŭm ilp'yŏndanshimilse
4. Yi kisanggwa yi mamŭro ch'ungsŏng-ŭl tahayŏ
　 Koerouna chŭlgŏuna nara saranghase

3. The National Flower

Rose of Sharon (*mugunghwa*)

In every characteristic of strength and beauty and profusion, the lovely rose of Sharon, is truly the national flower of Korea.

It flourishes in full abundance in every type of soil throughout the Korean peninsula. It first blossoms each year in early July, and the full glory of its profuse flowering continues into the autumn until its large and hardy shrubs are put to rest for the winter by October's frost.

Since time immemorial, the rose of Sharon has been loved and cherished by all Koreans. And because they found its inherent hardihood and persistence so symbolic of the national character, it was inevitable that they would take its lovely blossom to their hearts as their national flower, which they named *mugunghwa*, the flower of immortality.

4. The National Flag

T'aegŭkki

One of the world's most beautiful flags, that of the Republic of Korea, has in its center a circle of brilliant red and blue on a white background. Both the circle and the black bar designs in the corners are rich in symbolism.

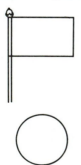

To begin with, the ground of the flag is white. White means purity. That is why Koreans are called the "white-clad people." Consequently, the white ground of the T'aegŭkki is the symbol of justice, humanity and peace.

The circle represents the Absolute, or the essential unity of all being. *T'aegŭk* (太極, great polarity) signifies the origin of the Universe.

The Universe is but one. All the phenomena are composed of one.

T'aegŭk is to be divided into two *ŭi*(儀, divine gender).

 The *yang*(陽) and *ŭm*(陰) divisions within the circle represent eternal duality; good and evil, male and female, night and day, life and death, being and not being, etc. The presence of duality within the Absolute indicates the paradox of life and the impossibility of ever comprehending it completely.

The bar designs in the four corners have many meanings. We call them four *kwae*(卦, divine diagram).

 called *kŏn*, stands for heaven or south;

called *kon*, stands for earth or north;

called *ri*, stands for sun or east;

called *kam*, stands for moon or west.

In the 19th year of King Kojong's reign in July 1882—when he dispatched Mr. Pak Yŏng-hyo to Japan as Korean envoy, this T'aegŭkki was hoisted on the boat Meiji Maru on which he and his suite traveled.

In the 24th year of the reign of the Emperor Kojong, in 1887, Mr. Pak Chŏng-yang was appointed Korean minister to Washington, and he embarked at Inch'ŏn (Chemulp'o) for the U.S.A. At that time the T'aegŭkki was hoisted aboard the American cruiser Oklahoma.

In this manner, this T'aegŭkki was hoisted in the east and the west, and was recognized accordingly as the Korean flag at home and abroad.

5. Character Discriminations

佳 가 佳作(가작)
往 왕 往來(왕래)
住 주 住宅(주택)

各 각 各種(각종)
名 명 姓名(성명)

間 간 間接(간접)
問 문 質問(질문)

干 간 干城(간성)
于 우 于今(우금)
千 천 千里(천리)

巨 거 巨大(거대)
臣 신 臣下(신하)

犬 견 忠犬(충견)
大 대 大小(대소)
太 태 太初(태초)

決 결 決心(결심)
快 쾌 快樂(쾌락)

拘 구 拘束(구속)
狗 구 走狗(주구)

考 고 參考(참고)
老 로 老人(노인)

苦 고 苦腦(고뇌)
若 약 若干(약간)

橋 교 橋梁(교량)
矯 교 矯正(교정)

起 기 起床(기상)
赴 부 赴任(부임)

技 기 技術(기술)
枝 지 枝葉(지엽)

開 개 開拓(개척)
聞 문 見聞(견문)

客 객 主客(주객)
容 용 容貌(용모)

斤 근 斤量(근량)
斥 척 排斥(배척)

營 영 營業(영업)
螢 형 螢光(형광)

薄 박 薄氷(박빙)
簿 부 名簿(명부)

郡 군 郡守(군수)
群 군 群衆(군중)

情 정 感情(감정)
清 청 清潔(청결)

須 수 必須(필수)
順 순 順從(순종)

挑 도 挑發(도발)
桃 도 桃李(도리)

俗 속 俗世(속세)
裕 유 裕福(유복)

燥 조 乾燥(건조)
操 조 操縱(조종)

婢 비 奴婢(노비)
碑 비 碑石(비석)

如 여 如意(여의)
奴 노 奴婢(노비)
好 호 好感(호감)

師 사 師弟(사제)
帥 수 將帥(장수)

思 사 思考(사고)
恩 은 恩功(은공)

飯 반 白飯(백반)
飲 음 飲食(음식)

象 상 象牙(상아)
衆 중 群衆(군중)

捨 사 取捨(취사)
拾 습 拾得(습득)

眠 면 多眠(동면)
眼 안 眼目(안목)

小 소 小隊(소대)
少 소 少年(소년)

栗 률 生栗(생률)
粟 속 粟米(속미)

免 면 任免(임면)
兎 토 兎皮(토피)

歎 탄 歎息(탄식)	刀 도 短刀(단도)	由 유 理由(이유)
歡 환 歡呼(환호)	刃 인 刃創(인창)	田 전 田畓(전답)
旅 려 旅客(여객)	曰 왈 曰可(왈가)	明 명 光明(광명)
族 족 民族(민족)	日 일 日課(일과)	朋 붕 朋友(붕우)
待 대 待機(대기)	午 오 午前(오전)	宣 선 宣布(선포)
侍 시 侍女(시녀)	牛 우 牛馬(우마)	宜 의 便宜(편의)
徒 도 學徒(학도)	句 구 句節(구절)	侯 후 諸侯(제후)
從 종 服從(복종)	旬 순 下旬(하순)	候 후 氣候(기후)
具 구 具備(구비)	己 기 自己(자기)	佛 불 佛敎(불교)
貝 패 貝物(패물)	巳 사 乙巳(을사)	拂 불 拂子(불자)
九 구 九拾(구십)	已 이 已往(이왕)	綠 록 綠色(녹색)
丸 환 丸藥(환약)	戊 무 戊種(무종)	緣 연 緣分(연분)
矛 모 矛戟(모극)	戌 술 戌時(술시)	墨 묵 墨畫(묵화)
予 여 予奪(여탈)	成 성 成功(성공)	黑 흑 黑幕(흑막)
深 심 水深(수심)	瓦 와 瓦解(와해)	栽 재 栽培(재배)
探 탐 探索(탐색)	互 호 相互(상호)	裁 재 裁斷(재단)
戀 련 戀慕(연모)	士 사 士林(사림)	恨 한 恨歎(한탄)
蠻 만 蠻勇(만용)	土 토 土木(토목)	限 한 限定(한정)
爪 조 爪甲(조갑)	亦 역 亦時(역시)	刑 형 刑罰(형벌)
瓜 과 瓜菜(과채)	赤 적 赤色(적색)	形 형 形象(형상)
摘 적 指摘(지적)	島 도 島民(도민)	搖 요 搖動(요동)
滴 적 餘滴(여적)	烏 오 烏口(오구)	遙 요 遙遠(요원)
適 적 適當(적당)	鳥 조 鳥獸(조수)	謠 요 民謠(민요)
陸 륙 陸地(육지)	甲 갑 甲兵(갑병)	粉 분 粉末(분말)
睦 목 和睦(화목)	申 신 申告(신고)	紛 분 紛爭(분쟁)
隣 린 隣近(인근)	今 금 今年(금년)	弦 현 弦月(현월)
憐 련 憐憫(연민)	令 령 命令(명령)	絃 현 絃樂(현악)

與	여	授與(수여)	書	서	書堂(서당)	功	공	功勞(공로)
興	흥	興亡(흥망)	晝	주	晝夜(주야)	巧	교	巧妙(교묘)
			畵	화	畵室(화실)	切	절	切斷(절단)
漸	점	漸次(점차)						
慚	참	無慚(무참)	浩	호	浩茫(호망)	代	대	代身(대신)
			活	활	生活(생활)	伐	벌	征伐(정벌)
衰	쇠	盛衰(성쇠)						
哀	애	哀歡(애환)	遣	견	派遣(파견)	辛	신	辛苦(신고)
			遺	유	遺産(유산)	幸	행	幸福(행복)
設	설	建設(건설)						
說	설	說敎(설교)	幣	폐	幣物(폐물)	閉	폐	閉門(폐문)
			弊	폐	弊端(폐단)	閑	한	閑暇(한가)
暑	서	避暑(피서)						
署	서	官署(관서)	頃	경	頃刻(경각)	何	하	如何(여하)
			項	항	項鎖(항쇄)	河	하	河川(하천)
享	향	享樂(향락)						
亨	형	亨通(형통)	遂	수	完遂(완수)	券	권	福券(복권)
			逐	축	驅逐(구축)	卷	권	卷數(권수)
玉	옥	玉石(옥석)						
王	왕	王家(왕가)	揚	양	揚名(양명)	北	북	北方(북방)
壬	임	壬午(임오)	楊	양	楊柳(양류)	比	비	比例(비례)
			場	장	場所(장소)	此	차	此後(차후)
分	분	分數(분수)						
兮	혜	耶兮(야혜)	堤	제	堤防(제방)	人	인	人口(인구)
			提	제	提携(제휴)	入	입	入口(입구)
末	말	末日(말일)				八	팔	八道(팔도)
未	미	未着(미착)	氷	빙	氷雪(빙설)			
			水	수	食水(식수)	兩	량	兩立(양립)
旦	단	元旦(원단)	永	영	永久(영구)	雨	우	風雨(풍우)
且	차	苟且(구차)						
			夫	부	夫君(부군)	毫	호	秋毫(추호)
壞	괴	破壞(파괴)	矢	시	弓矢(궁시)	豪	호	豪傑(호걸)
壤	양	土壤(토양)	失	실	失物(실물)			
懷	회	懷疑(회의)				壇	단	祭壇(제단)
			困	곤	疲困(피곤)	檀	단	檀君(단군)
墳	분	墳墓(분묘)	囚	수	囚人(수인)			
憤	분	憤怒(분노)	因	인	因習(인습)	堂	당	堂號(당호)
						當	당	當否(당부)

密 밀 密度(밀도)
蜜 밀 蜜語(밀어)

漫 만 漫評(만평)
慢 만 慢心(만심)

側 측 側近(측근)
測 측 測量(측량)

慮 려 考慮(고려)
廬 려 廬舍(여사)
虜 로 虜掠(노략)
盧 로 盧弓(노궁)

雄 웅 雄辯(웅변)
維 유 維新(유신)
唯 유 唯物(유물)
惟 유 思惟(사유)
雉 치 雉鷄(치계)

仰 앙 信仰(신앙)
抑 억 抑留(억류)

受 수 受容(수용)
愛 애 愛情(애정)

防 방 防衛(방위)
妨 방 妨害(방해)

騰 등 騰貴(등귀)
謄 등 謄寫(등사)
勝 승 勝利(승리)

殘 잔 殘額(잔액)
淺 천 深淺(심천)

陣 진 陣地(진지)
陳 진 陳列(진열)

官 관 官國(관민)
宮 궁 宮女(궁녀)

杳 묘 杳然(묘연)
早 조 早朝(조조)
旱 한 旱害(한해)

綱 강 綱領(강령)
網 망 網羅(망라)

每 매 每日(매일)
侮 모 侮辱(모욕)
海 해 海洋(해양)
悔 회 悔改(회개)

揮 휘 揮毫(휘호)
輝 휘 光輝(광휘)

賣 매 賣却(매각)
買 매 買收(매수)

寄 기 寄宿(기숙)
奇 기 奇異(기이)

續 속 續開(속개)
績 적 紡績(방적)

持 지 所持(소지)
特 특 特殊(특수)

飾 식 修飾(수식)
餘 여 餘暇(여가)

掘 굴 發掘(발굴)
拙 졸 拙劣(졸렬)

識 식 知識(지식)
織 직 織工(직공)
職 직 職業(직업)

幕 막 天幕(천막)
慕 모 追慕(추모)
募 모 募集(모집)
暮 모 暮雪(모설)
墓 묘 墓地(묘지)

能 능 能力(능력)
熊 웅 熊膽(웅담)
態 태 態度(태도)

冶 야 陶冶(도야)
治 치 政治(정치)

衝 충 衝突(충돌)
衡 형 銓衡(전형)

始 시 始作(시작)
殆 태 殆半(태반)

慨 개 慨歎(개탄)
概 개 概念(개념)
旣 기 旣往(기왕)

錦 금 錦繡(금수)
綿 면 連綿(연면)

觀 관 觀察(관찰)
勸 권 勸學(권학)

減 감 減少(감소)
滅 멸 滅亡(멸망)

平 평 平安(평안)
乎 호 斷乎(단호)

堅 견 堅固(견고)
腎 신 腎臟(신장)
賢 현 賢明(현명)

6. Characters with Multiple Readings

降 { 내릴   강   昇降 (승강)
     항복할   항   降服 (항복)

更 { 다시   갱   更生 (갱생)
     시각   경   三更 (삼경)

見 { 볼   견   見聞 (견문)
     드러날   현   見齒 (현치)

契 { 맺을   계   契約 (계약)
     나라이름   글   契丹 (글안)

句 { 글귀   구   句讀 (구두)
     귀절   귀   句節 (귀절)

龜 { 땅이름   구   龜浦 (구포)
     거북   귀   龜船 (귀선)
     터질   균   龜裂 (균열)

金 { 쇠   금   金銀 (금은)
     성   김   金氏 (김씨)

豈 { 어찌   기   豈敢 (기감)
     승전악   개   豈樂 (개락)

內 { 안   내   內外 (내외)
     여관   나   內人 (나인)

奈 { 어찌   내   奈何 (내하)
     어찌   나   奈落 (나락)

茶 { 차   다   茶房 (다방)
     차   차   茶禮 (차례)

糖 { 엿   당   糖分 (당분)
     엿   탕   砂糖 (사탕)

度 { 법도   도   制度 (제도)
     헤아릴   탁   度地 (탁지)

讀 { 읽을   독   讀書 (독서)
     귀절   두   吏讀 (이두)

洞 { 골   동   洞穴 (동혈)
     통할   통   洞察 (통찰)

樂 { 즐길   락   苦樂 (고락)
     풍류   악   音樂 (음악)
     좋아할   요   樂山 (요산)

率 { 비율   률   能率 (능률)
     거느릴   솔   統率 (통솔)

反 { 돌이킬   반   反擊 (반격)
     뒤칠   번   反畓 (번답)

復 { 회복할   복   回復 (회복)
     다시   부   復活 (부활)

否 { 아닐   부   否定 (부정)
     막힐   비   否塞 (비색)

北 { 북녘   북   南北 (남북)
     달아날   배   敗北 (패배)

射 { 쏠   사   射擊 (사격)
     벼슬이름   야   僕射 (복야)

邪 { 간사할   사   正邪 (정사)
     어조사   야   怨邪 (원야)

殺 { 죽일   살   殺生 (살생)
     감할   쇄   相殺 (상쇄)

狀	형상	상	狀態(상태)	刺	찌를	자	刺客(자객)
	문서	장	賞狀(상장)		찌를	척	刺殺(척살)
塞	변방	새	要塞(요새)	著	나타낼	저	著述(저술)
	막힐	색	語塞(어색)		붙을	착	著色(착색)
索	찾을	색	思索(사색)	切	끊을	절	切斷(절단)
	쓸쓸할	삭	索莫(삭막)		모두	체	一切(일체)
說	말씀	설	說明(설명)	齊	가지런할	제	整齊(정제)
	달랠	세	遊說(유세)		재계할	재	齊戒(재계)
省	살필	성	反省(반성)	辰	별	진	辰宿(진수)
	덜	생	省略(생략)		날	신	生辰(생신)
衰	쇠할	쇠	衰弱(쇠약)	車	수레	차	車庫(차고)
	상복	최	齊衰(자최)		수레	거	車馬(거마)
數	셀	수	數式(수식)	參	참여할	참	參席(참석)
	자주	삭	數數(삭삭)		석	삼	參等(삼등)
宿	잘	숙	投宿(투숙)	拓	열	척	開拓(개척)
	별	수	星宿(성수)		밀칠	탁	拓本(탁본)
拾	주울	습	拾得(습득)	則	법	칙	規則(규칙)
	열	십	五拾(오십)		곧	즉	然則(연즉)
氏	성씨	씨	姓氏(성씨)	沈	잠길	침	沈沒(침몰)
	나라이름	지	月氏(월지)		성	심	沈氏(심씨)
食	먹을	식	飮食(음식)	宅	집	택	住宅(주택)
	밥	사	疏食(소사)		댁	댁	宅內(댁내)
識	알	식	知識(지식)	便	편할	편	便利(편리)
	기록할	지	標識(표지)		오줌	변	便所(변소)
惡	악할	악	惡人(악인)	暴	사나울	포	暴惡(포악)
	미워할	오	憎惡(증오)		드러날	폭	暴露(폭로)
易	바꿀	역	交易(교역)	幅	폭	폭	大幅(대폭)
	쉬울	이	容易(용이)		폭	복	幅巾(복건)

合	함할	합	合邦(합방)	畫	그림	화	圖畫(도화)
	흡	흡	五合(오흡)		꾀할	획	計畫(계획)
行	다닐	행	行路(행로)	活	살	활	生活(생활)
	항렬	항	行列(항렬)		물소리	괄	活活(괄괄)

방위(方位)
DIRECTION

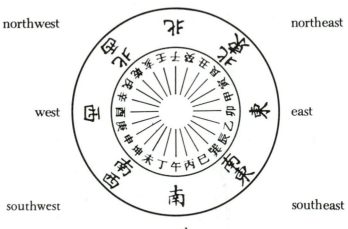

PHONETIC INDEX

Okp'yŏn. A Chinese-character word-book in which words are looked up by the radical and the number of strokes peculiar to the Chinese character.

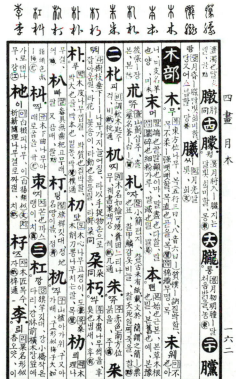

字音索引 Phonetic Index

(In *Han-gŭl* alphabetical order)

工 장인 61	鍋 노구솥	廣 넓을 141	絞 목맬	龜 땅이름 309
公 공변될 80	**[곽]**	匡 바를	較 비교할 312	具 갖출 223
孔 구멍	郭 성	光 빛 53	嬌 아름다울	柩 관
功 공 131	廓 클	狂 미칠	膠 아교	俱 함께
共 한가지 177	**[관]**	曠 휑할 94	橋 다리 83	救 구원할 314
攻 칠	官 벼슬 139	鑛 쇳돌 65	矯 바로잡을 140	球 지구 64
供 이바지 210	冠 갓 106	**[괘]**	**[구]**	溝 개천
空 빌 63	菅 왕골	卦 점괘 329	九 아홉 167	鳩 비둘기
恐 두려울	貫 꿸	**[괴]**	口 입 164	構 지을 230
恭 공경할 170	棺 널	怪 기이할	久 오랠 332	驅 몰 130
貢 바칠	款 정성스러울	塊 흙덩이	仇 원수	駒 망아지
控 당길	寬 너그러울	魁 괴수	區 나눌 76	鉤 갈고리 37
[과]	慣 익숙할 107	壞 무너뜨릴 332	丘 언덕 64	購 살
戈 창 270	管 대롱 67	**[굉]**	句 글귀 334	軀 몸
瓜 오이 194	關 관계할 209	宏 클	苟 구차할 332	懼 두려울
果 과실 192	館 객사 145	轟 수레모는소리	舊 옛 72	**[국]**
科 과정 163	觀 볼 53	**[교]**	臼 절구 308	局 판 61
菓 과실	罐 물동이	巧 교묘할 275	究 궁리할 201	國 나라 138
過 지날 217	**[괄]**	狡 교활할	灸 그을	菊 국화
誇 자랑할	刮 긁을	交 사귈 301	求 구할 114	麴 누룩
寡 적을 143	括 쌀	郊 들	拘 잡을 330	**[군]**
夥 많을	恝 소홀히할	校 학교 173	狗 개 124	君 임금 180
課 구실 55	**[광]**	教 가르칠 199	歐 노래할 253	軍 군사 262

金 성 141	念 생각 234	茶 차 70	**[답]**	**[덕]**
[나]	**[녕]**	多 많을 40	沓 물끓어 넘을 331	德 큰 78
奈 어찌 334	寧 편안할 219	**[단]**	畓 논 68	**[도]**
[난]	**[노]**	丹 붉을 334	答 대답 233	刀 칼 231
暖 따뜻할	奴 종 330	旦 아침 48	踏 밟을	圖 그림 207
難 어려울 80	努 힘쓸 156	團 둥글 108	**[당]**	到 이를 195
[날]	怒 성낼 279	但 다만	當 마땅할 259	度 법 232
捺 손으로 누를 37	**[농]**	單 홀 231	唐 나라	挑 끌어낼 330
[남]	農 농사 69	段 층계 151	黨 무리 81	逃 도망할 92
男 사내 177	濃 걸쭉할	斷 끊을 234	堂 집 213	倒 넘어질
南 남녘 254	**[뇌]**	短 짧을 236	棠 팥배나무	島 섬 113
[납]	惱 번뇌할	端 끝 116	糖 엿 62	徒 무리 286
納 들일 262	腦 머릿골 330	壇 제터 223	**[대]**	桃 복숭아 193
[내]	**[뇨]**	檀 박달나무 332	大 큰 245	途 길 133
乃 이에	尿 오줌 137	鍛 쇠불릴	代 대신 301	悼 슬퍼할
內 안 251	**[능]**	**[달]**	對 대답할 254	盜 도둑
奈 어찌 334	能 능할 35	達 사무칠	待 기다릴 298	萄 포도 283
耐 견딜 112	**[니]**	**[담]**	帶 띠 291	都 도읍 158
[녀]	尼 여승	擔 짐 313	袋 자루	陶 질그릇 333
女 계집 178	泥 진흙	膽 쓸개 333	貸 빌릴	渡 건널
[년]	**[닉]**	淡 물맑을 6	臺 돈대 281	跳 뛸 141
年 해 48	匿 숨을	談 말씀 284	隊 떼 264	道 길 77
[념]	**[다]**	曇 구름낄	戴 일	塗 진흙

稻	벼	凍	얼	等	가지런할 211	濫	물넘칠	梁	들보 155
導	인도할 269	桐	오동나무	燈	등불 141	藍	쪽	量	헤아릴 245
禱	빌 285	胴	큰창자	謄	베낄 333	**[랍]**		諒	믿을
蹈	밟을 281	動	움직일 161	藤	등나무	蠟	밀	輛	수레
[독]		棟	마룻대	騰	오를 333	**[랑]**		糧	양식
毒	독할 268	童	아이 110	**[라]**		郞	사내 269	**[려]**	
獨	홀로 253	銅	구리 22	裸	벌거벗을	娘	작은아씨	勵	근면할
督	독촉할 312	瞳	눈동자	羅	벌릴 40	朗	달밝을	呂	성
讀	읽을 36	**[두]**		**[락]**		浪	물결	梠	종려나무 87
篤	도타울	斗	말	洛	낙수 267	狼	이리 118	戾	어기어질
[돈]		豆	콩	落	떨어질 91	廊	행랑	侶	짝
沌	흐릴 52	讀	귀절 36	絡	이을	**[래]**		旅	나그네 146
豚	돼지 125	痘	마마	樂	즐거울 279	來	올 145	慮	생각 333
敦	도타울	頭	머리 77	酪	쇠젖	**[랭]**		麗	고울 160
頓	그칠 216	**[둔]**		諾	허락할	冷	찰 225	**[력]**	
惇	도타울	屯	모일	**[란]**		**[략]**		力	힘 61
[돌]		遁	달아날	亂	어지러울 251	掠	노략질할	歷	지날 200
突	우뚝할 125	鈍	둔할	卵	알 195	略	간략할 16	瀝	샐 208
[동]		**[득]**		蘭	난초	**[량]**		曆	책력 85
冬	겨울 218	得	얻을 107	欄	난간	兩	둘 116	**[련]**	
同	한가지 69	**[등]**		**[람]**		良	어질 148	戀	생각할 331
東	동녘 252	灯	맹렬한불꽃	籃	들바구니 172	亮	밝을	連	이을 209
洞	고을	登	오를 65	覽	볼 250	涼	서늘할	煉	달굴

蓮 연꽃	靈 신령 313	[롱]	淚 눈물	[률]
練 익힐 107	嶺 재	弄 희롱할	累 더할	律 법 313
憐 불쌍히여길 287	齡 나이	瀧 적실	樓 다락	率 셈이름 334
鍊 쇠불릴	[례]	聾 귀머울	漏 샐 75	栗 밤 193
聯 잇닿을 316	例 견줄 182	籠 새장 101	屢 여러	慄 쭈그릴
輦 임금의수레 103	禮 예도 152	[뢰]	縷 실	[륭]
[렬]	[로]	牢 옥	[류]	隆 성할
列 벌릴 113	老 늙을 27	雷 우뢰 247	柳 버들 229	[륵]
劣 용렬할 333	勞 수고로울 124	賴 힘입을	榴 석류 193	肋 갈빗대
烈 매울	爐 화로	瀨 여울	流 흐를 76	[릉]
裂 찢을 128	路 길 77	[료]	留 머무를 234	凌 얼음
[렴]	虜 사로잡을 333	了 마칠	琉 유리돌	菱 마름
廉 청렴할	魯 노둔할	料 헤아릴 183	硫 석유황	陵 능
斂 거둘 222	蘆 갈대	僚 동관	溜 물흐를	綾 무늬
[렵]	露 이슬 59	寮 작은창	類 같을 101	[리]
獵 사냥할 72	[록]	遼 멀	謬 속일	吏 아전 266
[령]	鹿 사슴 126	瞭 밝을	[륙]	利 이로울 186
令 하여금 265	祿 녹	療 병고칠 234	六 여섯 115	李 오얏 193
玲 쟁그렁할	綠 초록 91	[룡]	陸 뭍 83	里 마을 330
蛉 잠자리 136	錄 기록할 159	龍 용 120	[륜]	厘 티끌 109
鈴 방울	麓 산기슭	[루]	倫 인륜 260	狸 삵괭이
零 떨어질	[론]	壘 진루	綸 푸른실끈	梨 배 103
領 거느릴 80	論 의론할 266	陋 더러울	輪 바퀴 269	理 다스릴 148

沒 빠질 55	嘸 말우물거릴	彌 활부릴	薄 엷을 330	坊 고을
殁 죽을	撫 어루만질	眉 눈썹 160	**[반]**	邦 나라 252
[몽]	霧 안개 60	美 아름다울 275	反 돌아올 271	芳 꽃다울 26
夢 꿈 257	**[묵]**	迷 희미할	半 절반 113	防 막을 155
蒙 입을	墨 먹 331	媚 아첨할	伴 짝	妨 해로울 171
[묘]	默 잠잠할	微 작을 61	返 돌아올	肪 기름 25
卯 토끼 119	**[문]**	謎 수수께끼	畔 밭도랑	房 방 26
妙 묘할 241	文 글월 201	**[민]**	班 반열 118	放 놓을 232
苗 싹 70	吻 입술	民 백성 113	般 일반	倣 본받을
秒 벼가시랭이	門 문 221	敏 민첩할	絆 옭아맬	彷 방황할 146
描 그릴	紋 무늬 67	悶 민망할	飯 밥 58	紡 길쌈 25
猫 고양이	蚊 모기 135	**[밀]**	搬 옮길	旁 넓을
墓 무덤 84	紊 얽힐	密 빽빽할 170	頒 반포할	訪 피할 90
廟 사당	問 물을 208	蜜 꿀 332	磐 너럭바위	傍 곁
[무]	聞 들을 168	**[박]**	盤 소반 236	**[배]**
戊 다섯째천간 331	**[물]**	朴 성 101	**[발]**	杯 술잔 285
茂 무성할	勿 말	拍 손뼉칠	拔 뺄 168	拜 절 213
武 호반 270	物 만물 80	搏 칠	勃 발끈할	背 등 261
畝 밭이랑	**[미]**	泊 배댈	發 필 53	倍 갑절
務 힘쓸 92	未 아닐 332	迫 핍박할	鉢 바리때	俳 광대 277
無 없을 113	米 쌀 184	舶 당도리	髮 터럭 149	配 나눌 172
貿 무역할 133	尾 꼬리 120	博 넓을 200	**[방]**	培 북돋울 331
舞 춤출 281	味 맛 164	縛 묶을	方 모 249	徘 어정거릴

排 물리칠 251	範 법 40	竝 아우를 24	複 겹옷	扶 붙들
陪 모실	**[법]**	柄 자루	馥 향기	斧 도끼
輩 무리 116	法 법 249	病 병들 287	覆 돌이킬	府 관청 73
賠 배상할	**[벽]**	屏 병풍 31	**[본]**	附 붙을
[백]	碧 푸를	瓶 병	本 근본 55	阜 언덕 308
白 흰 119	僻 편벽될	塀 담	**[봉]**	負 짐질
百 일백 260	劈 쪼갤	餠 떡 276	奉 받들 316	赴 다다를 243
伯 맏 137	壁 바람벽 276	**[보]**	封 봉할	俯 구부릴
柏 잣나무 193	癖 버릇	寶 보배 30	俸 녹	剖 쪼갤 233
[번]	**[변]**	步 걸음 111	峰 산봉우리 60	浮 뜰
番 차례 259	便 오줌 335	保 보존할 139	逢 만날	釜 가마
煩 번거로울	邊 가 72	報 갚을 56	捧 받들	副 버금
繁 성할 99	辨 분별할 312	普 넓을	棒 몽둥이 236	婦 며느리 175
飜 뒤칠 259	辯 말잘할 166	補 기울	蜂 벌 135	符 병부
[벌]	變 변할 36	輔 도울	鋒 칼날 270	部 나눌 201
伐 칠 267	**[별]**	譜 족보 142	鳳 봉황새 103	富 부자 263
閥 문벌 142	別 다를 295	**[복]**	縫 꿰맬	腑 내장
罰 벌줄 188	瞥 눈깜짝할	伏 엎드릴	**[부]**	腐 썩을 235
[범]	撇 오른쪽삐칠 37	服 입을 102	父 아비 172	敷 펼
凡 무릇	**[병]**	復 돌아올 53	夫 지아비 174	膚 피부 291
犯 범할 147	丙 남녘 336	福 복 188	付 줄	賦 구실 56
帆 배돛	兵 군사 263	腹 배	不 아닐 140	簿 문서 330
汎 뜨울	倂 나란할	僕 심부름꾼 334	否 아닐	**[북]**

北 북녁 255	棚 사다리	**[빈]**	邪 간사할 334	辭 말씀 205
[분]	**[비]**	牝 암짐승	私 사사로울 187	飼 먹이
分 나눌 63	比 견줄 35	貧 가난할 98	社 모일 190	獅 사자
扮 꾸밀	妃 왕비	賓 손 145	使 부릴 54	賜 줄
霧 안개 163	批 손으로칠 312	殯 염할 145	事 일 69	謝 사례할 271
奔 분주할 252	泌 샘물흐를	頻 자주	舍 집 86	**[삭]**
盆 동이 282	沸 끓을	**[빙]**	俟 기다릴	削 깎을 151
紛 분잡할 152	肥 살찔 121	氷 얼음 232	思 생각 127	鑠 쇠녹일 143
粉 가루 184	非 아닐 314	聘 청할	査 사실할 264	**[산]**
焚 불사를	卑 낮을	**[사]**	砂 모래 334	山 뫼 65
噴 뿜을	脾 지라 166	士 선비 104	唆 부추길	産 낳을 67
墳 무덤 84	婢 여종 330	巳 뱀 331	射 쏠 271	散 흩어질
憤 분할 235	飛 날 104	四 넉 30	師 스승 199	傘 우산 230
奮 떨칠	匪 악할 267	司 맡을 265	捨 버릴 292	算 셈 206
糞 똥 123	秘 비밀 214	寫 베낄 202	斜 비낄	酸 실 174
[불]	備 갖출 59	史 사기 312	蛇 뱀 132	**[살]**
不 아니 112	悲 슬플	仕 벼슬	赦 죄사할 314	殺 죽일 267
弗 말 133	琵 비파 275	死 죽을 140	奢 사치할	撒 헤쳐버릴
佛 부처 60	費 허비할 146	絲 실 229	斯 이	薩 보살
拂 떨칠 240	扉 사립짝	寺 절 65	祀 제사 84	**[삼]**
[붕]	碑 비석 84	似 같을	詞 말씀	三 셋 260
朋 벗 331	鼻 코 162	伺 살필	詐 간사할	杉 삼목
崩 산무너질	譬 비유할	沙 모래 67	嗣 이을	參 석 335

森 나무빽빽할 90	桑 뽕나무 243	庶 뭇	先 먼저 82	齧 깨물
[삽]	祥 상서	婿 사위 181	宣 베풀 313	**[섬]**
卅 서른	商 장사 300	暑 더위 332	扇 부채 281	閃 번쩍거릴 53
挿 꽂을	象 코끼리 127	鼠 쥐 116	旋 돌이킬	纖 가늘
澁 떫을	裳 치마 228	瑞 상서	蟬 매미 135	**[섭]**
[상]	**[쌍]**	署 쓸 332	船 배 226	涉 건널 301
常 떳떳할 148	雙 쌍 110	嶼 섬 113	善 착할 78	攝 겸할 314
爽 밝을	**[색]**	緒 실마리	羨 넘칠	**[성]**
喪 상사	色 빛 116	誓 맹세 315	尠 적을	成 이룰 270
傷 다칠 75	索 찾을 331	薯 마	禪 중	聲 소리 273
想 생각할 127	**[생]**	曙 새벽	煽 불붙일	姓 성 330
詳 자세할	生 날 68	**[석]**	線 실 53	性 성품 85
像 형상 127	牲 희생	夕 저녁 58	選 가릴 292	城 재 208
嘗 맛볼	甥 생질	石 돌 74	膳 반찬 238	星 별 57
箱 상자	**[서]**	析 나눌	鮮 밝을 256	省 살필 232
賞 상줄 153	西 서녁 253	昔 옛	繕 기울	盛 성할 99
償 갚을	抒 물자아올릴	席 자리 145	銑 무쇠	聖 성인 48
霜 서리 62	序 차례	惜 아낄	**[설]**	誠 정성 78
上 윗 242	敍 지을 161	釋 놓을 139	舌 혀 25	醒 술깰
床 평상 70	徐 천천히 269	潟 개펄	屑 조촐할	**[세]**
狀 형상 296	恕 용서할	錫 주석 22	設 베풀 61	世 인간 156
尙 오히려 190	書 글 203	**[선]**	雪 눈 62	洗 씻을 313
相 서로 334	逝 죽을	仙 신선 103	說 말씀 200	細 가늘 167

稅	구실 185	騷	흔들릴	衰	쇠할 99	粹	순전할	肅	엄숙할 214
賞	세낼 56	蘇	깨어날	**[쇄]**		袖	소매	塾	글방
勢	형세 287	**[속]**		刷	인쇄할 240	授	줄 199	熟	익을 194
歲	해 134	束	묶을 239	碎	부서질	須	잠간 330	**[순]**	
[소]		俗	풍속 53	鎖	자물쇠 332	遂	드디어 267	旬	열흘
小	작을 246	速	빠를 238	殺	감할 334	隨	따를	巡	돌 219
少	적을 295	屬	붙일 283	**[수]**		愁	근심 299	苟	풀이름
召	부를 313	續	이을 333	水	물 331	數	셈 206	盾	방패 270
沼	못	贖	죄면할 313	手	손 151	睡	잠잘	殉	따라죽을 314
所	바 217	**[손]**		收	걷을 258	酬	술권할	筍	죽순 97
昭	밝을	孫	손자 181	囚	가둘 140	需	음식 262	純	순전할
消	꺼질 239	損	상할	守	지킬 144	穗	이삭	淳	순박할 201
素	바탕 66	遜	겸손할 298	壽	목숨 89	誰	누구	循	돌
笑	웃을 162	**[솔]**		秀	빼어날 185	樹	나무 77	順	순할 163
巢	새집 105	率	거느릴 334	受	받을 153	獸	짐승 148	脣	입술 119
掃	비질할 282	蟀	귀뚜라미 136	垂	드리울	輸	보낼 62	馴	말순할
燒	불사를	**[송]**		帥	주장할 330	豎	세울 37	瞬	눈깜작할
疏	성길 335	松	소나무 89	蒐	모을 108	髓	뼛속기름	**[술]**	
訴	송사할	蚣	베짱이 135	首	머리 158	繡	수놓을 333	述	지을
塑	허수아비	送	보낼	修	닦을 315	**[숙]**		術	재주 151
蔬	나물 87	訟	송사할	搜	찾을	叔	아저씨	戌	개 331
搔	긁을	頌	기릴 316	嫂	형수 176	宿	잘 248	**[숭]**	
韶	아름다울	**[쇠]**		殊	다를 226	淑	맑을	崇	높을 314

[슬]				
膝 무릎	是 이	識 알 268	沈 성 335	惡 악할 335
[습]	柿 감 193	**[신]**	沁 물이름	愕 놀랄
拾 주울 330	柴 땔나무	申 납 51	甚 심할	握 잡을
習 익힐 107	屎 똥 137	迅 빠를	深 깊을 331	**[안]**
濕 젖을	屍 주검	伸 펼 175	尋 찾을	安 편안 219
襲 엄습할	時 때 238	臣 신하 330	審 살필 314	按 누를 251
[승]	視 볼 159	身 몸 149	**[십]**	岸 언덕 64
升 되	豉 메주 191	辛 매울 174	十 열 260	案 기안할 207
丞 도울	詩 귀글 317	信 믿을 153	辻 네거리	眼 눈 109
承 이을	試 시험할 207	神 귀신 189	拾 열 331	顔 얼굴 120
昇 오를 242	豕 돼지 125	娠 아이 밸	**[아]**	贋 위조할
乘 탈 92	**[씨]**	訊 물을	牙 어금니 124	**[알]**
勝 이길 186	氏 성 176	紳 큰 띠	兒 아이 246	斡 돌
僧 중	**[식]**	愼 삼가할 16	我 나	謁 뵈올
蠅 파리 135	式 법 86	新 새 48	亞 버금 252	**[암]**
[시]	拭 씻을	腎 콩팥 333	芽 싹	庵 암자
示 보일 312	食 먹을 183	薪 섶	阿 언덕 20	暗 어두울 206
市 저자 82	息 쉴 219	**[실]**	俄 잠깐	闇 어리석을
矢 화살 268	熄 불꺼질	失 잃을 152	雅 맑을 205	巖 바위 74
侍 모실 331	蝕 벌레먹을	實 열매 192	餓 굶을	**[압]**
始 비롯할 289	植 심을 91	室 집 214	**[악]**	壓 누를
施 베풀	殖 날	**[심]**	樂 풍류 331	押 잡도리할 237
	飾 꾸밀 333	心 마음 148	嶽 큰메	鴨 집오리 255

[양]		冶	풀무 333	魚	고기 114	輿	수레	燃	불사를
央	가운데 248	**[약]**		漁	고기잡을 114	**[역]**		燕	연나라 102
仰	우러러볼 313	若	같을 75	語	말씀 166	亦	또 162	臙	연지 102
怏	앙심먹을 248	約	맺을 166	禦	막을	役	부릴 140	**[열]**	
昂	모시는차례	弱	약할 196	**[억]**		易	바뀔 133	悅	기뻐할
[애]		藥	약 75	抑	억제할 333	疫	염병 116	熱	더울 155
哀	슬플 279	躍	뛸 104	億	억	逆	거스릴	閱	볼 264
挨	밀칠	**[양]**		憶	기억할	域	지경 76	**[염]**	
涯	물가	羊	염소 122	臆	가슴	譯	번역할 259	炎	불꽃 163
愛	사랑 109	洋	큰바다 252	**[언]**		驛	역마	染	물들 287
隘	좁을	痒	가려울	言	말씀 166	**[연]**		焰	불꽃
曖	희미할	揚	드날릴 137	彦	클	沿	물따라내려갈	厭	싫을
[액]		陽	볕 85	諺	상말	延	뻗을	艶	예쁠
厄	재앙	楊	버들 332	**[엄]**		硏	갈 201	鹽	소금 68
液	진액	樣	모양 249	俺	나	宴	잔치 189	**[엽]**	
額	이마 290	養	기를 122	嚴	엄할 90	軟	부드러울	葉	잎사귀 91
[앵]		壤	고운흙 67	**[업]**		淵	못	**[영]**	
櫻	앵두 193	孃	아가씨	業	업 69	然	그럴 54	永	길 38
鶯	꾀꼬리	釀	술빚을	**[여]**		硯	벼루 202	迎	맞을
[야]		讓	사양할	與	더불 332	煙	연기 94	英	꽃부리 178
也	이끼	**[어]**		如	같을 56	鉛	납 22	泳	무자맥질할 66
夜	밤 92	於	어조사	汝	너	演	넓을 143	映	비칠 277
野	들 81	御	모실	餘	남을 331	緣	인연 114	榮	영화 99

營 지을 81	吾 나	窪 웅덩이	搖 흔들 172	于 갈 330
詠 읊을	娛 즐거울	**[완]**	腰 허리	又 또 305
盈 찰 80	悟 깨달을	完 완전할 216	遙 멀 331	友 벗 97
影 그림자 60	烏 까마귀 104	宛 정할	樂 좋아할 334	牛 소 117
穎 물이름 105	奧 깊을 241	玩 구경할	窯 기왓가마	尤 더욱
[예]	誤 그릇할 314	椀 주발	謠 노래 278	右 오른쪽 106
豫 먼저 55	**[옥]**	腕 팔뚝 151	曜 빛날 56	宇 집 52
曳 끌	玉 구슬 332	碗 그릇	**[욕]**	芋 토란
藝 재주 151	沃 기름질 68	頑 완악할	浴 미역감을 297	羽 깃 106
洩 퍼질	屋 집 242	緩 느즈러질 254	辱 욕뵐 62	迂 굽을
譽 기릴 99	獄 옥 140	**[왈]**	欲 하고자할 276	雨 비 59
詣 이를 221	**[온]**	曰 가로 331	慾 욕심낼 94	祐 도울
預 미리	溫 너울 71	**[왕]**	**[용]**	偶 짝 314
銳 날쌜	穩 편안할 241	王 임금 178	用 쓸 95	郵 우편 78
隷 종	**[옹]**	往 갈 330	勇 날랠 331	寓 부칠 119
叡 밝을	翁 늙은이	旺 성할	容 얼굴 133	遇 만날 175
[오]	擁 안을	**[외]**	庸 떳떳할 243	隅 모퉁이
五 다섯 317	**[와]**	外 바깥 80	湧 뭇	愚 어리석을
午 낮 60	瓦 기와 331	畏 두려울 268	茸 녹용 126	虞 염려할
伍 다섯사람	臥 누울	限 모퉁이	傭 품팔이	憂 근심
汚 흐린물고일	訛 거짓말	**[요]**	溶 녹을	優 광대 277
惡 미워할 335	渦 소용돌이	凹 오목할	踊 뛸 281	**[욱]**
吳 오나라	蛙 개구리 135	要 중요할 313	**[우]**	旭 빛날

郁 문채날	源 근원 71	謂 이를	儒 선비 124
[운]	遠 멀 314	**[유]**	諭 고할
云 이를	猿 원숭이 124	由 말미암을 161	濡 적실
運 옮길 60	願 원할 217	幼 어릴 314	癒 병나을 314
雲 구름 60	**[월]**	有 있을 217	**[육]**
韻 운	月 달 56	酉 닭 308	肉 고기 196
[울]	越 넘을 218	油 기름 288	育 기를 122
鬱 속답답할	**[위]**	乳 젖 190	**[윤]**
[웅]	危 위태할	幽 그윽할	胤 맏 131
雄 수컷 104	位 자리 99	柔 부드러울 234	潤 윤택할
熊 곰 115	圍 에워쌀 163	唯 오직 333	**[융]**
[원]	委 맡길	惟 꾀할 333	融 화할
圓 둥글	威 위엄 313	悠 멀	**[은]**
元 으뜸 48	爲 할 261	喩 비유할	恩 은혜 314
苑 나랏동산 126	胃 밥통 166	愉 기쁠	銀 은 22
垣 얕은담	僞 거짓	猶 잡을 313	隱 숨을
怨 원수 186	偉 클 238	裕 넉넉할 98	**[을]**
原 근본 288	尉 벼슬이름	遊 놀	乙 새 331
員 관원 144	萎 이울	愈 병나을	**[음]**
院 집 242	違 어질	維 버리 333	吟 읊을
媛 예쁜계집	慰 위로할 98	誘 꾈	音 소리 275
援 구원할 315	緯 씨 255	蹂 밟을	陰 그늘 85
園 동산 68	衛 호위할 274	遺 끼칠 197	飮 마실 188

蔭 덮을
[읍]
泣 울
[응]
應 응할 20
凝 엉길
鷹 매
[의]
衣 옷 228
醫 의원 286
依 의지할 72
宜 마땅 331
椅 교의
意 뜻 168
義 옳을 176
疑 의심 332
儀 거동 329
毅 군셀
誼 옳을
擬 비길
蟻 왕개미 136
議 의논할 214
[이]

證	증험할 139	肢	팔다리 147	塵	티끌 65	澄	맑을	察	살필 301
蒸	찔	智	지혜 268	震	진동할	徵	부를 127	擦	문지를
增	더할 158	蜘	거미 135	鎭	진정할 31	**[차]**		**[찰]**	
憎	미워할 335	遲	더딜	**[질]**		叉	깍지낄	參	참여할 187
贈	줄	識	기록할 335	叱	꾸짖을	此	이 332	慘	슬플
[지]		誌	기록할	帙	책값 31	且	또 332	慚	부끄러울 332
之	갈 79	**[직]**		迭	갈마들일	次	버금 159	斬	목벨
支	지탱할 250	直	곧을 232	姪	조카	借	빌 27	**[창]**	
止	그칠 155	織	짤 167	疾	병	差	어긋날	昌	창성할
只	다만	職	벼슬 298	嫉	시샘할 159	車	수레 250	倉	창고 212
地	땅 54	**[진]**		秩	차례	遮	가릴	唱	노래부를 200
至	이를 78	盡	다할 239	窒	막힐	**[착]**		窓	창 95
池	못 61	辰	별 335	蛭	거머리	着	입을 67	創	다칠 212
旨	맛	津	나루	質	바탕 296	搾	짤	脹	창증날
芝	지초	珍	보배	**[짐]**		錯	섞일	蒼	푸를 52
志	뜻 272	唇	놀랄	朕	나	**[찬]**		暢	화창할 191
枝	가지 330	振	떨칠 120	斟	짐작할 185	撰	지을	彰	빛날
知	알 73	晋	나라 131	**[집]**		贊	도울	槍	창 97
祉	복	眞	참 197	執	잡을 202	餐	삼킬	廠	헛간
指	손가락 236	陣	진칠 253	集	모을 108	纂	모을	**[채]**	
持	가질 217	進	나아갈 111	輯	모을 108	讚	기릴 316	采	일 308
紙	종이 122	陳	베풀	**[징]**		**[찰]**		彩	채색
脂	기름 288	診	맥짚을	懲	징계할 315	札	편지	採	딸 95

錐 송곳	忠 충성 84	治 다스릴 286	**[칭]**	濯 씻을
醜 추할	衷 가운데 169	値 맞날	稱 일컬을 314	**[탄]**
趨 달아날	衝 충동할 162	恥 부끄러울	秤 저울	呑 삼킬 169
雛 새새끼	**[췌]**	致 이를 166	**[쾌]**	坦 너그러울
[축]	悴 파리할	齒 이 165	快 쾌할 330	炭 숯 74
丑 소 336	贅 군살	稚 어릴 190	**[타]**	彈 탄환 273
祝 빌 48	**[취]**	痴 어리석을	他 다를 299	嘆 탄식할
畜 기를 220	吹 불	置 둘 219	打 칠 206	綻 웃터질
逐 쫓을 232	取 가질 292	**[칙]**	妥 편할	誕 탄생할 48
軸 굴대 249	炊 불뗄	則 법 335	舵 키	歎 탄식할 331
蓄 쌓을	臭 냄새 190	勅 칙령	墮 떨어질 314	灘 여울
築 쌓을 89	醉 술취할 148	**[친]**	惰 게으를	**[탈]**
縮 움츠러질 246	就 나아갈 116	親 어버이 142	詫 속일	脫 벗을 167
蹴 찰	翠 비취	**[칠]**	駄 짐실을	奪 빼앗을 266
[춘]	趣 뜻 108	七 일곱 59	**[탁]**	**[탐]**
春 봄 257	鷲 독수리	漆 옷	托 밀	耽 즐길 118
椿 참죽나무	**[측]**	**[침]**	拓 밀칠 335	探 더듬을 249
[출]	側 곁 333	枕 베개 31	卓 높을 183	**[탑]**
出 날 156	測 측량할 241	沈 잠길 233	託 부탁할	塔 탑 247
[충]	**[층]**	侵 침노할 254	啄 쪼을	搭 막을
充 채울 137	層 충층대 214	浸 잠글 315	琢 쪼을	**[탕]**
蟲 벌레 130	**[치]**	針 바늘 236	濁 흐릴 114	湯 끓을 132
沖 화할	侈 사치할	寢 잘 196	擢 빼낼	蕩 클

票 쪽지 224	**[하]**	**[할]**	海 바다 80	許 허락할 16
漂 뜰	下 아래 244	割 벨	害 해할 130	虛 빌 52
標 표할 84	何 어찌 334	轄 굴대빗장할	楷 해나무	噓 불
[품]	河 물	**[함]**	解 풀 233	**[헌]**
品 품수 217	夏 여름 73	含 머금을	蟹 게 136	軒 초헌
[풍]	荷 연꽃 212	函 함	該 마땅할	獻 드릴 201
風 바람 59	賀 하례 285	陷 빠질	骸 뼈	憲 법 263
楓 단풍나무	霞 놀	涵 젖을	鮭 어채	**[험]**
豊 풍년 289	嚇 웃을	緘 봉할 164	**[핵]**	險 험할 75
諷 욀	**[학]**	檻 난간	劾 캐물을	驗 시험할 164
[피]	學 배울 200	艦 싸움배 227	核 씨	**[혁]**
皮 가죽 291	虐 사나울	**[합]**	**[행]**	革 가죽 291
披 헤칠	鶴 두루미	合 모을 25	杏 살구 193	赫 빛날
彼 저	**[한]**	蛤 조개 136	行 행할 76	**[현]**
疲 피곤할 98	汗 땀	**[항]**	幸 다행 266	玄 검을 184
被 입을	旱 가물 333	巷 거리	**[향]**	弦 시위 331
避 피할 242	恨 한할 331	恒 항상 148	向 향할 249	縣 고을
[필]	限 한정 52	抗 막을 195	享 누릴 332	現 나타날 312
匹 짝	寒 찰 62	航 배 227	香 향기 87	絃 풍류줄 275
必 반드시 291	閑 한가할 332	港 항구 174	鄕 시골 299	賢 어질 333
筆 붓 202	漢 한나라 221	項 목덜미 332	響 소리울릴	顯 나타날 61
[핍]	翰 글	**[해]**	饗 잔치할	懸 매달
乏 다할 112	韓 한나라 254	亥 돼지 336	**[허]**	**[혈]**

繪 그림	**[후]**	**[휘]**	黑 검을 294	戲 희롱할
賄 선물	后 황후	揮 흔들 333	**[흔]**	希 바랄 312
懷 품을 332	朽 썩을	彙 무리	欣 기쁠	姬 계집
檜 전나무	侯 임금 331	輝 빛날 333	痕 흔적 272	喜 기쁠 279
[획]	厚 두터울	**[훤]**	**[흘]**	囍 쌍희 47
劃 새길 292	後 뒤 86	喧 지껄일	迄 이를	稀 드물
獲 얻을	候 기후 63	**[휴]**	**[흠]**	熙 밝을 16
[횡]	喉 목구멍	休 쉴 93	欽 공경할	犧 희생할
橫 비낄 36	**[훈]**	携 가질 332	**[흡]**	**[힐]**
[효]	訓 가르칠 220	**[흉]**	吸 숨들이마실	詰 꾸짖을
效 공효할 192	勳 공	凶 흉할 130	恰 흡족할	
肴 안주	薰 향풀	兇 사나울	**[흥]**	
曉 새벽	**[훙]**	胸 가슴 261	興 일 332	
酵 술밑	薨 죽을	**[흑]**	**[희]**	

BIBLIOGRAPHY

Braden, John. *Read Practical Japanese*. Japan: Kenkyusha Printing Company, 1976.

Budge, Wallis. *Egyptian Language*. New York: Dover Publications Inc., 1973.

Bullock, T. L. *Chinese Written Language*. Shanghai: Belly & Walsh, 1923.

Chang, Raymond, Margaret Scrogin. *Speaking of Chinese*. New York: Norton & Company Inc., 1978.

Chih, Yu-Ju. *Advanced Chinese Newspaper Readings*. New Haven, Conn.: The Institute of Far Eastern Languages.

Creel, Herrlee Glessner. Chicago: The University of Chicago Press, 1952.

Crowley, Dale P. *Manual for Reading Japanese*. Honolulu: The University Press of Hawaii, 1972.

Dykstra, Andrew & Dykstra, Yoshiko. *The Kanji ABC*. Los Altos: William Kaufmann Inc., 1975.

Geo, V. Strong. *Common Chinese-Japanese Characters*. Yokohama: Kelly and Walsh, 1911.

Hadamitzky, Wolfgan. *Kanji & Kana*. Rutland: Charles E. Tuttle Co., 1980.

Kang, C. H. & Nelson Ethel R. *The Discovery of Genesis*. St. Louise: Concordia, 1979.

Karlgren, Bernhard. *Grammata Serica Recensa*. Stockholm: Museum of Far Estern Antiquities, 1964.

Kennedy, George Alexander. *Serial Arrangements of Chinese Characters*. Yale University: Department of Oriental Studies, 1901.

Lai, T. C. *Animals of Chinese Zodiac*. Hong Kong: Swindon Book Company, 1980.

Lee, Cynthia. *Learn Chinese.* Toronto: University of Toronto, 1980.

Lee, James Zee-Min. *Chinese Potpourri.* Hong Kong: The Oriental Publishers, 1950.

Lin, Chao. *A Survey of Chinese Characters.* Hong Kong: Hong Kong University Book Company, 1968.

Mathews, R. H. *Chinese-English Dictionary.* China Inland Mission: Presbyterian Mission Press, 1931.

Murray, D. M. & Wong, T. W. *Noodle Words.* Tokyo: Charles E. Tuttle Company, 1971.

Osaka University. *The First Step to Kanji, and Second Step to Kanji.* Japan: Osaka University of Foreign Studies, 1969.

Pye, Michael. *Everyday Japanese Characters.* Tokyo: The Hokuseido Press, 1977.

Sakade, Florence. *Reading and Writing Japanese.* Tokyo: Charles E. Tuttle Company, 1959.

Tan, Huay Peng. *Fun with Chinese Characters.* Singapore: Federal Publications, 1982.

Tsang, O. Z. *A Complete Chinese-English Dictionary.* Shanghai: The Republican Press, 1926.

Vaccari, Oreste & Vaccari, Enko Elisa. *Pictorial Chinese-Japanese Characters.* Tokyo: Kasai Publishing Company, 1964.

Walsh, Len. *Read Japanese Today.* Tokyo: Charles E. Tuttle Company, 1969.

Well, H. R. (Rev.) *Chinese for Every One.* Hong Kong: The South China Morning Post, 1938.

Weiger, S. J. *Chinese Characters.* New York: Paragon Book Reprint Company, 1915.

Wiese, Kurt. *You Can Write Chinese.* New York: Viking Press, 1945.

高鴻晉, **中國字例**, 臺北：三民書局, 1936.

金益達, **故事成語辭典**, 서울：學園社, 1977.

金昌宜,　**韓國敎會文獻分類法**,　서울：성바오로, 1973.

藤堂明保,　**漢字語源辭典**,　東京：學燈社, 1965.

藤原鶴釆,　**和漢書道史**,　東京：二玄社, 1975.

羅振玉,　**殷墟書契前編 上・下**, 臺北：藝文印書館, 1934.

編輯部,　**常用漢字敎本**,　서울：理想社, 1977.

浜西正人,　**漢字學習字典**,　東京：角川書店, 1983.

姜舜植外,　**韓英大辭典**,　서울：時事英語社, 1982.

羅成均,　**書藝筆法敎本**,　서울：視聽覺敎育社, 1981.

吳絜寧,　**實用文字學 上・下**,　臺北：商務印書館, 1891.

王筠撰,　**文字蒙求**,　臺北：藝文印書館, 1964.

龍宇純,　**中國文字學**,　香港：崇基書店, 1968.

劉國鈞,　**中國書的故事**,　德證印務公司, 1956.

李家源・張三植,　**漢字大典**,　서울：裕庚出版社, 1973.

長沼直兄著,　**漢字帳**,　臺北：高塚竹堂書, 1951.

凟作民譯,　**象形文字**,　臺北：星光出版社, 1968.

蔣國國,　**中國文字之原始及其構造 上・下**,

曹先錕,　**文字學槪要 上・下**,　臺北：中文印書局, 1962.

曾連生,　**漢字爲寫裝飾**,　臺北：地質出版社, 1979.

朱盛科,　**常用形似字辨析**,　臺北：廣東人出版, 1982.

陳公哲,　**看圖識字一冊**,　香港：商務印書館, 1950.

陳冠學,　**象形文字**,　臺北：三民書局, 1934.

川嶋優,　**漢字をおぼえる辭典**,　東京：旺文社, 1975.

韓國改革主義信行協會,　**神學事典**,　서울：성광, 1981.

包明叔,　**說文部首通釋**,　臺北：漳洲, 1967.